ADVENTURES IN ARCHAEOLOGY

UNIVERSITY PRESS OF FLORIDA

Florida A&M University, Tallahassee
Florida Atlantic University, Boca Raton
Florida Gulf Coast University, Ft. Myers
Florida International University, Miami
Florida State University, Tallahassee
New College of Florida, Sarasota
University of Central Florida, Orlando
University of Florida, Gainesville
University of North Florida, Jacksonville
University of South Florida, Tampa
University of West Florida, Pensacola

ADVENTURES IN ARCHAEOLOGY

The Wreck of the *Orca II* and Other Explorations

P.J. CAPELOTTI

University Press of Florida

Gainesville · Tallahassee · Tampa · Boca Raton

Pensacola · Orlando · Miami · Jacksonville · Ft. Myers · Sarasota

This book may be available in an electronic edition.

23 22 21 20 19 18   6 5 4 3 2 1

Unless otherwise stated, all illustrations are courtesy of the author.

Chapters 4 and 14 are used with permission of Taylor and Francis, Inc., www.tandfonline
.com; chapter 5 is used with permission of *The Explorers Journal*; chapters 6 and 8 are used
with permission of Rutgers University Press; chapter 7 is used with permission of *EXARC:
The International Journal of Archaeological Open Air Museums and Experimental Archaeology*;
chapters 9 and 10 are used with permission of *Air & Space Smithsonian*; chapters 11 and 13
are used with permission of *Archaeology*; chapter 12 is used with permission of Cambridge
University Press; chapters 15 and 16 are used with permission of McFarland & Company, Inc.

Library of Congress Cataloging-in-Publication Data
Names: Capelotti, P. J. (Peter Joseph), 1960– author.
Title: Adventures in archaeology : the wreck of the Orca II and other
  explorations / P.J. Capelotti.
Description: Gainesville : University Press of Florida, 2018. | Includes
  bibliographical references and index.
Identifiers: LCCN 2018002630 | ISBN 9780813064840 (pbk. : alk. paper)
Subjects: LCSH: Underwater archaeology. | Coastal archaeology. | Space
  archaeology. | Aircraft accidents—History. | Jaws (Motion picture : 1975)
Classification: LCC CC77.U5 C37 2018 | DDC 930.1028/04—dc23
LC record available at https://lccn.loc.gov/2018002630

The University Press of Florida is the scholarly publishing agency for the State University
System of Florida, comprising Florida A&M University, Florida Atlantic University, Florida
Gulf Coast University, Florida International University, Florida State University, New College
of Florida, University of Central Florida, University of Florida, University of North Florida,
University of South Florida, and University of West Florida.

University Press of Florida
15 Northwest 15th Street
Gainesville, FL 32611-2079
http://upress.ufl.edu

Before our foolish faces
Lay lands we did not see;
Our eyes were in the places
Where we should never be.

—A. E. Housman, *A Shropshire Lad and Other Poems*

CONTENTS

PREFACE

Time and the River

The Old Colony Railroad line and its parallel acquaintance, the Shumatuscacant River, cut the street of my childhood from the remainder of
the quiet small town of Whitman, Massachusetts. Both river and rail
ran alongside a few immense shoe factories that throughout my youth
were dying or dead, like gigantic dinosaurs just after the meteor. A
paper factory briefly replaced one of the shoe factories, and after that
we could climb the stacked rolls of brown paper as if attacking near-
vertical mountainsides. One could make small boats and rafts of the
heavy paper and set them adrift, as in *Paddle to the Sea*, and imagine
they would reach the Atlantic Ocean. The imagination required to follow the water path to the ocean from my small town was considerable,
a deliberate thought experiment that no doubt assisted my later curi-
osities as writer and archaeologist.

Even so, it was not until I was fifty-seven and in a reminiscing mood
that I thought to inquire of a learned colleague the origin of the name
Shumatuscacant. He revealed it as a Native American name meaning
"Beaver River." I never saw a beaver in Whitman, so trappers must
have accounted for them ages ago. Neither was the Shumatuscacant
any part of a river. It was for the most part an unglorified trickle as it
wandered in and out of swamps, got held up for a spell in the old mill
puddle of Hobart's Pond, and was then funneled through a stone and
cement channel past old Gus's barber shop. In that tiny but hallowed
place, my first haircut cost twenty-five cents and a commitment of half
an hour of listening to old farts jabber about the good old days before

finally vacating Gus's chair. In summer the barber shop windows were open to let in fresh air and the sound of the Shumatuscacant as it dribbled along just below.

The river lolled past Gus's and departed Whitman to rejoin Nature in another swamp, on its way to a rendezvous with an unnamed puddle near North Hanson Station. There it emerged, rebirthed as the much more appropriately named Poor Meadow Brook. This honest stream wound into Robbins Pond to emerge to the west as the Satucket, a proper river, which in turn joined the Matfield and the Town rivers, which together flowed into the Taunton, another proper water flow on its perpetual course to Mount Hope Bay, an arm of the great Narragansett Bay, at Fall River. Any droplets originating in the Shumatuscacant would have one final stop in Rhode Island Sound before they could claim to be in the Atlantic Ocean proper.

Across the Old Colony tracks and the beaver brook stood the public park designed by Frederick Law Olmstead. I have yet to learn how the father of American landscape architecture and designer of New York City's Central Park found his way to my tiny hometown. A bit farther on, a man named Joe King in the early 1960s built King's Castle Land, a miniature fairy tale theme park that, after its purchase by Clarence Whitney and his family, added a toy store. Across the street my mother worked for many years as a waitress and hostess at the Wakefield family's Toll House restaurant, where Mrs. Wakefield in the 1930s invented the Toll House cookie by accident. The Toll House burned down in the 1980s, and King's Castle Land closed a decade later. A Wendy's replaced the famous restaurant, and the parking lot of a franchise grocery store obliterated any evidence of the theme park. The only surviving remnant of the vibrant otherworld on the opposite side of my hometown at the intersection of routes 14 and 18 is the "Toll House 1709" sign, now sited over a historical marker in the parking lot between the Wendy's and a Walgreen's.

I mention these random thoughts as they return to me now as some of my earliest impulses to search up and down creeks and shorelines for evidence of old factories and general wreckage and along backroads and intersections for the remains of roadside "attractions" and the signs that went with them. In other words, to become an archaeologist

Detail of an 1885 topographic survey of Whitman, Massachusetts.

and investigate any aspect of the past in any place from any time. In youth one races through such intersections, oblivious of time, stopping only rarely and recognizing the changing landscape only in deep hindsight.

This is probably to the good, as the Toll House, as one example among many, was never apparently an actual roadside tollhouse and was built not in 1709 but in 1817. So be it. If an artificial date affixed to an artificial restaurant enhanced the enjoyment of the patrons for authentically excellent service and original chocolate chip cookies, was that not all to the good? Whether Ruth Wakefield, Frederick Law Olmstead, or Joe King, all had transformed the natural landscape of my hometown into something they considered more authentic, more interesting, or simply more commercially attractive, in the roadside "attraction" sense of the word.

For archaeologists, was not everything in our field of study artificial? Artifact and artificial are practically the same word. Such transformations of the natural and cultural landscape from the mundane to the magical were essential to the escapism required to survive just about any childhood. Little did I realize, escaping to a dark theater in 1975 to witness the Hollywood spectacle *Jaws*, that one day I would travel as an archaeologist to Martha's Vineyard to survey the remains of one of its movie prop boats, the *Orca II*. Like Matt Hooper, the film's fictional and very wealthy marine biologist, I wanted my own flybridge research vessel complete with sonar, underwater lights, and a rack of scuba tanks. I reached the inlet where lay the wreck of the *Orca II* some forty years later, in possession of none of these things—just old sneakers, a notepad, and a measuring tape. One could do archaeology with very little.

The *Orca II*, a movie prop, no longer looked anything like a boat. Time and pillage had reduced it to a scatter of tubes and twisted metal. But of course it was not nor had it ever been a boat. It was a movie prop, virtually the definition of an artifice. Or, perhaps more appropriately—and pedantically—an artificial artifice, something created by humans yet never entirely real. This archaeological meaning—one that reverses upon itself—is hardly uncommon. And perhaps the best example can be found (or not) in a tiny English crossroads.

A few years ago, I found myself a few miles from the village of Piltdown in southeastern England. A colleague agreed to hunt the place down with me, and after some searching we came to this bump in a backroad that, a century ago, was the scene of the greatest discovery in the history of archaeology. A local lawyer by the name of Charles Dawson discovered what was soon announced to the world as *Eoanthropus dawsoni*, literally Dawson's Dawn Human, and the presumed missing link between humans and non-human apes. Piltdown instantly became the center of the scientific universe. A pillar to commemorate the great find was placed at the site in the 1930s, and the area was designated a national site of historic interest.

Then in 1953 the British Museum revealed that the whole discovery had been a fake, an artificial excavation of real bones fraudulently tampered with to create a false narrative of human evolution. As a lifelong seeker after historical markers—like the one solemnizing the "Toll House, 1709" in my hometown—I wanted to photograph the commemorative pillar at Piltdown. My colleague and I eventually found the drive leading to the now private estate (the "site of national interest" appellation was quietly dropped after the fraud was revealed). But the gate at the foot of the drive was locked and our entry blocked. How was this possible? How could public access be denied to such a historic site?

I was not, as they say in England, best pleased, to be stopped about a hundred yards short after a journey of more than 3,500 miles. However, as we left the site it finally dawned on me that nothing about Dawson's Dawn Man had ever been historic, not in any real sense. The bones were faked and the discovery a fraud. The marker, ultimately, commemorated an event that never happened. Even the local pub, once called The Piltdown Man, had reverted to its original name of The Lamb. The only evidence of the infamous past was a framed photo of the original 1912 excavation—tucked away in the men's loo.

Worse, the village of Piltdown offered none of the consolations of similar explorations of the American roadside: no T-shirts, no beer mugs shaped like primitive skulls, no souvenirs of any kind. This grievous neglect was an affront to American sensibilities. In the United States even the most seemingly insignificant roadside attraction can hold up for sale any manner of branded clothing, key chains, patches, and bumper stickers, along with an obligatory trifold tourist brochure.

At Piltdown Miles Russell, senior lecturer in archaeology at Bournemouth University, noted this glaring absence. In his excellent *The Piltdown Man Hoax: Case Closed*, he writes that "no indication is provided to the many visitors, travelers, tourists or passers-by as to why the village name appears to be so familiar. . . . If the story of Dawson and *Eoanthropus dawsoni* had occurred in the USA, there would, at the very least, be a theme park, museum or other acknowledgement of the discovery, but . . . a century on from the first announcement of Piltdown Man to the world, there is nothing."[1]

As this collection of essays on the adventure that is archaeology attempts to reveal, one struggles continuously to establish, for want of a better phrase, the reality of the artificial. In my own work, the earliest experiences from the artificial landscape of my small hometown seemed continually to find their way into the work. One seemed perpetually alongside some creek or river or along some shore or bay, or stuck on an island or, in the case of the waters that washed away our home in 1996, in the midst of a catastrophic flood. And nearly always in search of some technological chimera: an antique aeroplane or prehistoric raft, a prehistoric airship on an Arctic island, the ruins of a starship on the Moon, or a billboard by the side of the highway half hidden by trees and time. All these became raw materials for archaeological adventures, both in the field and in theoretical flights of imagination.

In the summer of 2017, after a quarter century of writing on the work and themes of archaeology, it seemed time to acknowledge this phenomenon. Even as we often deny their existence or their influence, it remains remarkable the degree to which the dreams and fantasies—the *artifices*—of childhood pursue us to adulthood.

ACKNOWLEDGMENTS

I am very grateful to the incredibly talented Lee Hartnup (Twitter @Goatboy667) for his re-creations of the vessel *Orca II* for the cover. John Galluzzo responded instantly to a request to track down the meaning of Shumatuscacant. I am further grateful to the excellent comments of peer reviewers for the University Press of Florida as well as those of the excellent editorial staff in Gainesville. C.L. Devlin contributed in a hundred different ways, including with excellent sketch maps and illustrations. This work was generously supported over many years by several excellent associate deans of academic affairs at Penn State University Abington College, most especially Drs. Leonard Mustazza, Peter Pincemin Johnstone, and Norah Shultz, and to continually supportive division heads Jim Smith, Gary Calore, Manohar Singh, and Fran Sessa.

Chapters 1, 2, and 3, appear in print here for the first time. For access to the site of the remains of *Orca II* and the other *Jaws* vessels I am grateful to Bret Stearns, director, Natural Resources Department of the Wampanoag Tribe of Gay Head (Aquinnah). My friend and colleague Col. Tom MacKenzie was instrumental in helping to make contact with Bret. For the story behind the long-term formation of the site, I am extremely grateful to Susan Murphy. Others in Menemsha, such as Donna Honig, also helped to point me in the direction of this terrific story. For chapter 2 I am grateful to the staff of Glen Foerd Estate in Northeast Philadelphia and to many former students who worked with me on that very challenging site from 1998 to 2001. For chapter 3 I am grateful to those who made our survey of the offshore wreckage we originally believed to be USS *Akron* possible (ranks and titles in 2002): Captain William Webster and Captain Jeffrey Karonis, U.S. Coast Guard; Lt. Rob Hanna and LCdr. Dennis McKelvey, skipper of the submarine *NR-1*, U.S. Navy; and Dr. Robert Browning, historian, U.S. Coast Guard. For the subsequent *Sea Hunters* film by Eco-Nova Productions, I am grateful to Mike Fletcher, James Delgado, John Davis, and Clive Cussler.

Chapter 4 is adapted with the kind permission of *Polar Journal* from "Extreme Archaeological Sites and Their Tourism: A Conceptual Model from Historic American Polar Expeditions in Svalbard, Franz Josef Land and Northeast Greenland," *Polar Journal* 2, no. 2 (2012): 236–55, www.tandfonline.com.

Chapter 5 originally appeared in *Explorers Journal* 75, no. 1 (Spring 1997). It is adapted here and reprinted with the kind permission of the *Explorers Journal*.

Chapter 7 originally appeared as "The Theory of the Archaeological Raft: Motivation, Method, and Madness in Experimental Archaeology," in *EXARC: The International Journal of Archaeological Open Air Museums and Experimental Archaeology* 8, no. 2 (2012). It is reprinted here with the kind permission of the journal.

Chapters 6 and 8 are adapted from *Sea Drift: Rafting Adventures in the Wake of Kon-Tiki* (New Brunswick, N.J.: Rutgers University Press, 2001).

Chapters 9 and 10 are reprinted with the kind permission of *Air & Space Smithsonian*. Chapter 9 originally appeared in *Air & Space* 9, no. 5 (December 1994–January 1995), and Chapter 10 in *Air & Space* 11, no. 3 (August–September 1996).

Chapters 11 and 13 are reprinted with the kind permission of *Archaeology*. Chapter 11 originally appeared in *Archaeology*, November–December 2006, and Chapter 13 in *Archaeology*, November–December 2004.

Chapter 12 is adapted from "A Preliminary Archaeological Survey of a Tupolev TB-3 (ANT-6) Aircraft on Ostrov Rudol'fa, Zemlya Frantsa-Iosifa, Russia," in *Polar Record* 43, no. 2 (2013): 173–77, and reprinted here with permission from that journal and Cambridge University Press. Special thanks are due the captain and crew, and especially the helicopter pilots, of the icebreaker *Yamal* for enabling this reconnaissance and survey to take place. Victor Boyarsky of the Russian State Museum of Arctic and Antarctic led the expedition, which was organized by Alexei Mironov of Poseidon Arctic Voyages in Moscow. This survey could not have been attempted without positioning data provided by Dr. Susan Barr from her visit to the area in 1990. I am also grateful to Gordon Kilgore and Christine Reinke-Kunze for their photographic documentation of the site. Great thanks are also due to Magnus Forsberg, Andreas Umbreit, and Mike Hewitt for their discussions of Soviet polar history in general and the expeditions at Rudolf Island in particular.

Chapter 14 is reprinted with permission from "Surveying Fermi's Paradox, Mapping Dyson's Sphere: Approaches to Archaeological Field Research in Space," in *Handbook of Space Engineering, Archaeology and Heritage,* edited by Ann Garrison Darrin and Beth Laura O'Leary (Boca Raton, Fla.: CRC Press–Taylor and Francis, 2009), 857–69.

Chapters 15 and Chapter 16 are adapted and updated from *The Human Archaeology of Space: Lunar, Planetary and Interstellar Relics of Exploration*, by P.J. Capelotti (Jefferson, N.C.: McFarland & Company, 2010).

Finally, with love and thanks to C.L., Jeremy, Jenny, to Patricia McMillan-Barclay, and to Beowulf, Grendel, and Monty for all the long walks that distracted me long enough to think through many of the ideas expressed herein.

I

Shoreline and Shallows Archaeology

1

The Last Logbook of the *Orca II*

The building blocks of archaeology are the artifacts made or modified by humans. Seldom, however, do such artifacts of past behavior arrive in the present unaffected by time and the host of changes time carries with it. This is as true—and in many cases much more so—for an artifact created just forty years ago as it is for a stone tool fashioned millions of years ago. The actual artifacts from a Hollywood movie seldom survive as long as the celluloid movie in which the artifacts appear.

Major artifacts and support vessels from the filming of the 1975 Hollywood blockbuster film *Jaws* were purchased after the production by a local boat captain and taken to a remote stretch of shoreline opposite the small fishing village of Menemsha on the island of Martha's Vineyard, Massachusetts. Key among these items used in the movie was the fiberglass copy of the fishing boat *Orca*. This copy, called *Orca II*, remained on the shoreline for decades, becoming the object of increasingly brazen predation by rabid fans of the movie, who eventually stripped the site to near non-existence. The local captain and his wife who originally purchased the movie remnants tried for decades to preserve the artifacts but in 2005 eventually removed the remaining visible segments of the hull of *Orca II* to be recycled as small souvenirs of the movie. What survives *in situ* from the original movie production is almost completely covered by sand or shallow water, as recorded during a survey in May 2017.

These represent the final stages in the archaeological transformation of a Hollywood icon. *Note: citations from Internet fan sites are direct, uncorrected quotes and contain offensive language.*

The motion picture *Jaws*, filmed largely on the island of Martha's Vineyard in the summer of 1974 and released to an almost unprecedented media frenzy in the summer of 1975, still exerts an outsized influence on American popular culture nearly half a century later. That significance was not immediately apparent. Peter Benchley, author of the best-selling novel that became the basis for the film, wrote in 2001 that none of those involved in the film project "knew that we were involved in the birth of a phenomenon that would retain a strange resonance in the culture for a *quarter of a century* . . . and in the worldwide debut of a director [Steven Spielberg] who would go on to influence the film industry like no other."[1] Carl Gottlieb, who both co-wrote the screenplay and acted in the film, subsequently wrote a best-selling account of the making of the movie and noted that "Jaws made film history as the highest-grossing movie of all time, and established a business model and release pattern for large-scale summer movies that persists to this day."[2]

The decision by director Spielberg to film the movie's central conflict—between an obsessed shark hunter named Quint, played by English actor Robert Shaw, and a great white shark (*Carcharodon carcharias*)—with a mechanical shark in actual waters required both specific location attributes and a diverse fleet of watercraft. The location attributes required an island in the northeastern United States surrounded by sheltered, shallow waters and a sandy bottom that was in close proximity to support areas for a large film unit and cast, one that included an array of shore locations to serve as stand-ins for the towns and beaches of a fictional island called Amity. The variety of watercraft included an actual fishing vessel that would be converted for on-screen work as Quint's shark-hunting fishing boat called *Orca*, as well as a small fleet of waterside support vessels to enable the filming and to operate and maintain what became several versions of a mechanical shark.

The film's producers eventually found their location on the island of Martha's Vineyard off the coast of Cape Cod. A temporary mock-up of a Hollywood version of Quint's fisherman's shanty was erected at the head of the small and picturesque fishing village of Menemsha on the southwestern corner of the island, and local waterman Captain Lynn Murphy and his wife Susan were hired to drive the various support vessels throughout the production.

The key vessels required for filming, as Carl Gottlieb writes, were "a submersible platform with a track, on which rode a crane-like attachment with a bucket-pivot on top [to hold and operate the mechanical shark; and] a model of a fishing boat with flotation barrels supporting a realistic superstructure."[3] In addition the production required an actual fishing boat, enhanced to appear even more "nautical" for a general movie audience, that would serve as the original to a copy used for stunts. Various other shuttle and support boats included a large tugboat out of Vineyard Haven called *Whitefoot*; a fleet of small boats to be used in a scene depicting an armada of local fishermen out to hunt the shark and including a small fishing boat skippered by a character named Ben Gardner (played by a local and legendary islander by the name of Craig Kingsbury; and perhaps most critically, additional support barges for the mechanical shark, half a dozen inflatable runabouts, and a large floating camera and miniature studio barge eventually dubbed the SS *Garage Sale*.

The actual fishing boat was found in a shipyard near Marblehead, Massachusetts. According to Gottlieb, this was "a forty-two-foot Nova Scotia lobster boat named *Warlock*."[4] This all-white vessel, a type derived from the Cape Islander lobster boats designed on Cape Sable Island off the southern coast of Nova Scotia since the beginning of the twentieth century, was driven to Martha's Vineyard. Once the vessel arrived, movie production designer Joe Alves transformed it into the dark and menacing *Orca* through the application of "gallons of burgundy and black marine paint."[5] Oversized windows all around the cabin enhanced the sensation of being at or even below the surface of the sea and therefore directly within the realm of the shark. The effect was heightened through the addition of an oversized bowsprit more typical of a swordfishing boat, a rack for similarly oversized yellow

Actors Richard Dreyfuss and Roy Scheider at the transom and Robert Shaw on the flybridge try to hang onto the operational *Orca* as it heels from the actions of a monster shark in the 1975 blockbuster movie *Jaws*. The need for an *Orca II*—a non-functioning copy of the *Orca* that could repeatedly sink and heel—became evident, as Susan Murphy relates, when the tug *Whitefoot* almost pulled the working *Orca* apart in the course of filming these stunts. Courtesy of Universal Studios Licensing LLC.

kegs for use in harpooning sharks, and most notably, an almost absurdly oversized mast. The overall effect was to make the *Orca* a sort of Disney version of a maritime hunting vessel, or what an audience of landlubbers might believe a fully laden shark-fishing vessel should look like.

An identical but non-operational, motorless copy of this wooden vessel was created (the "model of a fishing boat with flotation barrels or drums supporting a realistic superstructure") out of fiberglass and then fitted with a metal framework beneath the hull that could be manipulated by the addition or subtraction of air to the barrels to simulate heeling or even sinking. Painted exactly as was the working *Orca*, this stunt boat was named the *Orca II*.

To operate the variety of vessels involved in the film in the ever-changing sea and weather states in and around the harbors of Martha's Vineyard required local watermen skilled in mechanics who could also afford to participate in a project that eventually stretched to nearly five months from early May 1974 through the summer and into the early fall. Chief among these watermen was Captain Lynn Murphy, at the time a forty-six-year-old local maritime legend.

One of the key figures in the successful completion of the film production, Captain Murphy has been described as a man "whose reputation for mechanical skill is matched only by his well-known temper,"[6] someone who "will boil and rage and from time to time he will burst, and someone will be catapulted into Menemsha Harbor."[7] He became a local hero two decades earlier at the age of twenty-six through his actions in assisting boaters in and around Menemsha Harbor when Martha's Vineyard was struck by Hurricane Carol on August 31, 1954.[8] A young U.S. senator named John F. Kennedy even stopped by Murphy's boathouse to commend his heroism. In the spring of 1974 Murphy became the principal boat driver for the production of *Jaws* and, in the process, one of the local models, along with Craig Kingsbury, for the character of the profane shark fisherman Quint. Murphy was soon joined in his movie support work by his wife Susan.

Menemsha Basin and the fishing village of Menemsha on Martha's Vineyard, as seen in the summer of 2016 and little changed from its appearance during the filming of *Jaws* in 1974.

To heel and "sink" the *Orca II* successfully and then raise it again—
and to accomplish this feat innumerable times to get the filming completed from support vessels in accordance with the director's vision for
the movie—was a considerable combined feat of movie prop engineering and manufacture, small boat handling in a saltwater environment,
and cinematic perseverance in a highly unfavorable environment for
movie making.

In addition to being without any working machinery from the keel
upward, *Orca II* was also constructed without a transom so that a temporary balsa wood transom could be fitted to it. This false transom
would break away in the climactic scene when the mechanical shark
leapt from the sea and onto the stern of the boat. As profiled by Christopher Balogh in 2015 in the magazine *Marlin*: "*Orca 2* was created out
of fiberglass that came from the mold made from the original boat.
There was no motor attached and several breakaway sterns were built
into the replica. In the infamous scene where the shark chomps on
Quint as Chief Brody throws a scuba tank into the shark's mouth," this
was all filmed on board the *Orca II*.[9]

When fitted with a false transom, and with the resulting film foot-
age subsequently edited through the use of extremely quick scenes cut
at strategic points throughout the sea chase with the shark, *Orca II*
became, to a movie-goer, indistinguishable from its operational twin.
As Susan Murphy recalled: "The shot of the shark leaping onto the
back of *Orca II* [required] a number of balsa wood sterns that were all
lined up and ready to go [because] we ended up doing an awful lot of
takes. . . . That was one of the most dangerous effects we did all summer because if [we] failed to let go of the line at just the right time,
we'd have pulled the shark all the way through the [*Orca II's*] cabin."[10]

Both the on-screen vessels, the wooden operational *Orca* and the
fiberglass copy *Orca II*, took continued hard use and exposure to pun-
ishing conditions and by the conclusion of the production had been
thoroughly worn out. They had, after all, been intended only as temporary props in a rapidly executed production schedule set in demanding saltwater conditions. As Susan Murphy remembered: "How *Orca II*
didn't completely come apart in the water is beyond me. She was just
a prop—a hollow, fiberglass shell that was designed to hold together

just long enough to run through a few takes. [In the end], she was put through a lot more stress than she was built to withstand."[11]

For props that would one day be as famous as the ruby slippers of *The Wizard of Oz*, the maritime vessels from the production of *Jaws* suffered ignominious fates. Following the production of the film, the working fishing vessel *Orca* and the small boat belonging to the character of Ben Gardner both found their way to the West Coast, where they ultimately became part of a new tourist attraction at Universal Studios, the corporation responsible for the production of *Jaws*. Constructed on the banks of a shallow water filming area formerly known as Singapore Lake, the "existing Southeast Asian–style houses were redressed to look like [*Jaws'*] New England beach town."[12] The attraction became the key part of a studio tram tour and included signature elements from the film, among them the billboard welcoming visitors to Amity Island, a mechanical shark, and the working *Orca* and the Ben Gardner small boat.[13]

According to one Internet site, after the production of the film the *Orca* "was purchased by a special-effects technician, who restored the boat and later used it for sword fishing up and down the California coast. After the film was released and became a huge box-office success, the studio approached the former tech and purchased the boat back from him for use at the Universal Studios Tour. This is the original *Orca*, the boat used during all the major scenes requiring a moving, floating boat. The *Orca* was on display in the Amity lagoon." Apparently Steven Spielberg himself would occasionally take his lunches on board the *Orca*, where he would "just sit inside [and] reminisce and look back to that movie that launched my career. But I would go there alone and spend time on it and not tell anybody."[14]

Over time the wooden vessel deteriorated to the point where it could not be salvaged or repaired. According to Spielberg, during one return visit to the *Orca* he discovered the boat missing. "And I called up the head of the backlot and I said, 'What happened to the *Orca*?' He said, 'Well, it was just rotting there so we just took an ax and a couple chainsaws and cut it up for timber and shipped it out.'"[15] There is, however another slightly different version of the loss of the working *Orca*. "The pond wasn't that deep and when the wood rotted the boat sank in the shallow water, which flooded the lower cabin where the bunks/ head was and the engine room. In 1996 Universal apparently tried lifting the *Orca* out with a harness and the hull was so rotted that the boat simply broke in half."[16]

As for Ben Gardner's boat, the same Internet site reports that in 1981 it was repainted white from its original blue and that in "May 2005 [it] was removed for unknown reasons and binned in a skip during a major refurbishment of the area. . . . The boat was the last remaining piece of authentic *Jaws* movie history featured in the attraction."[17] As John Murdy, creative director for Universal Studios Hollywood, noted: "The *Orca* and Ben Gardner's boat are gone now. That's the thing about when you make something for a movie. It isn't built to last. It's built to last for the life of the production."[18]

From this perspective, both the *Orca* and Ben Gardner's boat far outlived the useful lives that could have been foreseen for them in the absence of routine and continuous maintenance that any long-lived maritime vessel must receive. By neglecting to remember that these movie and studio props were in fact originally constructed as working fishing vessels, and therefore in need of routine maintenance, Universal Studios condemned them to the same fate of any watercraft abandoned on any shore—to be slowly weathered, worn, rotted, and ultimately destroyed entirely.

As for the *Orca II*, the fiberglass copy of the working *Orca*, it was not an actual boat converted to movie use but instead a specifically created movie prop intended for temporary use during a rigorous film schedule in the spring and summer of 1974. As Susan Murphy noted, it was a miracle that it survived the hard use it received in the end. It was used for all the film's scenes requiring the *Orca* to heel or sink, and it then survived on the southern shore of Menemsha Creek, at the entrance to Menemsha Pond on Martha's Vineyard, for a decade longer than its working namesake. The story of its three decades of transformation from a movie prop to an outline of a hull in the sand to a series of metal flanges protruding from the sandy beach at low tide is a tale of looting, souvenir hunting, and transformational archaeology.

By September 21, 1974, as Matt Taylor writes in his pictorial history of the effect of the movie on the people of Martha's Vineyard, "all outward signs of *Jaws* had disappeared from the island."[19] This was not strictly the case. On that same day, after Captain Murphy sold one of his boats—a Formula boat called *Gotcha*—to an individual involved in the production of *Jaws*, he simultaneously purchased from Universal Studios the *Orca II*, along with three of the mechanical shark support barges and the filming platform, the SS *Garage Sale*.[20]

Murphy towed this mass of props and support vessels to his private strip of gently sloping sandy beach on Menemsha Creek, opposite the fishing village of Menemsha itself. When his original intent to use the materials to construct a new shed on his property was blocked by local authorities, the small fleet of *Jaws*-related vessels remained on his shoreline property for the next thirty years. There, as the natural environment took its toll, and as the movie grew into its present cult status, they also became the target of increasingly rabid souvenir hunters.

A forum post on the website Woodenboat.com, from a user named CrosbyStriper, presented three images of the *Orca II*, ostensibly taken

Three decades after the filming of *Jaws*, the remains of *Orca II* as they appeared in May 2005. Picked apart for years by souvenir scavengers, the remaining fiberglass hull was finally removed from the Menemsha Inlet shore by Lynn Murphy soon after this picture was taken. Photo by Bill Greene, *Boston Globe* via Getty Images.

during the 1980s. CrosbyStriper wrote that the *Orca II* "was abandoned in Menemsha Pond after the movie finished, and was left to rot, before being totally destroyed in 2005."[21] In fact these images show a clearly written notice on the starboard aft quarter of the boat that reads: "No Trespass." The flybridge is gone, the mast is broken and canted off the starboard gunnels, the breakaway balsa transom is long gone, yet the vessel is clearly identifiable as a copy of the *Orca*. David Hamblen's stepfather visited the site in the 1980s and the *Orca II*, with its broken mast and absent transom, was nevertheless largely intact, its bow facing eastward in Menemsha Pond and pointed at the remains of the SS *Garage Sale* about fifty feet away.[22]

Lynn Murphy himself is seen boating to the remains along Menemsha Creek and discussing them in a 1995 Universal Studios documentary called "The Making of Steven Spielberg's *Jaws*." This interview was incorporated into a 1997 British Broadcasting Corporation documentary, *In the Teeth of Jaws*.[23] As he drives to the site, Captain Murphy first describes the ruins of a metal framework as the remains of the SS *Garage Sale* that acted as a floating film studio and controlled the compressor and other machinery operating the shark.

As Murphy comes to the remains of the *Orca II* embedded in the sandy beach, he passes a larger white wooden vessel on the water side of the *Orca II* remnants. This is the *Far Star*, a vessel salvaged by the Murphys but which was not a part of their small fleet of *Jaws* watercraft. The remnants of *Far Star* became important in later years as the target of souvenir hunters who mistook it for the *Orca II*. As Murphy noted: "Just behind [the white vessel, the *Far Star*] is the *Orca*, what's left of her." Going ashore, Murphy places himself inside the *Orca II*, now filled with sand. "We're standing right inside of the *Orca*. This is the one that could sink on command. It had rows of barrels under here—they're still under here. They stood on end, on an angle. You pulled a lever and they would tip up, sections of them, so we could sink the corners of the boat, could level it [back] up and get it into position, so the shark could come up and take a bite out of the stern, smash it, and then we could do it again, until we got it right."[24]

A fortieth anniversary notice of the release of the film, published on the website Boston.com in 2015, included a photograph of the *Orca*

II remains as they appeared in 2005. The caption on the image read: "What is left of the *"Orka"* [*sic*], the boat featured in the filming of *Jaws*, lies rotting on the shore of Menemsha Creek. Owned by Lynn Murphy, the boat has been picked apart by souvineer [*sic*] scavengers over the years. Several [*sic*] *"Orkas"* were used in the filming of the movie, but only one remains on the island. This one was used in the sinking scene where Quint was eaten by the shark."[25] In this image all that remains of the *Orca II* is the bare hull attached to the barrel sinking framework underneath the hull, and even these remains show evidence of being cut away by saws. The dark paint of the lower hull has weathered away, leaving a white-gray lower hull with the still-surviving burgundy paint along the gunnels.

Prior to a direct visit to the remains, it was necessary to fix its location on the shores of Menemsha Creek. This was accomplished through the use of Google Earth images, which employ aerial and satellite data from the late 1990s to the present day. This progression of aerial imagery was extremely valuable not only in fixing the location of the *Orca II* but also for the variety of other watercraft and barges purchased by Lynn Murphy and towed to his private stretch of beach in the fall of 1974. It also enabled the documentation of the latter stages of the decay *of Orca II*.

In the earliest such image, from December 30, 2000, the remaining hull of the *Orca II* and the largely intact *Far Star* next to it are clearly visible, just north of the submerged remains of the SS *Garage Sale*. A sandy and now largely overgrown access pathway to the shoreline leads about two-thirds of a mile from the paved West Basin Road.

By April 29, 2005, the *Orca II* was visible only as a bare outline of a bow in the sand, while the *Far Star* next to it was still nearly intact. The submerged remains of the SS *Garage Sale* were much reduced but still fully visible.

By May 20, 2010, the *Orca II* still remained as the outline of a hull in the sand, and likewise the *Far Star* next to it had been reduced to a wreck of a boat. The submerged remains of the SS *Garage Sale* had begun to be broken up or covered by sand. Over the next five years aerial images reveal the site progressively covered in sand, until the most recent Google Earth image, from May 23, 2015, shows mere traces of

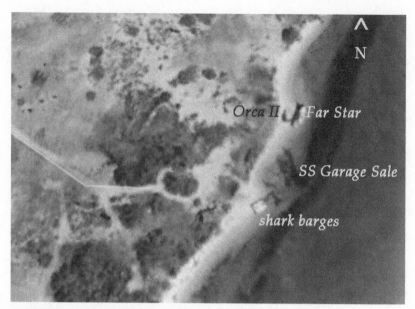

Google Earth image of the *Orca II* site from December 30, 2000.

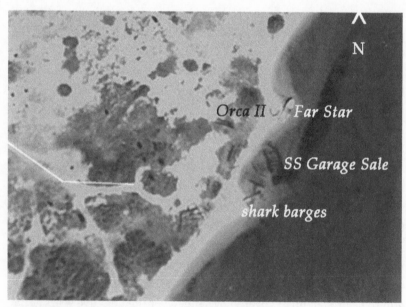

Google Earth image of the *Orca II* site from April 29, 2005.

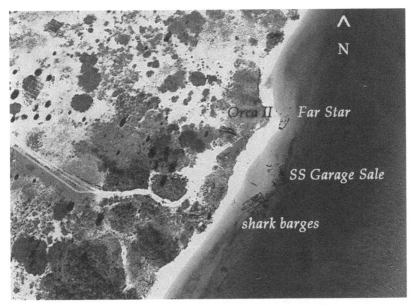

Google Earth image of the *Orca II* site from March 11, 2012. The *Orca II* has nearly disappeared, while the shark barges have been broken up and scattered, and the SS *Garage Sale* has largely disintegrated into the surf.

the *Orca II*, while all that remains of the *Far Star* adjacent to it is the outline of a hull in the shoreline sand. In this image the submerged remains of the SS *Garage Sale* can barely be seen at all.

Local historian Matt Taylor extensively documented the interactions of the local islanders with the cast and crew from Hollywood and made a brief reference to the fate of the remains purchased by Captain Murphy. "In 2005, Murphy moved the weather-beaten *Orca II* to a more secure location, free from the elements and unremitting torrent of souvenir hunters who for decades had picked away at the relic's most identifiable features."[26] In fact in that summer of 2005 the remains of *Orca II* were cut away from the metal structure that originally held the barrel mechanism, and some of those fiberglass segments were further reduced to small squares for sale as part of a limited edition hardcover of Taylor's book and for private sale.

The reasons for this somewhat drastic measure can be understood through the three-decade-long defense of the site by the Murphys. The necessity of such a guard can be glimpsed in a sampling of Internet sites related to Hollywood films, and in particular horror movies, populated by the fans who seek out and collect souvenirs of such films. At HorrorDomain.com, a site that self-describes as a place "horror fans, collectors, and producers all call home," there is a forum space specifically for discussions of horror movie collectibles.

In 2009 a visitor to the site with the username "Ryan" began a forum on the topic "Does anyone know anything about boats??? 'Jaws Question.'"[27] A seemingly innocent question about the kinds of boats used in the filming of *Jaws* quickly descended into a desire to reach the *Orca II* remains quickly so as to strip them for souvenirs. The user Ryan posted images taken by a friend on a visit to Martha's Vineyard with the comments: "My buddy . . . seen this boat on a land stripe across some river so I *geuss* and asked a boating guy there what it was. He said that it was the Orca from the movie Jaws. . . . When they were done shooting the film they drug it up on the sand and left it there to rot."[28]

The images showed Ryan's friend actually standing next to the *Far Star* that Lynn Murphy had positioned next to the remains of *Orca II*. Further images show the friend removing nails and even an entire plank from that vessel, in the mistaken belief that he is taking souvenirs from *Orca II*. In fact, as he pillaged segments from the *Far Star*, the remains of *Orca II* were right next to him in the sand. One image is captioned: "Pulling out a nail for collectors sake . . . lol He grabed me a chunk of wood from the back of the boat."[29] Not realizing that his friend was removing pieces of the wrong boat while the remains of the actual *Orca II* lay at his feet, the user Ryan was ecstatic, laying plans to accompany his friend on another visit to the island.

> If you noticed, there still is 1 "O" Screw [eyebolt] in the top de of the boat that at one time had a cable attached that lead up to the crows nest. It just kept the pole from falling over . . . lol. . . . When he goes again, I'm going along with and I am bringing a Crow Bar and a Hammer. . . . I'm going to stick that crow bar through the "O" and turn that fucker out of there. . . . It's comming with me provided nobody else nails it first. . . . I am also going to pull out about 10 nails and I am going to grab that ladder if it's still there along with a few boards from the back or de of the boat. . . .

I plan on making a HUGE DISPLAY with those pieces . . . I can't freaking wait!!! As far as I can tell, nobody claims the boat. . . . Not to many people know about it, so I would geuss otherwise it would all be gone by now. . . .

I just wish I could have either gotton the shark Jaws from it, or better yet, the steering wheel. . . . That would have been AWESOME!!! Someone out there has it and they are lucky as piss. . . . When he told me he found the boat, I nearly SHIT in my pants. . . . I shit even more when he told me he got me a piece of the wood from it.[30]

Six months into the back and forth on the subject of the remains of *Orca II*, a visitor to the site by the name "jlt13th" enters the discussion. He corrects the existing forum misunderstandings regarding the origin and the fate of both the *Orca* and *Orca II*, and then adds:

In 2005 the owner of Orca 2 (lynn murphy) cut up the boat with a chainsaw right before "Jawsfest" in order to keep Jaws fans visiting the island off his property. The Orca 2 is now completely gone. The white boat you have in the pics Ryan was a boat used to haul camera equipment and other stuff they needed for filming. It never appeared in the movie and unfortunately is not the Orca. The Orca 2 once sat right next to it though. You can see in the pics I attached below the two boats sitting together. The white boat is directly behind the Orca. As you can see the white boat still had its cabin at the time the pics were taken and is clearly not the Orca. Sorry to disappoint you. . . . In the pic you posted, you can see in front of where the two people are standing that there are sharp rusted bent metal things sticking up. Thats where Orca 2 once sat. If you look at the pic I posted you can see those same pieces of bent metal inside the hull of orca 2.[31]

While satisfied that the mystery of the remains of the *Orca II* had been solved, the forum user Ryan responded:

I am so glad to actually know for sure now, but in the same breath. . . . Damn thats a bummer. . . . That seriously hits the spot for me. . . . *Jaws* is my favorite Horror movie and I thought

I really had a piece of that boat. . . . Man that sucks . . . It just hurts. . . . Why do people have to fuck it up for others all the time? Why would they cut up the Orca 2 just because someone doesn't want people on there property? It's not like those people are there to fuck shit up. . . . The're just looking at the boat. I'll never understand why people do what they do . . . OR why they would neglect an important piece of movie history and just let the Orca 1 Rot . . . It's just not fair.[32]

Of course, these comments of dismay at the fate of Orca II were written by someone who earlier in the forum had proclaimed he was preparing to visit the site with "a Crow Bar and a Hammer" and that it was going home with him "provided nobody else nails it first."[33] The final statement of regret came in the forum about two years later, when a user named "joor" mentioned that he had purchased a piece of the white boat being offered on eBay, "certified" as coming from the Orca II. As joor lamented: "I m afraid i own a piece of wood now from a boat next to the remains of Orca 2. I bought it on e bay and he whas sure it is from the Orca boat, but i'm not anymore!"[34]

Reaching the site of Lynn Murphy's Jaws beach today involves first the special permission of the Natural Resources Department of the Federally Acknowledged Wampanoag Tribe of Gay Head (Aquinnah), which now manages the land. Ordinary access is restricted to tribal members only. One must then correctly time a forty-five-minute ferry ride from Woods Hole, Massachusetts, to the port of Vineyard Haven on the island of Martha's Vineyard, in order to arrive on the island about two hours prior to a low tide, when the remains of the Jaws vessels are most exposed. It takes another forty-five minutes to drive from Vineyard Haven to the remote segment of West Basin Road opposite Menemsha and then a further forty-five minutes to hike around a salt marsh and across some high white dunes to the shore.

It is a bit odd to apply for permission to visit a maritime archaeological site in order to locate and survey remains of a vessel that was not really a vessel from an event that was not really an event. The Orca II was not an actual maritime vessel engaged in typical maritime activities during an actual historical process. It is, rather, an artificial vessel from an imaginary story. In this, my journey to the shoreline suddenly felt similar to my attempted visit to the site of the Piltdown Man "discovery" in Sussex in the United Kingdom. The Piltdown Man was the most infamous hoax in the history of archaeology—probably the greatest in the history of science—so the real monument to the "discovery" of the Piltdown fossils commemorated a historical event that had never actually been. Small wonder then that the current property owners were anxious to keep at bay the curious—no matter how far they had traveled.

Like the historical Piltdown marker, the *Orca II* was not real in the sense of ever having been a functioning maritime vessel. Like the faked Piltdown Man fossils, the *Orca II* had been a copy of a real boat, a prop employed in a Hollywood sea adventure. In this way both sites bore something of a relationship to one of the many cautions offered by archaeologist Michael B. Schiffer in his seminal *Formation Processes of the Archaeological Record*.[35] Since "children formed a major part of the social unit[s]" examined by archaeologists, it is important to keep in mind the possibilities of child's play in the deposition of artifacts at an archaeological site.[36] As archaeologists reflexively search for the material cultures and the meanings behind the work of adults, they can in the process miss the remains of the activities of children and the often incomprehensible meanings behind them. The same can perhaps be said of the *Orca II*, a prop employed in the fictional representation of a sea hunt itself created by the interplay of a novelist, screenwriter, director, and a team of actors and crew.

The prop vessel nevertheless survives in an actual environment. Low tide in Menemsha Creek on Friday, May 19, 2017, occurred at 0924. The weather at the site was better than fine for a mid-May day on the island, with mostly sunny skies and temperatures in the mid-60s and rising rapidly. The creek was near calm, with a slight current running out to Menemsha Bight, and the shallow water at the *Orca II* was clear and warm. The winds were light and out of the southwest, the same direction toward which the bow of the remains of the *Orca II* point.

All that remains above the sand of the *Orca II* are six stanchions from the metal framework that was once fixed beneath the hull. The

The remains of the *Orca II*, aligned in a southwest–northeast line, as they appeared on May 19, 2017, at low tide. The remains of the *Far Star*, its bow awash and pointing northeast, can be seen on the left.

remains from "bow" to "stern" make up a rectangle 18'6" in length by 8' wide. Aft of these are four short lengths of pneumatic tubing that allowed the hull to simulate heeling or sinking. Three feet to port of the *Orca II* are the remains of the *Far Star*, much reduced and decaying into the sand but possessing very much the appearance of the actual working vessel that it once was. The *Far Star* had taken its place next to the *Orca II* some years after the production of *Jaws* and can be seen briefly in the 1997 BBC documentary *In the Teeth of Jaws*, as Lynn Murphy takes the film crew to a visit to the remains of *Orca II*.

The avaricious fans clamoring for a piece of the *Orca* could be forgiven for mistaking the remains of the *Far Star* for those of the *Orca II*. Whereas nothing identifiable as a vessel remains from *Orca II*, the *Far Star* still retains its aspect as the wreck of a working fishing boat. This, combined with its length of 37', are both close enough the original 42' *Warlock* to fool any trespassing fan of the movie unaware of the history of the site and the 2005 removal of the surviving remains of the *Orca II*'s fiberglass hull. Aside from a metal fuel tank still fixed into the hull of *Far Star*, only the ribs of that vessel remain—with the exception of

Low tide, Menemsha Creek, May 19, 2017. The remains of the SS *Garage Sale* are in the foreground. In the middle distance are the remains of the shark barges and, in the distance, the remnants of a car, possibly a dune buggy.

an 8' length of its deck that has been detached from the main wreckage, either by normal tidal or storm action or by humans in search of what they believed to be a piece of *Orca II*.

Sixty feet southwest of the *Orca II* are the remains of the SS *Garage Sale*. These remnants consist of metal frames covering an area 20' wide by 40' long and are largely awash in the light surf. They are aligned with the "bow" of the rectangular barge pointing in toward the shore and facing toward the northwest. Some of these frames have been removed from the *Garage Sale* and lie exposed in the sands farther up on the beach. There they have been entangled in a modern cable, perhaps in an attempt to chain them in place or to drag them off the beach.

Farther to the southwest along the beach, the remains of the frames of the shark barges are nearly entirely submerged and scattered in several segments in shallow water. Some of these frames appear to have been dragged above the high water mark and into the dunes, perhaps in Lynn Murphy's early attempts to transform his *Jaws* vessels into a shoreside hut. Farther yet along the beach and nearly 200' from the *Orca II* are the remains of a vehicle—possibly the remnants of a four-wheeled dune buggy—and perhaps the vehicle that towed what are now the remains of a boat trailer that exist farther up on the dunes

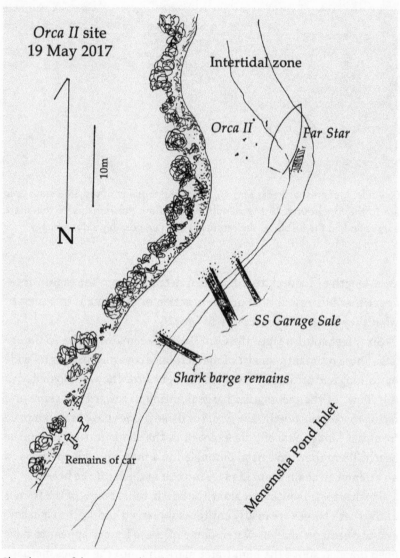

Orca II site
19 May 2017

N

10m

Intertidal zone

Orca II

Far Star

SS Garage Sale

Shark barge remains

Remains of car

Menemsha Pond Inlet

Sketch map of the *Orca II* shoreline from May 19, 2017. Courtesy C.L. Devlin.

alongside the now overgrown sandy pathway from West Basin Road to the *Jaws* beach.

The desire to possess a fragment of Hollywood archaeology has only intensified as *Jaws* and other iconic motion pictures have developed cult-like followings. A site on Facebook called Jaws Finatics has over three thousand members. Many of these "finatics" can deconstruct the original movie frame by frame, while others have intense interest in any form of art, artifacts, or souvenirs from or related to the film. On Twitter, @Jawscast75 has more than 3,200 followers, @thedailyjaws nearly 10,000.

With such legions of fans, artifacts that remain after the completion of a motion picture have become in many cases objects of particular cultural relevance and reverence. At least seven museums in the United States maintain large collections of such material culture. To be considered for acquisition by the Natural History Museum of Los Angeles County in Los Angeles, California, a Hollywood artifact "must be a signature piece from a major film or a significant piece of equipment—'something that defines the progression of the technology and the industry,' says collections manager Beth Werling."[37]

Likewise, the private auction market for movie artifacts has reached levels the original writers, actors, and directors probably never imagined as they organized their productions and constructed their props. A 2011 auction of Hollywood artifacts produced sales for single production cels (transparent celluloid sheets) from movies such as *The Empire Strikes Back* and *Sleeping Beauty* of nearly $50,000, while the crystal ball of the Wicked Witch of the West in *The Wizard of Oz* sold for $125,000. The entire auction resulted in nearly six million dollars in sales.[38]

A movie prop artifact that could be considered more on the level of an entire vessel, like the *Orca II*—in this case the car from the movie *Chitty Chitty Bang Bang*—sold at this same auction for more than $800,000. It offers an indication of what *Orca II* might have been worth had it somehow survived four decades of transformation processes both cultural and natural. The remains of *Orca II*, however, exist only as traces of metal and rubber in the sand. Even these, with the exceptions of the pneumatic rubber hoses that could survive another century, will soon disappear.

The *Orca II* can at least vanish alongside the remains of an actual maritime vessel. Fate has permanently intertwined the *Orca II* and the *Far Star*, in ways Lynn Murphy likely could never have foreseen. Both vessels are awash at high tide and both completely exposed at low water. Now fixed in place in their sandy cradles, they have nevertheless migrated to multiple places in time. The *Far Star* has been transformed from a working vessel to a salvaged, beached reclamation project, to a vessel mistaken for a Hollywood prop, and now to an outline of a vessel in the sand.

The *Orca II* has made a similar arc. It has transformed from Hollywood prop to shoreline curiosity, to a target for looters and souvenir hunters, to some salvaged fiberglass cut into souvenirs by its owners, and at the end to a few bits of metal protruding from the sand at low tide. In these closely related transformations, the two vessels face in opposite directions while heading to the same place: a gradual diminution to oblivion, one for years with its identity mistaken for its archaeological neighbor, the other famous but, in this last entry in its logbook, now nearly invisible.

2

The Throwaway Society
in the Mudflats

In the early 1970s archaeologist William Rathje began a study of land-fills in and around Tucson, Arizona. Le Projet du Garbàge, or the Tucson Garbage Project, pioneered the field of "Garbology" and showed that modern human waste disposal could be as revealing of human behavior as a prehistoric midden thousands of years old. Among the project results: Tucson residents threw out 10 percent or more of the food they brought home to consume, and middle-income households wasted more of their food than either the poor or the wealthy. This chapter relates a modest project to uncover the waste disposal patterns of some of Philadelphia's nouveau riche.

Poquessing Creek, like Menemsha another small tidal stream, forms the geographic boundary between the City of Philadelphia and Lower Bucks County, Pennsylvania. Before reaching its confluence with the Delaware River, the creek runs under Interstate Highway I-95 and the adjacent Amtrak northeast corridor rail line. In the 1990s a dense stand of old growth trees and new scrub foliage hid an old estate from those who, like my son and I, paddled the creek at high tide. In 1994, while kayaking into Poquessing Creek, my five-year-old son noticed a bottle eroding out of the mud bank below the estate, so we paddled over, pulled the bottle out, and washed off the mud to uncover a turn-of-the-century patent medicine bottle. After that we landed and found more intact bottles, along with plate fragments and the beginnings of what would become seven years of occasional explorations in the mudflats.

The Poquessing is the middle of three once-well-known Philadelphia-area creeks, with the Neshaminy on the north and the Pennypack on the south, purchased from local Native American Lenape Indians in 1683 by William Penn.[1] Dutch vessels cruised past the mouth of the creek as early as 1624, on their way upriver on the Delaware, to be followed over the next half-century by the Swedes and the British. A hinterland of Philadelphia until well into the twentieth century, the Poquessing empties into the Delaware River on the north side of a large nineteenth-century estate called Glen Foerd. Built as Glen Garry in 1850 by Charles Macalaster, a financial advisor to several U.S. presidents, the estate was purchased in 1893 and renamed and rebuilt over the next decade by U.S. Congressman Robert H. Foerderer, owner of a Philadelphia leather tanning concern. Foerderer planned the modifications of several of the structures on the estate, including—apparently in the early years of the twentieth century and around the time of Foerderer's death in 1902—changing the Macalester gas works along the Poquessing Creek into a boathouse. This structure was remodeled again, in 1915, into a cottage for one of two Foerderer daughters, Caroline, upon her marriage to a William Tonner. A large addition on the north side of the main estate building was added in the early 1930s.

Following on this sequence of occupation, one can divide the history of the estate into three convenient periods: Macalester (1850–93); Foerderer (1893–1930); and Tonner (1930–71). Given to the city of Philadelphia in the 1970s by Foerderer's descendants, the estate is maintained today by a local non-profit organization as part of Philadelphia's Fairmount Park. It is the last surviving publicly accessible riverfront estate in Philadelphia and a historic site listed on the National Register of Historic Places.

Situated on a high bank above the Poquessing Creek, Glen Foerd in the 1990s was hidden behind dense growth of foliage. This foliage also

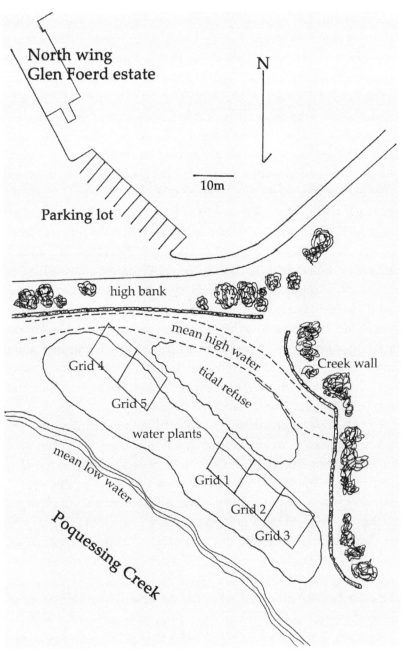

North wing
Glen Foerd estate

N

10m

Parking lot

high bank

Creek wall

mean high water

Grid 4

tidal refuse

Grid 5

water plants

Grid 1

mean low water

Grid 2

Grid 3

Poquessing Creek

Sketch map of the mud bank site below the estate of Glen Foerd in northeast Philadelphia. Courtesy C.L. Devlin.

shielded the estate from sight of refuse as it floated in and out of the brown waters of the muddy creek on each successive tide. At low tide a large mud bank spanned the distance between a partly crumbled and unused set of granite stairs, leading from the estate to a river wall at the mouth of the creek, and the end of the river wall up the creek some one hundred yards away. At high tide the creek reaches to the river wall, while during spring tides the mud bank is gradually uncovered until one can walk nearly halfway across the creek and even several hundred feet onto the uncovered bed of the Delaware River itself.

In a sense, the estate had faded behind its wall of scrub and foliage much as the Gilded Age had itself faded nearly a century earlier. Then the ugly concrete State Road bridge span covered the creek from the view of the daily commute of thousands of Philadelphians. Across the creek a tired apartment complex occupied the opposite bank, filled with working-class commuters unlikely to have received invitations to a Glen Foerd party had they lived a century earlier in the estate's heyday. We had moved into this complex in the early 1990s, and it was from the stony "beach" on its Delaware riverfront that my son and I launched our inflatable kayak on miniature adventures up Poquessing Creek, in search of whatever archaeological detritus the daily tides and recent rains might have revealed.

Indeed, these informal kayak surveys of the mud bank at low tide with my young son led to the discovery of numerous old bottles. This in itself was not especially noteworthy. Such bottles could be found at low tide along much of the Delaware. It was when we located several examples of turn-of-the-century Limoges porcelain, along with other fine examples of ceramics and glass, that it became evident we had very likely located the creekside dump of the Glen Foerd estate. If we could land and study a representative slice of the bank near the historic slipway leading to the estate's boathouse, we might locate enough of the estate's discarded glassware and flatware to be able to examine life on the estate in the late nineteenth and early twentieth century.

We had to consider other possibilities as well. There is a great and general downwash of debris coming down the creek, including most prominently in the late 1990s a quantity of shopping carts. These we

The author and Penn State Abington student Brad Ostrov attempt some stratigraphic archaeology on the edge of Poquessing Creek using a small water pump.

could tell from their plastic handles had marched down the creek from a pharmacy located about a mile away at a nearby mall. The carts—so numerous that we decided to name the sand bank that emerged every day at low tide "Shopping Cart Shoal"—extended, in the creek bed, from the bridge at State Road half a mile up the creek to nearly halfway across the Delaware River itself. The rise and fall of tides, the variable outflows of the creek, the rush of waters—especially during springtime floods—all pushed these shopping carts farther down the creek bed and into the Delaware. These moving artifacts were silent testimonials to the acquisition and discard of objects along this creek at the junction of a major U.S. city and its northeastern exurbs, a confused agglomeration of roadways and pathways, of houses and businesses both planned and seemingly random, and of forests and scrub and litter and mud.

It is the kind of place the British writer Marion Shoard describes as "edgelands," a space between urban and rural "characterized by rubbish tips and warehouses, superstores and derelict industrial plant, office parks and gypsy encampments, golf courses, allotments and fragmented, frequently scruffy, farmland. All these heterogeneous elements are arranged in an unruly and often apparently chaotic fashion against a background of unkempt wasteland frequently swathed in riotous growths of colorful plants, both native and exotic."[2]

The Glen Foerd estate is preserved in part as an example of "turn-of-the-century wealth and industry," or what the wealthy of a century ago believed was important. As we began a more intensive examination of the mud bank in the late 1990s it was with the goal of learning something of the objects tossed away by "turn-of-the-century wealth and industry" and its servants.

The mud bank below Glen Foerd is underwater for more than half the day. When the tide goes out much of the bank is uncovered, but even this uncovered segment is difficult to access because of loose mud and, in summer, a thick foliage of water plants making the mud surface inaccessible. However, these same environmental factors seem also to have acted to preserve and protect the artifacts embedded within the mud bank. The area is not easily accessible from landward, and to land from the creek or river requires a shallow draft boat such as a kayak, canoe, inflatable, or jon boat.

Climbing down to the mud bank in the spring of 1998, we found that the turn-of-the-century bottles and ceramics found in 1994 at the creek edge of the mud bank could also be found closer inshore, or in other words nearer to the Glen Foerd estate itself. In fact we found several examples of intact bottles with embossed brand names. This discovery led to additional visits over the next three summers, always at low tide, and now with undergraduates from my introduction to archaeology courses at Penn State Abington College. We laid out a baseline and placed five grid squares along it. This completed, we began to record and recover hundreds of artifacts of glass and porcelain and metal.

We also placed a smaller grid near a large semicircular log or board, one end of which was always exposed at low tide. We considered the possibility that it might be part of either a dock works or a vessel, as the confluence of the Poquessing and the Delaware has been described as an "historic graveyards of vessels."[3] So it was not outside the realm of possibility that we were looking at the remains of such a vessel.

Digging down into this smaller grid produced four artifacts, including a clay pipe bowl covered by a thin layer of surface muck. Clay pipe bowls are catnip to archaeologists, as a series of them can serve as an accurate calendar with which to date a site. We then found a collection of connected metal hooks and two pieces of a rubber strap, wrapped around a semi-circular length of wood or log exposed on the surface but deeply buried into the mud toward the creek. The rubber strap seemed to toss out any possibility of the wood being from a vessel—at least an early historic vessel.

The intact clay pipe bowl, on the other hand, with its stem diameter indicating a possible date of A.D. 1700, gave us pause, because it was wildly out of time sequence with the other artifacts associated with it. It was more than enough to trigger further archival research on historic activities on the creek.[4] In the end, we never could find a definite origin for the clay pipe bowl, as it is completely without identifying markings.

An early historic association with the lone clay pipe took another blow as we dug farther down into the tidal mud. There we found fourteen separate artifacts of a machine we later identified as a Bissell Carpet Sweeper, patented in 1880. Other artifacts included three intact early twentieth-century bottles, a shard of Depression-era Rock Crystal, and a glass bottle stopper of the type usually seen in salad dressing bottles. Nothing here to suggest the cargo of a Colonial-era vessel!

Below these, the ever-present water became a continuous problem and began to infiltrate the test pit, so we held off further exploratory work until we could bring a water pump to the site to allow more time in the pit. Unfortunately, nothing can hold back the tide, and certainly not the small and quickly overmatched water pump we lugged down to the mud bank.

As we ended our third summer of occasional visits to the site in August 2001, we had collected hundreds of glass and porcelain fragments as well as a remarkable number of intact bottles. The presence

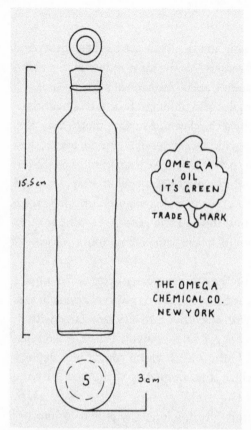

Sketch of the Omega Oil bottle recovered from Poquessing Creek and an Omega Oil advertisement recorded on the side of a New York City building in 2001.

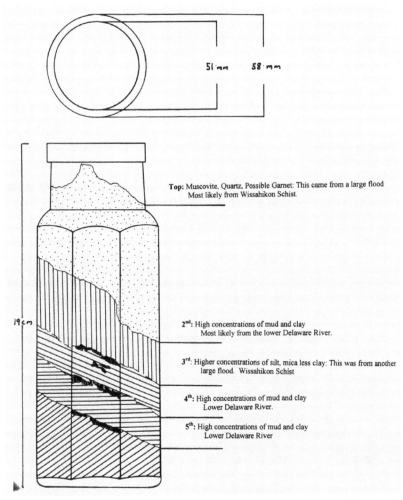

The apparent Heinz pickle bottle, recovered upright and intact, with its sedimentary record of flood events along the Poquessing Creek.

of so many intact bottles strengthened our feeling that we were at a dump site, as it would be unlikely for so many bottles to have traveled downstream and survived the turbulent tumbling of the tides along the mud and sand of the creek without fracturing.

Among these intact bottles was an apparent Heinz pickle bottle that was either placed upright in the creek or assumed an upright position after being discarded in the water and mud. It then remained in this upright position, so far as we could tell, for a century, recording in its narrow confines a remarkable stratigraphy of the passage of sediment-bearing floods.

We shifted the many bottles and plate and cup fragments to a make-shift archaeology lab at Penn State Abington. There it soon became clear that most of the surface finds, as well as those from the test pit, date from approximately 1900–1939, with the majority dating to the 1920s and 1930s.[5] This seems to place the surface and near-surface artifacts recovered from the end of the Foerderer period and beginning of the Tonner era at Glen Foerd. Artifacts as recent as 1998 came from a lone McDonald's Happy Meal cup that drifted into the mud bank just after the new Animal Kingdom theme park opened at Disney World in Florida in April 1998, as this logo is printed on the cup. With some notable exceptions, the bottlework recovered from the surface survey reflects summer party use, as it includes numerous Heinz ketchup and pickle bottles. The apparent Heinz pickle bottle found upright in the mud, filled with a variety of flood sediment, was typical.

The other significant number of intact bottles seems to indicate a concern with personal health and well-being on the part of people living on the estate. Among these are a Kruschen Salts bottle (a laxative used in the 1930s); an Omega Oil bottle (a kind of turn-of-the-century cure-all); a jar of Chesebrough petroleum jelly; an apparent make-up jar from the Menley & James company; and two as yet unidentified bottles, one with a strange "3xii" symbol, which appears to be a medicine bottle; and another with the name "Maggi" embossed on it, apparently the size and shape of a perfume bottle.

Taken together, these bottles and jars seem to indicate a turn-of-the-century lifestyle of gatherings and parties, one clouded by concerns for personal appearance along with apparent measures to ensure constitutional regularity and relieve the stresses of that lifestyle. Or, as one of my students put the hypothesis more succinctly: "Rich people are full of it." It would be interesting indeed to learn whether this dichotomy between status as reflected in the European porcelain and concerns for health as reflected in patent medicine bottles is a local or general phenomenon on similar archaeological sites of American wealth.

The plate fragments found during our surface survey carried the maker's mark of GDA, or Gérard, Dufraisseix and Abbot, a porcelain maker in Limoges, France. GDA produced porcelain for export to the upscale American consumer market between 1902 and 1941. This export Limoges was sought after for wedding gifts of turn-of-the-century debutantes. Finding it combined with a single shard of clear and downscale Depression-era Rock Crystal, we can hypothesize the situation in several ways. The Limoges would seem to indicate turn-of-the-century wealth, while the Rock Crystal could reflect downscale living during the Great Depression. On the other hand, the Rock Crystal can also be seen as a cheap, almost disposable ware for outdoor functions, indicating that a party lifestyle flourished even in the Depression. What seems most interesting is that both styles seem to have been discarded at the same time, and from associated artifacts, this deposition seems to have taken place in the mid-1930s.

The mud bank near the confluence of Poquessing Creek and the Delaware River is an extremely complex archaeological site in terms of formation processes. It is both riverine and tidal, both a wet site and alternately a dry land site. In extremely cold winters, ice from the upper Delaware can career into the river wall. In dry summers the water levels can drop so low that at low tide one can walk nearly halfway across the Delaware River. Below a layer of coal or coke near the surface, with its associated limestone or calcium carbonate, is a thick layer of organic matter, suggesting that the creek was much cleaner before the turn of the century, when a shad fishery is believed to have existed at the mouth of the Poquessing until at least 1891. If the coal/coke/limestone is associated with the estate, and the artifacts associated with it point to such a conclusion, then it could be residue from the gas production facility said to have been located in the current Swiss-style house on the estate during the Macalester years.

Our basic investigations of the site had left us with innumerable questions. What were the artifactual transitions between occupation eras at the estate and the human behaviors within those eras? What is the role of water plants in artifact retention in or movement within the mud bank? What is the exact stratigraphy of the various layers of the mud bank? Could these layers be probed for evidence stretching back to potential Native American occupations of the area? What were the precise movements and disposition of artifacts down the creek and out to the river? One of my students even found and photographed a surviving Omega Oil advertisement on the side of a building block in New York City, opening the door to all sorts of advertising and branding research related to the artifacts at the site.

These were all promising areas of inquiry as we wrapped up our final visit to the site in late August 2001. Two weeks later, as I paddled my canoe along the creek, my mobile phone rang in my pocket. Terrorists had attacked the World Trade Center in New York City—not very far, as it happens, from that surviving Omega Oil advertisement. I was being called to active duty in the U.S. Coast Guard Reserve. As I turned the canoe around, I thought I would paddle back to Poquessing Creek within a few weeks, perhaps a month at most. In the end, I remained on active duty for a year and a half.

When I finally returned home and had a chance to return to the creek, I found there a new sea wall. The site of much of our mud bank research had been excavated with a large dredge, cleared and scattered. I returned to the college, to teaching and to my Arctic research, which I expected to complete within a few months and then return to the creek. Fifteen years later, that research in the High North is still not complete. As for the bottles and plate fragments recovered from the mud of Poquessing Creek, they remain locked in a closet next to my office at Abington College. There they await a final determination of whether the very rich really *are* "full of it."

3

Airship Underwater

In Search of the USS *Akron*

Sometimes a project you have given up hope of achieving gains new life in seemingly random and unexpected ways. A project to locate the massive remains of a U.S. Navy lighter-than-air dirigible was one such. In a further irony, though it brought to bear the world's most sophisticated undersea survey machine, we failed to find a single trace of one of the largest artifacts ever created by human hands.

It would be nearly two years before I returned to my college and, so it seemed then, to any further archaeological explorations. Then, in the natural irony of events, one project dormant for nearly a decade was given new life. When the USS *Akron* (ZRS-4), a giant U.S. Navy airship, crashed and sank off the coast of New Jersey in 1933, it was the greatest air disaster to that moment in U.S. history. It had long been a goal to discover and document the wreckage of the *Akron*, submerged somewhere in New York Bight, but the project never materialized. When an offer came to do some post-9/11 historical and archaeological liaison work between the U.S. Navy and the U.S. Coast Guard, I jumped at the chance to propose a joint service operation.

14 June 2002: 0224

It's midwatch on board the submarine NR-1. Sitting alone in the small two-person mess surrounded by twin computers, book-shelves, and a condiment rack. Before turning in the captain said the sub would run some more side-looking sonar sweeps over-night before we surface at 0630 for a rendezvous with the sub's mother ship *Carolyn Choest*. I've been on board for thirty-nine hours, and will be for another eight, as we collect more visual and sonar data from the reported last location of the *Akron*. This we will analyze and use to plan for direct scuba dives to the site.

The giant lighter-than-air vessel USS *Akron* was designed for a single purpose: to scout the vast reaches of the Pacific Ocean for the U.S. Navy's Pacific fleet. Early in the interwar period of 1919–39, the navy sensed potential pressure in the western Pacific from the Japanese navy and planned its annual "Fleet Problems" exercises accordingly. During the early 1930s *Akron* was both state-of-the-art technology for long-range aerial scouting and a practical component of the develop-ing U.S. Navy strategy for the American defense of the Pacific, where the unique capabilities of an airship were a geographic necessity. If in fact "airships were paradigms of the men and nations that built and flew them," then *Akron* reflected the advance guard of naval doctrine building in the inter-war period, and that doctrine revolved around a victory at sea over the naval forces of Imperial Japan.[1]

Commissioned at its namesake city in Ohio in the fall of 1931, *Ak-ron* thereafter suffered a series of accidents, some minor, one fatal, and the final one catastrophic, that conspired to make her operational career very brief. In early 1932 a gust of wind at the Naval Air Station in Lakehurst, New Jersey, crumpled the lower fin of the ship as it sat at its mooring, preventing the dirigible from making a scheduled voy-age to Hawai'i in March. There her purpose was to have been to inter-cept and thwart the primary component of Grand Joint Exercise No. 4, Fleet Problem XIII: a carrier-based attack on Pearl Harbor from the northwest. With its participation in this eerily foreshadowing exercise canceled, *Akron* after repairs at Lakehurst did participate in scouting force exercises that June, impressing the fleet with her potential as a

USS *Akron* (ZRS-4), moored near the airship hangar at Naval Air Station Lake-hurst, New Jersey, circa 1931–33. U.S. Naval History and Heritage Command Photograph, catalog #NH 44098.

long-range scout in operations west of Hawai'i. But this was not before an attempt to moor the airship in San Diego killed two sailors.

The heavier-than-air component of *Akron* as a "flying aircraft carrier" made significant strides as well. The airship was large enough to carry three F9C Sparrowhawk aircraft in her interior hangar, and improvements in scouting technique by lieutenants D. Ward Harrigan and Donald M. Mackey enabled *Akron* to reconnoiter a path some 200 nautical miles wide and 10,000 nautical miles long. But *Akron* never had the chance to deter or provide early warning of hostile naval maneuvers in the Pacific at that most critical moment in American history on December 7, 1941.

In early April 1933 the airship departed Lakehurst on what was intended as a routine cruise northeast to New England to calibrate radio direction beacons. The light duty no doubt led to the presence of numerous supercargo on board. These included Rear Admiral William A. Moffett, medal of honor recipient and chief of the Bureau of Aeronautics from 1921 to 1933, and his aide, Commander Henry Barton Cecil, along with the commanding officer of the Naval Air Station at Lakehurst, Commander Fred T. Berry. The vice-president of Mack Trucks, a man fascinated by the potential of rigid airships to accomplish civilian cargo work, was also on board the flight. Altogether, the *Akron* left Lakehurst with seventy-six officers, crew, and passengers. About the only naval personnel not on board were the pilots of the scout aircraft squadron, who, along with their aircraft, had been left behind for this particular mission.

The *Akron* passed over the New Jersey coast and maneuvered out to sea in an attempt to avoid a patch of severe weather. It was unable to outrun this area of low pressure, and the altimeter in the ship's control gondola gave a false indication that the *Akron* was much higher in the sky than it actually was. As lightning flashed, strong wind gusts buffeted the ship. Just after midnight, as a violent updraft lifted the ship and was followed immediately by a similar downdraft, the *Akron's* commander, Commander Frank T. McCord, ordered ballast dropped and full speed ahead.

The lifting of the airship's bow had forced the tail into the ocean. As the *New York Times* described it the next morning, these combined actions had the effect of grinding the ship in the ocean. In an examination of the crash for the Naval Institute's *Proceedings* a year later, Lieutenant Commander Charles E. Rosendahl noted similarly that "the sudden arrest of a 200-ton mass going forward at a speed of over 100 miles an hour [and] slapping [it] down onto and into the incompressible unyielding water. It might as well have been concrete."[2]

A German ship called *Phoebus* was cruising in the area of the *Akron's* flight when its crew saw lights descending into the ocean just after midnight. The *Phoebus* altered course and within thirty minutes found itself in a wide sea of twisted wreckage and drowning men. All but three of the seventy-six on board, and including Rear Admiral Moffett and all his guests, were lost. *Phoebus* recovered the executive officer, Herbert V. Wiley, alive but unconscious, as well as three sailors, one of whom, Chief Radioman Robert W. Copeland, never regained consciousness and died on board the German vessel. Not until Wiley regained consciousness at about 0130 in the morning did the crew of the Phoebus learn that they had cruised into the wreckage of the USS *Akron*.

The search and rescue that followed was both difficult and dangerous. The *J-3*, a navy blimp sent out to join the search, also crashed, with the loss of two men. The first American vessel on the scene, the Coast Guard cutter *Tucker*, arrived at 0600 and took on board the survivors and the body of Chief Copeland. Among the other vessels that combed the area for any other possible survivors were the Coast Guard cutter *Mojave*, the Coast Guard destroyers *McDougal* and *Hunt*, and two Coast Guard aircraft. They were joined by the navy's heavy cruiser *Portland* and the destroyer *Cole*.

One of the survivors, Boatswain's Mate 2nd Class Richard E. Deal, brought ashore to the Brooklyn Naval Hospital, recalled to a fellow patient how the drowning crew called out "cheery farewells to each other as, one by one, they gave up their fight against the rough sea and drowned after the crash. 'Well, good-by!' he said he heard them say. And: 'Good luck to you—wherever you're going.'"[3]

Two weeks later the U.S. Navy salvage vessel *Falcon* located the wreck in one hundred feet of water, about thirty nautical miles east of the Barnegat Lighthouse. Navy divers and the *Falcon's* grappling hooks salvaged the starboard side and bottom of the control car, along with a few of the duralumin girders, all returned to the giant hangar at Lakehurst. As the search for wreckage continued, a congressional investigation began.

The *Akron's* loss spelled the beginning of the end for the rigid airship in the U.S. Navy. Franklin Roosevelt, inaugurated as president just one month prior to the crash, commented that morning: "The loss of the *Akron* with its crew of gallant officers and men is a national disaster. . . . Ships can be replaced, but the nation can ill afford to lose such men."[4] In fact an airship with the size and capabilities of USS *Akron* was almost impossible to replace in these years prior to the invention of air defense radio detection and ranging systems.

It is difficult today to conceive of a flying machine on the scale of *Akron*. An officer in the control cabin could relay messages to crew along the upper keel more than thirteen stories above, or call to crew at the stern control station, a seventh of a mile away. At ten tons and nearly eight hundred feet in length, the airship was virtually the same size,

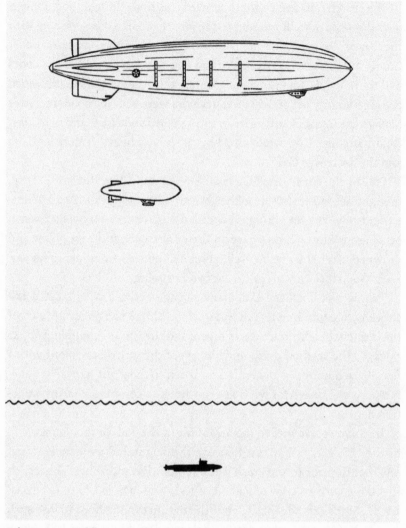

Relative sizes of the USS *Akron*, the blimp *J-3* lost while searching for *Akron*, and the submarine *NR-1*. Herman Van Dyk.

if hardly the same weight, as RMS *Titanic*, and as with *Titanic*, her size and advanced design touched boundaries of technology that held both promise and terror for society. The wreck of the airship went undisturbed for more than half a century until 1986, when a team led by adventure novelist Clive Cussler announced that they had relocated the site.

Six years later, during doctoral work in archaeology at Rutgers University, the presumed location of the *Akron* wreck off the coast of New Jersey made it an inviting target for both primary research and studies in public history and historical archaeology. Combined with fieldwork at the site of Walter Wellman's airship base in arctic Norway, these projects offered entry into larger themes within the archaeologies of exploration and aerospace technology and the growing societal awareness that such cultural resources were both inherently fragile and increasingly in need of protection if they were to survive as testaments to human endeavor.

A 1994 Department of Defense cultural resources workshop at the Naval Air Station in Pensacola, Florida, offered the perfect venue to talk about this research. I left Pensacola after several days with a notebook full of contacts within the navy's impressive historical and cultural resource agencies. One of these contacts was with the team that managed the navy's secretive nuclear research submarine, the *NR-1*. Over the next few years, as I wrote up the fieldwork from the Wellman airship site in Norway and searched for something approximating a regular job, I continued to bounce proposals to the Naval Submarine Base in Groton, Connecticut, to use the *NR-1* to search for the remains of the *Akron*.

In late 2000, about when it seemed time to give up on the project and move on, I received a call from the *NR-1's* executive officer. Plans were afoot to drive the submarine in the fall of 2001 from Groton to North Carolina to survey the site of the famous Civil War iron-hulled steamship USS *Monitor*. The presumed *Akron* site was more or less *en route*, and the submarine's Simrad side-looking sonar should allow it to locate the wreckage and then record it with the sub's high definition CLD video cameras.

The terror attacks of 9/11 further delayed this work for nearly a year. By then I was on active duty myself, with the U.S. Coast Guard Reserve, documenting the Coast Guard's response to 9/11 at the service's history office led by Dr. Robert "Doc" Browning. When the navy decided to take up the *Akron* search again, in June 2002, Doc and I were welcome to come on board—provided we could find our own transport off the sub as it resumed its southward course toward the wreck of the

Monitor. Fortuitously, during our 9/11 work we had interviewed dozens of active duty personnel. These people include some of the most highly trained, intensely motivated problem solvers anywhere. One of these was the director of operations for the First Coast Guard District in Boston, Captain William R. Webster. Captain Webster possessed an intense love of maritime history and had been trying for years to organize a search for the wreck of the cutter *Bear*, perhaps the Coast Guard's most famous vessel and one lost in the Atlantic in 1963 after a long and remarkable career in the polar regions. If we could demonstrate the ability to locate the *Akron*, we could propose the wreck as a potential National Underwater Preserve, to be managed as an important ground for both scientific research and submerged cultural resource management practices. The next logical target would then be the *Bear*.

Captain Webster recognized that a survey of the *Akron* site by *NR-1* offered an opportunity for operational liaison between the submarine, its surface tender, and a Coast Guard patrol boat. So, at the conclusion of the underwater archaeology survey, the submarine would surface and transfer Doc Browning and me to a Coast Guard patrol boat from Cape May, on board which we could document the run from the site to shore, data crucial to the ultimate protection of the site. This liaison also offered a chance to demonstrate that close cooperation between the Navy and Coast Guard in maritime archaeology research could help both services in the protection of their unique submerged cultural resources.

That is how, on June 11, 2002, Doc Browning and I found ourselves on board the *NR-1's* support vessel, *Carolyn Choest*, as it towed the submarine from Groton toward the area where *Akron* was lost. At noon the following day I hopped onto the *Choest's* rigid hull zodiac for the transfer to the submarine. This involved some fine small boat handling, with choppy seas lifting the zodiac alongside the sub as the same waves broke over the sub's decks. I climbed onto the sub with a dry bag containing my own cameras, some extra batteries and digital video tape, some medicine for one of the crew, and the last coordinates of the wreck of the *Akron*.

Few inanimate objects attain beauty in the pursuance of their courses, and yet, to me, at least, the flight of this ship was far lovelier than the swooping of a bird or the jumping of a horse. For it seemed to carry with it a calm dignity and a consciousness of destiny which ranked it among the wonders of time itself.

It was the *Akron* . . .

I wondered if it were only the beauty of the ship which aroused my emotions so keenly or if it were because I vaguely realized that our lives would become so involved in her fate.

Widow of an *Akron* officer, writing in 1934[5]

I am not sure what I expected as I climbed down into the cramped and private world of the small submarine—probably that submariners were as highly strung and boisterous as were stereotypical aviators. But quite the opposite was true. The sub was intensely close and dark and lit with the low glow of red lamps and panel lights. The voices of the captain and crew were so low, almost whispers, that one had to strain to hear them. It was as if one had entered some strange high tech underwater chapel. The nuclear reactor, which took up two-thirds of the length of the sub, was off-limits behind a secure hatch. The space that remained was reduced to a narrow passage separating the minuscule mess and berthing areas for the crew of a dozen from the even smaller head and a "galley" that was little more than a tiny microwave oven, a small refrigerator, and an even smaller sink. A set of rules and regulations posted at the entry hatch offered instructions for, among other scenarios, the boarding of the sub by pirates.

Near the bow of the sub was the driving station with its dozens of instruments, and underneath this was a cramped floor where two prone observers could peer from small portholes into the undersea gloom. Submarine captain Lieutenant Commander Dennis McKelvey's "cabin" was a sleeping bag rolled out directly behind the seats for the sub drivers. The captain's sleep amounted to brief catnaps, as he would often be awakened by a gentle touch from one of the drivers if there was any doubt as to the sub's attitude, positions, movements and, especially, potential obstructions.

As the sub descended, I briefed Captain McKelvey on the history of the *Akron* site and we speculated on what might remain of the airship after seventy years. The list was long and included the tail section—separated from the rest of the airship during the crash—as well as crew effects and potential crew remains, the remains of the partly recovered control car, and the hangar from which *Akron's* aircraft were launched.

The *Akron* site presented special problems for the *NR-1*. The submarine was designed and built as a deep submergence vessel to conduct operations near the depth limits of the world's oceans—though precisely how deep it could go was a closely guarded naval secret, as were most of its operations. At 150 feet long and nearly fifteen feet high, the submarine would be searching for the wreckage of an airship thought to be sticking up perhaps ten feet from the bottom of the ocean and resting in little more than eighty feet of water. It was a very tight fit and so our search for *Akron* was necessarily slow and extremely cautious.

We began in deep water some thirty nautical miles from the presumed coordinates of the wreck and proceeded to crawl "uphill" at about four knots toward the shallow waters around the wreck. In a few hours the powerful side-scan sonar was switched on as the sub cruised along with about sixty feet of water above its decks and just thirty below its keel. The *NR-1* passed directly over the coordinates given for the *Akron* wreckage in the National Oceanic and Atmospheric Administration's wreck database and found nothing. Neither did we find wreckage with the navy's own coordinates from its 1933 salvage of parts of the airship.

13 June: 0200
Midwatch. The submarine commenced an expanding box search, outward from the NOAA coordinates, each box drawn at the limits of the sub's side-scan sonar. I listen in on snippets of banter passing back and forth from an observer stationed at the small viewports to the XO and the helmsman at the conn. The skipper is asleep in his "cabin." We are either circling the area of the wreck or it is just outside the box search area. Or else the girders have been so compressed and flattened into the sand that they are

no longer distinguishable with sonar from the surrounding sand waves. The duralumin evades the magnetometer.

By the closure of the third box in the survey, the *NR-1* was fully a nautical mile east from the presumed coordinates of *Akron*. It was here that the sonar picked out what could have been a debris field, but one apparently covered with sand. We noted a similar anomaly during the fourth box search, but again it was difficult to make any real determination of a collection of longitudinal girders from the surrounding sand and the noise in the readings coming from the surface waves just a few feet above us.

The midwatch concluded in frustrating fashion, and I retreated at 0800 to a narrow bunk to sleep. My eyes had barely shut when a petty officer jostled me awake. Sonar had picked up an anomaly to the east— and it was a big one.

I arrived at the conn to find the captain discussing the find with the men who had made it: LCDR Lawrence D. Ollice Jr., and Chief of the Boat Michael C. Uherek. The *NR-1* had slowed to a two-knot crawl to record an outline of twisted metal and what even appeared to be remains of giant gas bags. The submarine was in water twenty feet deeper than the recorded depth of the *Akron* wreckage. But the debris field was approximately two hundred feet long, just the right length for the tail section presumably broken from the ship as it struck the ocean.

Captain McKelvey turned the sub around and slowed it to less than two knots in an attempt to bring the wreckage into the sight of the observer in the viewport station. He sent me into the observation deck in the hope that I might see some recognizable feature in the mass of wreckage. In fact, a pile of what appeared to be twisted metal soon appeared directly under us. We hovered just above the wreckage, but with just a foot or two of visibility. The skipper brought the sub to a full stop to prevent its entanglement in the chaotic jumble of debris.

After this hopeful beginning, we turned along the axis of this wreckage to see if we could pick up a debris trail that might lead us to the main body of *Akron* wreckage. Even if we had found the tail section, there was another nearly 600 feet of wreckage still out there somewhere. We picked up speed, moving at three knots, but over the

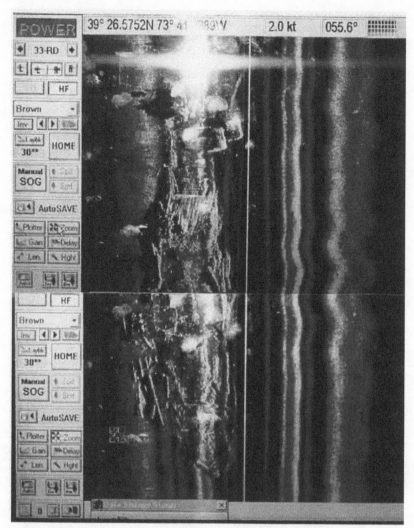

The hard sonar anomaly recorded by *NR-1*, 13 June 2002: 0930.

course of several more hours of searching found nothing. No further traces of debris. Once again, the weird squiggles in the sand produced by the action of water made it nearly impossible to differentiate between these natural formations and anything like the long, twisted girders of a wrecked airship.

After four hours *NR-1* returned to the initial debris field for three more passes along it. The submarine spent another day on the site, but we soon concluded that any further observation would require the presence of scuba divers. We surfaced at 0630 on June 14 for Doc Browning to come on board for several hours to receive a briefing from Captain McKelvey on the mission to this point and to confer with him on the potential of future missions of mutual interest to both the U.S. Navy and Coast Guard.

Doc and I soon found ourselves in the tower of the sub as the cutter *Mako*, the Coast Guard coastal patrol boat Captain Webster in Boston had arranged to retrieve us, stood off the submarine. A zodiac from *Mako* plucked us from *NR-1*, and in a few hours we were ashore in Cape May, not far from the point where *Akron* had left the coast of New Jersey on its final flight nearly seventy year earlier.

A few months later I wrote a brief note describing the *Akron* search for *Naval History* magazine. The note was prudently restrained in celebrating the apparent discovery and described what we *"believed* to comprise the stern of the airship. If this supposition is borne out by direct scuba surveys, then further study of this section of the wreck,

I took this blurry image through the *NR-1's* viewport. This direct view of the wreckage, combined with the hard sonar return, fit neatly how one might think a pile of airship girders might appear after seventy years on the bottom of the ocean and led us to think we might have located the site of the USS *Akron*.

as well as further searching for the remaining forward section of the airship, will be required."[6] This prudence whenever an apparent archaeological discovery was made with remote sensing technology was increasingly difficult to maintain in a world of 24/7 cable news (and was destined to become virtually impossible in the hyper-driven social media markets that lay just a few years into the future). But there was no getting around the fact that the highly suggestive wreckage was both a nautical mile from where it was supposed to be and in substantially deeper water—and when data do not add up neatly, it is always wise to double check the math. The only way to verify the *NR-1* survey was to put divers down on the site.

Our caution was quickly rewarded. Only a few days after the *Naval History* note appeared, a Canadian diver and film producer named Mike Fletcher contacted me and asked about our plans to put human eyes on the *Akron* site. Well, at the time, we had none, so Mike, along with film producer John Davis of Eco-Nova Productions in Halifax, Nova Scotia, suggested a collaboration to dive to ground truth the remote *NR-1* data. Mike and John had just begun the production of a television series called *The Sea Hunters*, based around the global shipwreck adventures of the same Clive Cussler who had identified the area of the *Akron* wreck in the 1980s. My enthusiasm doubled when I learned that the archaeological diver and advisor to the series was James Delgado. I had not met Jim Delgado personally, but he had an international reputation as one of the finest maritime archaeologists around and we had many colleagues in common, including Doc Browning.

Mike and John and their film crew were soon set up in my living room, filming the introduction to our episode: a phone call from me to Clive Cussler asking his Sea Hunters to renew the search for *Akron*. This completed, Mike and John traveled to the New Jersey shore to interview local scallop dredger captains about where they had noted obstructions in the area where *Akron* went down. With this additional detail, along with the precise position of the wreckage provided by *NR-1*, Mike and John, along with Jim Delgado and sonar expert Vince Capone set off in a charter vessel, the *Venture III*.

Two hours later, just an eighth of a mile from the *NR-1* coordinates, *Venture III* slowed its course so that Vince's side-scan sonar could go to work. Within seconds he located the same suggestive collection of wreckage we had recorded from the submarine. It was at this point that Jim Delgado's long experience with maritime surveys came to the fore. As everyone excitedly looked at what they believed to be *Akron*, Jim offered an immediate caution.

"That's a real hard return [on the sonar image]. That's not what I'd expect from aluminum." The pieces of wreckage were about twenty feet long and sticking up above the surface of the ocean about five to ten feet. "That kind of a reflection, that's not some light piece of aluminum girder. It looks like it could be, but of course you don't know until you go."[7]

Mike and Jim suited up for a direct dive to the site. As they descended to the debris, the evidence was at first encouraging. The metalwork certainly appeared to be girders. Then the two divers came across the reasons for the hard sonar target: large heavy pieces of sheet iron near two gigantic Scotch marine boilers—most definitely *not* the kind of equipment carried on board a lighter-than-air vessel! It was as if someone had shredded an entire freighter to pieces and then dumped the fragments into the ocean.

These direct observations instantly eliminated the wreckage we had seen remotely from *NR-1* from being in any way connected with the USS *Akron*. This, of course, led to multiple additional questions. Just what was this strange and unconnected wreckage, and more important, just where was the *Akron*? Days of further sonar surveys, with Mike Fletcher diving to inspect each promising site directly, produced not a trace of evidence we could link to the airship.

Mike and John and I went back to the beginning and studied the original crash and salvage records, the record of the congressional hearings, a scallop dredger's chart of wrecks in the *Akron* area—anything that we might have overlooked or that might offer a new search area. This work produced a new sonar survey area and more scuba dives but still no evidence of one of the largest pieces of aeronautical technology ever produced.

One hypothesis is the total corrosion of the light duralumin structure in the heavily scoured and turbulent saltwater shallows where the airship went down. Duralumin is an alloy consisting of 94% aluminum,

4% copper, 1% magnesium, and some small amounts of manganese and silicon. A National Advisory Committee for Aeronautics report produced while *Akron* was under construction studied the corrosion embrittlement of duralumin and found that the magnesium in the alloy would lead to accelerated corrosion in saltwater.[8] *Akron* of course was designed to fly high above any saltwater and did—until its final and fatal mission.

Another potential hypothesis is that the wreck, torn apart by both the original crash and subsequent partial salvage, has simply been dragged over by heavy scallop dredges for so long that it has been reduced to small fragments now lying under waves of shifting sand. This, perhaps in combination with an accelerated corrosion of the duralumin, might account for our inability to locate it today.

Over the next decade Mike Fletcher and I would touch base every few months to bounce around ideas for new expeditions, and each time we would return to the mystery of the airship under the sea. Surveys off the coast of California of the remains of the *Akron's* sister ship, USS *Macon*, documented an enormous debris field complete with the remains of the airship's patrol aircraft. The survival of the *Macon's* wreckage, albeit in vastly deeper waters, offers some hope that the *Akron* may yet be located.

The *Macon* site was entered into the National Register of Historic Places in 2010. As for the crash site of the *Akron*, with its enormous loss of life, no such memorial has occurred, as it continues to elude even the most detailed searches. In a final irony, the submarine *NR-1* itself was decommissioned in 2008 and cut up for scrap. Several years later the navy announced that small bits of *NR-1* would be preserved in the Submarine Forces Library and Museum in Groton, where Doc Browning and I joined the sub so hopefully back in the summer of 2002.

4

The Archaeological Shorelines of the High North

Global climate change has forced archaeologists to initiate intensive rescue missions at sites around the world where rising seas threaten to destroy many sites and put others underwater. Nowhere is this issue more acute than in the Arctic, where I began my fieldwork a quarter century ago and where archaeologists are in a race to study and save historic sites from a combination of environmental shifts and pressure from extreme tourism.

My interest in archaeological sites along tidal creeks like the Poquessing and saltwater inlets like the entrance to Menemsha Pond, as well as the whole history and archaeology of lighter-than-air technologies, began with studies of the history and archaeology of polar exploration sites. While upland sites do exist in the High Arctic, most are located within a few feet of a shoreline. However, the issues in the North are an order of magnitude greater than those at small local sites like Poquessing or the fan-looted Hollywood artifact shoreline at Menemsha. Differing levels of scholarly study and protection by national cultural resource management regimes, wide geographic dispersal, tourist visitation and the casual looting that sometimes accompanies it, all had left large gaps in both the scholarship and even the possibilities for scholarship at archaeological sites from the history of arctic exploration. Add to this the growing awareness that shoreline sites in the High Arctic are increasingly under threat from rising seas on account of global climate change. In fact, in late summer of 2017, as this volume of essays was in final preparation, a team of Russian archaeologists announced a rescue mission at the site of Evelyn Briggs Baldwin's East Camp Ziegler on Alger Island in Franz Josef Land. The shoreline at the site, which has seen massive erosion over the past decades, will soon undermine the archaeological remains completely and destroy the site.

This essay, adapted from a 2012 article in *Polar Journal*, summarizes some twenty years of research into the history of seven American arctic expeditions, the actual and potential archaeological remains they left behind, and the historic and contemporary use of these sites in arctic tourism. I then propose an idea that has been kicking around these same twenty years: the remote monitoring of archaeological sites combined with episodic fieldwork, a model for an international scholarly architecture for the interactive study of polar archaeological sites tourism.

Seven failed American polar expeditions to the European and Russian High Arctic in the years 1898–1905 left behind a large variety of archaeological remains and documentary records. These remains span the distance from Bass Rocks in North East Greenland to Wilczek Island in Franz Josef Land, and their associated records lie in the newspaper accounts and archives in countries from the United States to Russia. The widely scattered nature of these sites and their documentary records accounts in large measure for the absence until recently of both a modern synthesis about these expeditions and a comprehensive archaeological survey of their remains. The combination of national failure and international geographic dispersal is further complicated by the historic and contemporary interaction of these heritage sites with international polar tourism, with global climate change, and with the resulting formation processes both cultural and natural. These latter factors may be the most difficult of all when it comes to the study and preservation of these areas. There is at present no workable regime for the continuous monitoring of sites beset by wider access on account of global climate change and the increased tourist traffic such change enables.

The American attempts to reach the North Pole from the European and Russian High Arctic include five expeditions led by journalist Walter Wellman (1894, 1898–99, 1906, 1907, 1909); one led by meteorologist Evelyn Briggs Baldwin (1901–2); and one headed by photographer Anthony Fiala (1903–5).[1] The 1898–99 Wellman expedition, as well as those of Fiala and Baldwin, all staged from the Russian arctic archipelago of Franz Josef Land. Wellman's four other expeditions all took place in the Norwegian arctic archipelago of Svalbard. Baldwin additionally had relief encampments for his expedition constructed in North East Greenland.

These expeditions, all undertaken in the decade and a half before the North Pole was claimed from the North American side of the Arctic in 1909 by naval engineer Robert Peary, left behind a substantial body of archaeological remains in the European and Russian Arctic. These include two shipwrecks (one each in Svalbard and Franz Josef Land); three balloon inflation sites (one each in North East Greenland, Svalbard, and Franz Josef Land); the remains of two airships in Svalbard; innumerable balloon buoy communication devices scattered across the Arctic; and numerous base camps, temporary shelters, relief stations and supply depots, along with thousands of scattered and isolated artifacts. Each of these sites is located near, alongside, or under the sea.

Wellman's 1894 expedition led to the destruction of the expedition ship, *Ragnvald Jarl*, near the western shore of Waldenøya in Svalbard. Some cargo and remnants salvaged from the ship itself before it sank provided the materials necessary for the construction of an emergency shelter on Waldenøya. In 1898 Wellman's second attempt to reach the North Pole staged from Franz Josef Land, which, like Svalbard during Wellman's career as an explorer, was also a *terra nullius*, a place owned by no one. The expedition created a base camp at Cape Tegetthoff on Hall Island, in part by the reuse of huts removed from the Jackson-Harmsworth base camp at Cape Flora on Northbrook Island. An advance hut consisting of stones collected from the surrounding landscape was built by members of the expedition at Cape Heller in the fall of 1898, and it was in this hut that a Norwegian member of the expedition died during that same winter and was later buried at the site.[2]

In 1901 Evelyn Briggs Baldwin, Wellman's second-in-command from the 1898–99 expedition, returned to Franz Josef Land to lead his own polar expedition. With an enormous budget provided by an American corporate sponsor, the expedition constructed twin base camps on the southern shore of Alger Island. Baldwin soon consolidated these sites into a single main base camp at the easternmost site. The expedition also constructed an advance hut, Kane Lodge, on Greely Island. On a rough line from Alger Island north to Rudolf Island—the northern-most island in the Franz Josef archipelago—and with Kane Lodge in the approximate middle, the expedition created numerous other supply depots. In addition to these Franz Josef Land sites, Baldwin chartered a second, separate expedition to construct relief stations in North East Greenland in the event the expedition returned in that di-rection from the North Pole. These were eventually built on Bass Rock and Shannon Island and included facilities to generate hydrogen gas for the sending of message balloons. A similar hydrogen-generating facility was also built at the Alger Island site, and in June 1902 Alger Island was the scene of more than a dozen launches of hydrogen bal-loons carrying message buoys.[3]

When Baldwin's expedition returned to the United States in the fall of 1902 without meaningful results he was replaced as leader by a fel-low expedition member, Anthony Fiala. Fiala returned to Franz Josef Land to continue the American polar effort from the Russian High Arctic in 1903. Favorable ice conditions allowed the expedition ship, *America*, to steam and sail all the way to Teplitz Bay on Rudolf Island. Fiala's camp there made use both of his own cargo and of materials left behind by an earlier Italian expedition under the duke of the Abruzzi. When pack ice threatened the expedition ship with destruction, Fiala further enhanced his base camp with materials salvaged from the ship. The vessel finally vanished into the bay during a winter storm early in 1904.

After the shipwreck Fiala made two half-hearted attempts to reach the pole, but mostly he plied along Baldwin's depot route from Rudolf Island to Alger Island and from there to Cape Flora. Like Wellman and

Baldwin before him, he expended much effort in placating recalcitrant crew members. After seven years the American futility in Franz Josef Land ended in 1905, not before Fiala's discouraged relay teams created numerous additional sites where supplies and other artifacts were discarded, lost, or deliberately cached for later use or retrieval.[4]

In 1906, in the summer after the American exploration of Franz Josef Land ended, Walter Wellman returned to Svalbard, where he built a large base camp complete with an airship hangar on the shoreline of Virgohamna on Danskøya. There both Wellman and S. A. Andrée—who attempted his own fateful balloon flight to the Pole from Virgohamna in July 1897—left behind remnants of some of the strangest polar expeditions ever attempted. In Wellman's case the site included an expedition headquarters, a machine shop, and a hydrogen-generating facility along with the massive airship hangar.

Wellman used the Virgohamna airship base over three summers (1906, 1907, 1909), enlarging and improving the airship's design and performance each time. He abandoned his pursuit of the North Pole when, in September 1909, fellow Americans Frederick Cook and Robert Peary both claimed to have reached the Pole, Cook in 1908 and Peary in 1909. When Wellman made this decision, he also abandoned his base camp and the discarded remnants of his three airships.

The collective remains left behind by these American polar expeditions provide a wealth of material evidence for the archaeological analysis of the history of polar exploration. The surface of this wealth has only been glimpsed and may never be fully explored before these sites are claimed by rising sea levels. Virgohamna has received attention,[5] and the Baldwin expedition relief camps in North East Greenland as well as the Wellman base camp on Hall Island in Franz Josef Land have received preliminary surveys.[6] But many of the potentially most significant sites, both underwater and on land, have yet to be located, much less examined archaeologically. These undocumented sites include the wreck of Wellman's *Ragnvald Jarl* off the shore of Waldenøya, the hut built from the salvaged remnants of the ship on the island's shore, and the wreck of Fiala's *America* that presumably lies either in or somewhere in the vicinity of Teplitz Bay. Nor has the potentially major American site of Kane Lodge on Greely Island in Franz Josef

Land been positively identified or surveyed—although the German arctic guide Andreas Umbreit may recently have discovered its rapidly vanishing remains.[7]

These American sites have faded into an obscurity that requires some examination. There is the problematic geographic isolation of most of the sites, of course, which does not lend itself to easy access for historical archaeology field research. At the same time, this isolation exists for the European and the even more remote Russian High Arctic, thereby further limiting access of American studies scholars and historical archaeologists from North America. Franz Josef Land, in particular, was closed to Westerners during the entire Soviet period, and even now its visitation is limited to Russian military and science operations along with infrequent (but increasing) high-end polar tourism cruises. One notable exception was a successful joint Russian-Norwegian expedition to visit heritage sites in 1991.[8]

The legal status of the American sites is another contributing factor in their relative and continuing obscurity, even in an age of heightened economic, political, and scholarly interest in the polar regions in a time of global climate change. Each of the sites was abandoned fifteen to twenty years before formal national claims were made in the 1920s on Svalbard (by Norway) and Franz Josef Land (by Russia). As Russian explorers of Franz Josef Land in the 1930s made clear, the absence of any kind of cultural resource protection on these historic sites meant that they had become regular looting places for other expeditions, both scientific and military.

In Svalbard, where arctic tourism was well established by the turn of the century, sites like Wellman's camp at Virgohamna became regular points of interest by summer tourist cruises which, along with hunters, trappers, and scientific expeditions, caused remains on the site to be carried away as souvenirs or as the raw materials for other camps or structures elsewhere in the archipelago. Today the northwest corner of Svalbard holds a large concentration of tourist visitation sites, a legacy of its long history as the staging area for numerous expeditions and resource extraction enterprises. Each of these cultural formation processes, along with a natural environment that combines both corrosive and corrasive elements and occasional trampling by wandering

Landing sites used one or more times by tourist ships in the period 2006–2009. Source: Norwegian Polar Institute.

populations of reindeer and polar bear, led to the reduced archaeological remains that exist now as firmly protected sites (Svalbard), sites with variable protection and reconstruction (North East Greenland), and sites where protection, preservation, and study have only begun to be seriously considered (Franz Josef Land).

These remains, in addition, include not just the archaeological materials abandoned or lost but also the numerous contributions to geographic nomenclature made by these expeditions. Almost regardless

Greely Island in Franz Josef Land, detail of a survey by R. W. Porter in 1903–1905.

of the vast archaeological possibilities, the nomenclature of American polar patriotism evident at such sites as Greely Island—identified and surrounded as it is by locations named for American presidents, explorers, and corporate barons—should have tailor-made these expeditions and sites for a profound examination by scholars of both American studies and the heroic age of polar exploration.

Perhaps much of this obscurity can be traced to a leitmotif of material evidence of multiple American polar exploration failures. These expeditions were all private ventures undertaken at a time when American capital was making itself felt around the globe. In the High Arctic, American capitalist John Munroe Longyear visited in 1901 and established the Arctic Coal Company in Adventfjorden in 1906. In

Franz Josef Land corporate magnate William Ziegler put millions of dollars into attempts to reach the North Pole. Evidence that private American capital had sponsored so many failed attempts to reach the North Pole did not fit well with the ethos of American capitalism then (or now). When the last American attempt to reach the pole from the European side failed in 1909, followed a few years later by the sale of the Arctic Coal Company to Norwegian interests, American interest in the European and Russian High Arctic dwindled almost to invisibility. With it went interest in the remains left behind by the American polar expeditions.

Besides the potential archaeological significance of this rather massive cultural database, still substantially unexplored—either archaeologically or "archivally"—the remains of the American polar sites in the European and Russian Arctic have also provided both a historic and a more recent magnet for arctic tourists. In the absence of a systematic program of material and cultural studies aimed at these sites, the alternative for some of them, like Virgohamna, has been as a destination for adventure tourists.

Polar tourism overall now amounts to more than 40,000 visits to Antarctica per year and millions of visitors to the Arctic and sub-Arctic.[9] These tourists and their ships have access, on account of global climate change, to areas of Svalbard and elsewhere once considered all but impossible to reach. Inevitably, such increasing numbers will come into more or less predictable contact with the remains of the American polar expeditions that until now have largely been spared such contact.

To the casual tourist, the human imprint on Svalbard can seem small indeed, with many relatively small explorations and industrial operations placed against the overwhelming beauty of stark mountains and enormous glaciers. Viken writes that the "tourist experiences offered on Svalbard are all related to nature," an error of significant proportions.[10] The seemingly marginal evidence of human behavior can take on an entirely magnified aspect when it is viewed as standing out boldly from the natural environment, announcing as it does a human presence in an otherwise seemingly overwhelming natural environment.

As early as the summer of 1906 tourists were already arriving in Virgohamna not mainly or even primarily to see ice or polar bear or walrus. They were there to see if humans could fly to the North Pole. Walter Wellman, who was not unsympathetic to the requirements of profitable business operations, noted that in each of the summers at his Virgohamna base camp he was deluged by tourists. Wellman writes that tourist steamers disgorged "hundreds of visitors descending upon us with their cameras, their autograph hunting and their innumerable questions."[11] In 1907 two of Wellman's own daughters raced to Virgohamna on board a tourist steamer in hopes of seeing their father off to the North Pole.[12]

The visitors to Wellman's polar airship operations were hardly the first tourists to Svalbard. No sooner had Andrée established his base camp on the shore of the harbor and begun construction of the hangar for his balloon in 1896 than a small tourist steamer named *Express* arrived.[13] The tourists, in this case, were rewarded with an extended stay, as a storm forced the vessel to lie in the harbor for nearly a week. Martin Conway, who carried out extensive explorations in the islands in 1896, describes his surprise when, after a month in the field, he returned to Advent Point (near the present-day capital of Longyearbyen) to find a tourist hotel being built there. "Presently a German tourist steamer came in and emptied its passengers upon the shore. We felt that we had returned from the wilderness to a centre of advanced civilization."[14]

Even these Germans were not the first tourists in Svalbard. By the time of Conway's expedition, tourists had been visiting Svalbard for at least a quarter century. In his seminal history of the islands, *No Man's Land*, Conway notes that the first tourists arrived in the islands in the summer of 1871 on board "a small Hammerfest steamer."[15]

By the time Fridtjof Nansen visited Virgohamna in 1912, Wellman's camp in just three summers had completed its transition from an active exploration base camp to an archaeological relic. As such, it had become "a regular looting place for tourists and others looking for souvenirs."[16] Nansen thought that anything of what he considered real value had already been taken away from the site. But much was still left to entice others over the following century. As Nansen sardonically

"The tourists trooped ashore to see the sights . . . amazed at the magnitude of our operations and surprised at the comfort and cleanliness of Record-Herald House . . . the porcelain tub . . . and sleeping bunks [with] clean white sheets." Walter Wellman, *Chicago Record-Herald*, September 1, 1906.

wrote, the "trappers and the tourists did not have time to get it all yet."[17]

The other archaeological sites created by Wellman in Svalbard—the *Ragnvald Jarl* shipwreck and hut at Waldenøya—have not been located. One tour guide related to me that tourist vessels operating in this area are usually on their way to Sjuøyane—the more northerly Seven Islands—and are reluctant to spend any valuable time attempting surveys or landings at or near the isolated Waldenøya, which is often surrounded by ice. It remains largely unexamined by historical archaeologists.

Similarly, the Baldwin relief station sites in North East Greenland, recently surveyed by Mikkelsen, also exist far off the usual pathways of the arctic tourism. In Greenland the National Museum has responsibility under Home Rule for historic structures dating to before 1900.[18] The Baldwin camps fall just outside this remit and were also reused several times by subsequent expeditions and so have seen significant formation processes since their initial occupation. Arctic cruise ship tourism as defined by Thomson and Thomson remains outside the area of North East Greenland and away from the usual arctic itinerary themes of the Northwest Passage or the popular "trail of the Vikings" tours.[19]

In Franz Josef Land, the situation is substantively more complex. Discovered in 1873 by the Austro-Hungarian expedition of Karl Weyprecht and Julius Payer, the archipelago is the site of one of the most dramatic events in the history of exploration: the survival in a small stone hut over the winter of 1895–96 by Fridtjof Nansen and his companion, Hjalmar Johansen. The two men escaped from the islands in the following summer in part by an extremely fortunate meeting with the British Jackson-Harmsworth expedition then exploring the archipelago. Franz Josef Land is also unique in the history of arctic exploration and American studies as it holds the remains of three separate American expeditions under three different leaders all within a tightly defined geographic and temporal space. As such, the archipelago has the potential to provide dramatic comparative data on how the American experience in the Arctic evolved.

The Soviet Union claimed Franz Josef Land in 1929 and soon closed the islands to outsiders. Occasional tourist visits took place, but these were rare. Barr writes of the Norwegian vessel *Isbjørn* arriving in the islands in 1931 with a French count on board.[20] During the Cold War Franz Josef Land became a kind of stationary aircraft carrier, positioned a short bomber flight over the North Pole from targets in North America. The practical effect of this long history of closure to outsiders from the West meant that the American polar base camps were only occasionally visited or studied by Soviet military or science expeditions or relief expeditions. The sites therefore remained substantially—but by no means entirely—intact into the 1990s.

Yevgeny Fedorov visited Franz Josef Land in the early 1930s. He had the chance to visit the remains of the base camps of both Fiala and Baldwin. He found both in states of confusion but both filled with artifacts and intact structures. In a fascinating chapter in his *Polar Diaries* entitled "Summer in a Museum," he describes the archaeological remains in and around Teplitz Bay on Rudolf Island as "a museum telling about the race to the North Pole at the turn of the century." Seeing the disarray of the remains, he urged that this unique "museum should be put in order."[21] Fedorov later participated in the momentous Soviet North Pole adventures of 1937–38, when more structures and an aircraft base were built on Rudolf Island and at least one aircraft wrecked near Teplitz Bay. He writes: "I did not know then [1933] that in a mere four years I would also take part in creating the last exhibits of that museum, in the final conquest of the North Pole by Soviet people."[22]

Similarly, when a Russian expedition searched Baldwin's East Camp Ziegler site on Alger Island site in 1930, they found that it had been heavily disturbed. A number of buildings were explored, and inside the visitors found a wealth of expedition gear, medical supplies, and cans of spoiled food. The Russians decried the looting apparent at the site and implored their government to protect the artifacts that were "of great historical interest."[23]

Today the Alger Island base camp remains a large and complex archaeological site, heavily disturbed by tourists, scientists, and hunters as well as polar bears and severe arctic weather. The rate of erosion at the shoreline site is a worrying sign that it will not long survive rising sea levels.

For modern tours plying the waters of Franz Josef Land—usually on the way to or from the North Pole—the search for profit predictably outweighs more cultural considerations such as the search for and study or preservation of historical sites. In the rush to reach the North Pole, sites of historic interest are often stricken from itineraries or skipped. Even tours within the islands can miss or pass over important sites from a lack of knowledge by the tour operator. As a tourist from a 2005 Franz Josef Land tour wrote to the author: "We were ... tantalizingly near to Alger Island, spending about 3 hours in the Negri Strait and in the vicinity of Alger Island looking at walruses. We asked for a landing [on Alger Island] but were told that there was not much to see!"[24] Such a situation creates two distinct but interrelated problems: the lack of visibility of the pressures the current wave of polar tourism is placing on polar archaeological sites, and the current absence of a data cloud that makes readily accessible all available archaeological and documentary records related to the expeditions that created the sites in the first place.

The character of arctic tourists themselves has also changed little across the past century, since Walter Wellman signed autographs for visitors to his base at Virgohamna. In the summer of 2006 two icebreaker voyages to the North Pole by way of Franz Josef Land provided me with the opportunity to observe such tourists both at the historic sites in the archipelago and at the Pole itself, and to compare these tourists with similar groups observed in 1993 at Virgohamna. The gaps in our knowledge of such behavior became immediately apparent.

At the very least, most have exchanged guns for cameras, to the relief of both wildlife and, in the following vignette, other camera operators. Martin Conway describes the many tourists who arrived in Advent Bay in 1896 and disported themselves strangely during the few hours that the weekly tourist boat would anchor there. "They always brought rifles with them, under the impression that bears, or at least reindeer, herded at every point along shore. There being nothing to shoot, they nevertheless fired off the rounds of ammunition ... aiming at birds, or merely into the air. . . . One foolish creature is said to have mistaken a photographer with his head under a dark cloth for a reindeer, and put a bullet through his hat."[25]

The tours that made their way north to Virgohamna in 1906 would eventually leave Wellman's airship base camp with their personalized souvenirs and then voyage even farther north to the edge of the polar ice pack itself. There, at about 80° north, they would have reached a more northern point than would Wellman himself in his airship—and best the marks of all but a small handful of nineteenth-century polar explorers. With the introduction of the Russian nuclear icebreaker into the arctic tourist market, tourists can now journey in comfort all the way to the North Pole and back in less than two weeks.

Some things have changed, of course. One display in particular that Walter Wellman probably never witnessed: a sixty-year-old French woman arrived at the Pole during one of the 2006 icebreaker journeys and, once there, claimed it as her mission to channel energy streams and bring peace to the world. To accomplish this noble feat, she performed a strip tease around a metal pole the icebreaker crew had set up to represent the North Pole. The woman then proceeded to strip nude and dance and roll happily in the snow. There was no appreciable change observed in the cause of world peace, but the ceremony certainly bemused, bewildered, and appalled the 150 bystanders.

The North Pole tour has become a popular one, much more so than the more localized tours of Franz Josef Land, even though it can be as much as four times more expensive. In large part, the wealthy tourists who purchase places on these tours want something radically different from a tropical holiday or continental river cruise. They want to lay claim to membership in a somewhat exclusive club of people who have been to the North Pole. The trip to the Pole allows them to add a very special extra to their usual itineraries.

Thomson and Thomson write of typical passengers on small-ship cruises to cold water islands who "are relatively well-off, highly educated and ecologically aware people who feel they have 'done it all . . .' They are seeking experiences on less-traveled ground."[26] Many of the passengers on the North Pole voyages, by contrast, exhibited only marginal interest in ecology or history. There were a few for whom the tour was a chance to learn something of arctic history and archaeology of the historic sites of Franz Josef Land. For most, however, the attainment of the Pole while eating and drinking well along the way seemed to be the predominant characteristics on a tour priced at more than $50,000 per couple.

Tours to selected historic sites within Franz Josef Land often had the feel of tour "filler," something to complete a tour advertisement but far from the main point of the "expedition." These tours used the Nansen-Johansen stone hut at Cape Norvegia and the remnants of the Jackson-Harmsworth huts and the Benjamin Leigh Smith overwintering site at Cape Flora as their primary historic sites. One tour visited the Wellman base camp at Cape Tegetthoff, but neither tour landed passengers at the other American sites at Cape Heller, Teplitz Bay, or Alger Island.

The decision not to visit the site of Wellman's "Fort McKinley" at Cape Heller seems to have been an arbitrary one on the part of the tour operator. Alger Island, as noted earlier, seems to be skipped because it is believed that there is not much there to interest passengers, especially when the famous round rocks of Champ Island are close by and offer better photographic possibilities. As for Teplitz Bay, the reluctance appears to have as much to do with attitudes about revealing the remains of a former Soviet installation to outsiders. In all these decisions, it is also necessary to take into consideration the requirement of the security of more than one hundred generally elderly passengers from the threat of polar bears, uneven terrain, and uncertain weather. There was additionally a sense of having to "balance" historic site visits with opportunities for observation of nature. If the tour threatened to "list" too heavily to one or the other theme, then this imbalance would be "corrected" with the next landing.

Attempts to educate passengers about proper routes to walk around fragile historic sites were frustrated by the multilingual collection of passengers (one cruise had distinct populations of German, French, English, Italian, Russian and Luxembourgish speakers) as well as the apparent feelings of a wealthy, already privileged class of tourists who in some cases felt that they had paid for the further privilege to walk anywhere they liked. One tourist at Cape Tegetthoff stepped directly upon and nearly through the fragile floorboards of Walter Wellman's main hut. In his defense, no wayside panels or any other historic markers or pathways existed to guide tourist progress around the site or otherwise inform them of its history.

Where small signposts have been placed, at Cape Flora and at Cape Norvegia, their placement alongside the cultural remains often has the effect of drawing tourists onto fragile areas rather than keeping them at a distance. In addition to the ongoing removal of artifacts from unprotected sites—documented in conversations with several tourists, tour guides, tour operators, and cultural resource professionals— some sites have gained notable additions. Someone placed a scattering of walrus bones alongside the Nansen hut, ostensibly to give the small area a more "authentic" look for tourists who expect to see a rough and ready survival encampment. Subsequent visitors to the site reported that these bones had been removed, presumably as souvenirs, or perhaps as items for sale on eBay, similar to the "authentic" pieces of the *Orca II* that were in fact fragments of the adjacent *Far Star*.

Passenger indoctrination into either polar history or cultural resource protection for the historic sites visited during the 2006 cruises was minimal and, as observed, largely ineffectual. Beginning with the tour operator's website, tourists received little in the way of pre-experience information to enhance their appreciation of the sites on the tour agenda. The website, since heavily redacted, misidentified three of the six major early expeditions to Franz Josef Land. Benjamin Leigh Smith and his research vessel *Eira* were referred to as "Lee Smith and "*Aira*"; Evelyn Briggs Baldwin as "A. Baldwin"; and the Wellman expedition became the "Welle expedition."[27] No reading list was provided that might have served as a foundation of historical and cultural knowledge to prepare passengers for what they would see. It was little wonder, then, that passengers arrived on board the tour cruise with little in the way of historical background and expected such gaps to be filled in by on-board lectures.

In 2006 the tour operator was reluctant to allow passengers to do anything not previously programmed for the tour. We made a special archaeological expedition to Teplitz Bay to locate and survey the wreck of a Soviet-era aircraft. We helicoptered to the site in the middle of the night, and the mini-adventure was kept secret even from passengers who might be inclined to pay extra for the privilege of accompanying the brief archaeological excursion.[28]

There were obvious solutions to some of these local site issues. At a minimum, wayside panels such as those placed at Virgohamna would seem a natural progression of cultural resource protection in Franz Josef Land. The current collection of memorials and occasional informative markers—such as those at Cape Flora and Cape Norvegia—do not serve to guide the tourist around the more fragile historic areas of these sites. As noted, tours to Franz Josef Land have the additional complication of being multilingual. Based on the 2006 cruise experiences, any such panels proposed for the historic sites of Franz Josef Land would need to include text in Russian, German, English, Norwegian, and French, to enable the widest possible comprehension by a diverse international tourist clientele.

Even the issue of such panels at archaeological sites is not as clear as one might hope. While helping to preserve a site and guide tourist traffic around it, such panels can often seem a modern distraction to the "authentic" experiencing of the past. As Robert Finch noted in his travels around Newfoundland when he came upon an unmarked but nonetheless historic site: "The sense of the past lives lived here was more vivid and present because of the lack of labels, signs, and official tours."[29] He puts this down to a Canadian "proclivity to allow and encourage people to discover and interpret places on their own."[30] Such an attribution of a national "proclivity" is admirable but perhaps less well suited to sites visited by an international collection of individuals of such means, in many instances, as to consider themselves above local rules and regulations.

In twenty-six days on board the icebreaker, shore visits at historic sites in Franz Josef Land accounted for a total of five hours. Other than the unifying goal of the North Pole, these tours offered little to attract the serious heritage tourist. Unlike similar tours of the Arctic or sub-Arctic—the Northwest Passage, for example, or the route of the Vikings theme tours—the North Pole voyages can be described as an oxymoron, a comfortable form of extreme tourism, making little attempt at historical thematic coherence. As such, they represent lost opportunities to contribute to the awareness of an elite class of

Tourists in the summer of 2006 march toward the small memorial to Nansen and Johansen at Cape Norvegia on Jackson Island in Franz Josef Land.

tourist to the presence, heritage, and fragility of the archaeology of polar exploration.

The situation on the large-scale North Pole cruise has echoes in my experience in 1993 while conducting archaeological research for several weeks at Wellman's camp at Virgohamna in northwest Svalbard. This was just as tourism was beginning its astounding boom in the Norwegian Arctic and before the digital revolution changed the world. Cultural resource management officials in the Office of the Sysselmann in Longyearbyen were concerned enough about the site to request a survey of tourist traffic there. Some of the archaeological remains (those predating 1900) had already been designated a "cultural monument" in 1974 by the government of Norway. The Wellman 1906–9 site at Virgohamna came under blanket protection in 1992 when the government extended protection to all historic remains in Svalbard from prior to 1946. Regulations prohibited camping within three hundred feet of archaeological remains, but tourists were at that time free to land on the shore and walk around the remains without much in the way of guidance.

The 1993 survey demonstrated the popularity of the archaeological remains at Virgohamna for tourists. Over eighteen days, 250 tourists came ashore from six different vessels. Extrapolated over a 10- to 12-week tourist season, this averaged 84 visitors per week and between 840 and 1,000 tourists per season.[31] This figure was seemingly a large one for a remote island site barely 600 miles (965 km) from the North Pole. It would have been far higher still but for the shallow water entrance to Virgohamna from Smeerenburgfjorden, rendering it too dangerous for larger cruise ships such as the *Polaris*, which passed Danskøya twice during our stay but did not stop or discharge passengers on the island.

The tourists on board the vessels that did call at Virgohamna were ferried ashore by zodiac and began a circuit that started with the Andrée monument and continued around the Wellman remains. (In this sense the Virgohamna tour had changed little since Wellman's activity drew tourists there nearly ninety years earlier.) In 1993 there were no defined pathways around the archaeological assemblage or wayside panels to inform visitors as to the identity and history of what they were seeing, nor any pamphlet to explain the site's history in some detail. Artifacts were picked up and cast down, the soft wood of the hangar was walked upon, and metal debris from the machine shop was trodden upon. After their wanderings many tourists gathered along the shoreline to share champagne and peanuts, and one part of Wellman's hydrogen-generating apparatus was in reuse as a garbage bin for bottles and plastic wrappers.[32]

I envisioned then, and believe even more firmly nearly a quarter century later, that a remote reporting station, emplaced high on the cliffs above this important site and combined with some kind of international data access architecture via cloud computing, would be an ideal vehicle to study, manage, and educate on the metatheme of polar archaeological sites tourism. The need for these three areas—archaeology, cultural resource management, and tourism—to operate at some level of international cooperation if not coordination is increasingly required by the numbers of tourists visiting the Arctic.

There are fundamental reasons for this. As Hall and Saarinen write, "numerous gaps remain in our knowledge base."[33] Stewart, Draper, and Dawson write that there exists a "basic lack of information on cruise tourism activities, alongside limited monitoring, lack of formal regulations and poor surveillance capability of cruise ship activities."[34] There is no centralized—much less comprehensive—source of data on just what all this activity is doing, either intrinsically or as a causal factor in the rapidly changing polar regions. Roura further makes the point that "it can be difficult to differentiate unambiguously actual traces of tourism behaviour from those caused by other contemporary or historic cultural processes, by nature, or by a combination of processes."[35]

Stopgap measures have served as a bridge from the early "Wild North" days of polar tourism to the current multiplication of cruises and tours. Partly in response to the data on the frequency of the tourist traffic at Virgohamna, a series of pathways around the archaeological remains was mapped, a wayside panel placed on the site with an explanatory map, and a brochure using the 1993 archaeological survey produced and distributed by the Sysselmann in 1996. Soon thereafter, a more detailed and well-illustrated booklet was produced in both English and Norwegian to explain briefly but comprehensively the history, archaeology, and heritage of the site and to caution visitors to be aware of its fragility.[36] This publication explicitly delineated the "travel forbidden areas" of the site, which include all the structures associated with Wellman's activities there, and speculated that over the previous century the site had been visited by "nearly 100,000 adventure-seeking tourists."[37]

Currently, in a further attempt to preserve the multilayered heritage at the site, landings require the special permission of the Sysselmann's office. Even with this, we only have self-reported landing statistics and little to no idea of the actual behavior of tourists once on site. We lack both objective data on tourist behavior and comprehensive access to site histories and archaeologies. Given the lack of visibility of both site visitation and historical data matrices, combined with recent developments in remote monitoring technologies and cloud computing, the time would seem right to create integrated site study and access schemes that operate on more globalized terms.

The Norwegian Polar Institute has established a preliminary model of this sort, with its *Cruisehåndbok for Svalbard* available in both print and online formats. The *Cruisehåndbok* seeks to provide "quality-assured information about the natural environment, history and cultural heritage sites along the coasts of the archipelago."[38] This information includes current cultural resource protection regimes for sensitive sites like Virgohamna. The *Cruisehåndbok* warns that: "The cultural treasures must not be handled, moved or destroyed," and walking upon them is forbidden:

> The cultural heritage of Virgohamna is significant, vulnerable and worn from traffic. . . . The wooden remains of Wellman's collapsed hangar were walked upon, as were the remains of the airship *America*. The piles of iron filings around the hydrogen works were trampled to a mush. This is why from 2000 onwards regulations on traffic have been put into effect in Virgohamna. Anyone wishing to alight here must apply for permission from the Governor of Svalbard, who will be strict in granting it. The criteria for landing here are listed in a folder which can be obtained from the Governor of Svalbard. The regulations control who alights and sets conditions on the visit.[39]

As a guidebook for visitors, the *Cruisehåndbok* serves its purpose brilliantly. However, it and the other Norwegian measures also point to the overall gaps in knowledge related to tourism both at Virgohamna and across the polar regions. The Norwegian cultural resource management model in Svalbard has succeeded somewhat in buffering its historic sites from the inevitable and increasing pressures from the ongoing transition from an industrial resource extraction economy to a combined industrial/post-industrial scientific research and tourism economy. In addition, new museums and cultural programs in Longyearbyen serve to educate visitors, one hopes before they venture far afield.

These measures, however, are not structured toward several major areas of interest related to these sites. These can be defined in three broad categories. First, there is no real-time reporting from these sites during the summer tourism season in the form of remote monitoring stations. Second, there is no interactive mechanism to the digital edition that would enable real-time feedback from tour operators and tourists themselves on the current state of cultural sites (numbers of visitors, condition of remains, etc.). And third, there is no integrated data cloud containing the archival records related to these sites that would further the understanding and study of them.

To take these one at a time, we note first that the study of tourist behavior at extreme sites like those in Svalbard, North East Greenland, and Franz Josef Land suffers from several structural impediments. It is a highly irregular human and cultural phenomenon, whereby tours can land at a heritage site at any time in the summer season, in numbers from a single kayak to a vessel ferrying a hundred or more passengers ashore by helicopter. Given these brief but intense and unpredictable visitations, it would not be practical to station a human monitor at such sites.

The solution is to emplace remote monitoring stations that would be self-powered (batteries with wind and/or solar recharging capabilities). These would record images at a predetermined rate, for example one image every minute. Such a collection, recorded over the course of a twelve-week summer season, would amount to an unprecedented database of over 120,000 images that would allow for the study not just of absolute numbers of tourists but also of the pathways taken by such tourists as they make their way around the site. Another benefit would be the automatic recording of wildlife disturbances on site, such as from polar bear and reindeer.

Bradford and McIntyre pioneered such remote monitoring of human usage for park areas in Canada. In this research, visitor responses to nature reserve signage were collected on video by remotely operated cameras placed inside bird boxes to conceal the cameras.[40] To alleviate privacy concerns, the images collected were deliberately blurred to conceal the identity of the humans being recorded, and no audio data were recorded. The data were then used to evaluate hypotheses regarding human behavior and the preservation of wilderness areas.

At the same time, while such remote stations record their etic data, there needs to be an architecture of emic communication with the tourists themselves. This can take the form of site-specific blogs where visitors and tour leaders can record impressions of the site, upload their own imagery, and interact with scholars and resource managers, informing all constituents in the site preservation and study imperative. At its most basic, an online architecture could be constructed around Wordpress-style blogs for individual sites, integrated with a Facebook-style page combined with site-specific metadata hashtags for tweets to produce real-time reporting from tourist visits. My colleague Urban Wråkberg has initiated such interviews, and his preliminary data indicate that a majority of polar tourists prefer "comfortable and only modestly demanding fieldtrips. Most tourists like variety and are curious about nature as well as culture, especially history, but also geo-economics and social living conditions up north."[41]

Lastly, all the remotely recorded data, the tourist blogs, and the prevailing cultural resource regimes and site cautions would reside in a cloud database alongside historic archival materials related to the expeditions that created the heritage sites in the first place. Ideally, such a cloud would be managed by the national research institutes of the polar nations where the sites are located.

Taken together, this layered approach has the potential to join all the interested and affected parties—scholars, managers, visitors, and tour organizers—in a unified platform that functions to maximize the knowledge, study, and preservation of heritage sites in extreme environments. In Franz Josef Land—given the lack of a permanent cultural management presence and the uneven prospects for a central museum or even a designated landing place where the story of the discovery, exploration, and use of the islands can be told and visitors educated—such a digital architecture could serve in their place.

Museums, wayside panels, and brochures are all essential. However, by themselves they are unlikely to succeed in the absence of an internationally accessible database related to the particular historic expedition sites such cruises visit. This is where a "one-stop" cloud computing archive of historical documents, imagery, and motion film from historic sites will offer real-time access for scholars, managers, and site visitors alike. Even with such a virtual architecture, in light of the increasing tourist traffic in the archipelago since its opening to the West after 1991, Fedorov's eighty-year-old idea of transforming Teplitz

Bay, or another place in Russia's vast new Arctic National Park, into a museum of polar exploration, is one Russian cultural authorities are now considering.[42] Such a museum, based at the abandoned station at Teplitz Bay, for example, would have the effect of creating a magnet for both tourists and scientists, and a cultural center that would encompass almost all forms of arctic travel: maritime, overland, over ice, and aeronautical.

As for Virgohamna, its history of expedition base camps and contemporary and current tourist visits can serve neatly as a microcosm of polar tourism at large in the development of the research plan of the international polar heritage sites cloud. Between 1997 and 2006 tourist visits to Svalbard nearly doubled, from 15,437 to 28,787.[43] At Virgohamna an average of over 800 visitors land each summer season.[44] But these figures are self-reported by the landing vessels themselves. There are no independent data on these numbers, much less what such visitors, like the naked lady at the North Pole, actually do while on site. While the existing rules stipulate where and how these tourists can interact with this site, no method currently exists for evaluating how effective such measures are in the control of tourist pathways around the site or in preventing direct damage in the form of trampling, looting, polluting, or rearranging artifacts.

The emplacement of remote monitoring stations at sites like Virgohamna would provide near real-time reporting data on the numbers of visits and visitors and also qualitative data on what humans are doing while on site. As Roura correctly points out, "it may only be possible to attribute an impact to visitation by direct observation."[45] Given the problematic nature of direct human observation of these sites, remote stations are the logical alternative. Remote monitoring of an archaeological site such as Virgohamna, with its existing longitudinal visitation figures, would provide both cultural data and technological expertise to enable the deployment of such technologies across the polar regions.

II

Transoceanic Archaeology

5

The Elusive Island

Norwegian explorer and anthropologist Thor Heyerdahl's *Kon-Tiki* expedition single-handedly opened the world's waterways to archaeological experiments—both eminently rational and exceedingly bizarre—about prehistoric human expansion around the globe. The drifting raft became an essential component of a bewildering array of theories of possible human migrations or prehistoric contacts between widely scattered human groups as well as of theories of individual human endurance.

As soon as I had, as it were, squeezed out my doctorate in archaeology, it was time to get to work, writing and publishing every scrap of research done over the previous decade. Almost as soon as this had begun, a flood destroyed our home and more than a dozen others on our small Pennsylvania street and drowned our elderly neighbors. The waters also took with them my library, research files, boxes of artifacts collected along the Delaware River, and dozens of hours of audio tapes recorded in the Arctic in 1993. Government flood recovery paperwork buried us for nearly two years. On the horizon lay little beyond academic adjunct work, especially with a research career seemingly demolished. If ever there were a time to escape to those intensively carefree days along the Shumatuscacant, dreaming of rafts and rivers and oceans, this was it. I began to assemble the story of every transoceanic raft expedition I could find. Then came a call from an editor by the name of Edward Burlingame. He had been publisher at Harper and Row and had worked with some favorite writers like the great Jonathan Raban before suffering something akin to a devastating flood in the publishing business. He had just founded the Adventure Library in order to reprint classic stories of exploration and sell them by subscription. He was in search of ideas and, reaching into my growing collection of transoceanic raft expedition files, *Kon-Tiki* was the obvious choice. The fiftieth anniversary of the famous 1947 balsa raft expedition was fast approaching and a perfect time for a new edition. When Ed asked who could write a foreword, I suggested Raban, or the great Tim Severin. Ed suggested me. This was extremely flattering—especially if one chose to ignore the facts that the book could not wait on a famous author-adventurer to produce an intro and my work would come cheap. Free, in fact. Nevertheless, the Adventure Library's fiftieth anniversary edition of *Kon-Tiki* was produced beautifully and published bang on time in April 1997, with my modest introduction treated to pride of place. It was also the highlight of five years of research into the stories of transoceanic explorers, a journey that would lead to contact with many such explorers and culminate in the 2001 publication of *Sea Drift: Rafting Adventures in the Wake of Kon-Tiki*.

On April 28, 1947, six men—two of them heroes of the Norwegian Resistance during the Second World War—drifted away from Callao, Peru, in a re-creation of a pre-Incan balsa wood raft named for the ancient god-king Con-Ticci Viracocha. One hundred and one days and 4,300 miles (6,000 km) later, against all odds, the raft smashed into the reef at Raroia in the Tuamotu Islands. One of the greatest sea epics ever, the voyage was recorded in brilliant prose in a best-selling book and in an amateur film created with a handheld 16mm camera—a film that won an Oscar.

That expedition's leader, a thirty-three-year-old Norwegian explorer named Thor Heyerdahl, earned international fame that continued to shine through subsequent maritime expeditions with reed boats and archaeological digs on Polynesian atolls and at coastal South American pyramids.

The adventure and romance surrounding the *Kon-Tiki* expedition, exciting a world wearied from almost two decades of Depression and war, has tended to obscure the serious nature of Heyerdahl's purpose. By linking pre-Columbian South America with Polynesia via the balsa raft, Heyerdahl had at a stroke used ocean currents to transform a seemingly impenetrable barrier of ocean separating the two areas into a convenient cultural conveyor belt. And a debate was joined that continues today.

Of Modern Voyages and Ancient Diffusions

For nearly a decade after a yearlong stay in the Marquesas Islands in the 1930s, Thor Heyerdahl followed intently the trend of academic discussions relating to the peopling of Polynesia. These discourses dismissed the idea that pre-Incan maritime cultures of South America influenced Polynesia. Especially disparaged was the idea that pre-Incan balsa wood rafts could remain afloat long enough to reach even those islands of eastern Polynesia, such as the Marquesas, closest to the South American coast.

Heyerdahl, in the Marquesas to conduct research into the question of the zoological populating of the scattered islands of the Pacific, recognized in various archaeological and oceanographic patterns an opportunity to turn his attention from animals to Indigenous peoples. As weeks and months passed and turned into the complete cycle of a year, Heyerdahl became more and more transfixed by the endless succession of waves breaking from the east, accompanied by a seemingly endless procession of clouds driven by southeast trade winds. The continuous physical procession of southeast winds and waves took on a psychological permanence in his mind, until he began to imagine these same physical processes carrying cultural elements from the South America coast, four thousand miles away, into the eastern rim of Polynesia.

Heyerdahl's search for cultural connections and patterns led him on a ten-year archival odyssey that began with the chronicles of the European discoverers of the Pacific, led to the myths of native Polynesians, and continued to such practical questions as, for example, how long a coconut can remain afloat and viable in salt water. After assembling mountains of anecdotal, botanical, and linguistic evidence bearing on his hypothesis, Heyerdahl nevertheless found it rejected out of hand for the aforementioned skepticism of the water-tightness of balsa logs. If a raft could not float for more than a few days or weeks, all the historical or circumstantial evidence in the world suggesting otherwise was meaningless.

As early as 1941 Heyerdahl put forth the idea of a dual migration into Polynesia from the Americas. The first migration, he reasoned, was led by a "pre-Incan civilization, with its centre near Lake Titicaca and along the Peruvian coast below, [which] seems to have swept the islands at a comparatively early period, via Easter Island," while a second wave arrived from the northwest coast of North America via northeast trades and currents.[1] Not then a sailor, nor in any way very familiar with balsa rafts, Heyerdahl based his conclusions "wholly on the observation that certain culture plants had been brought across the sea from Peru to Polynesia in prehistoric time together with a conspicuous series of man-made cultural elements and traditions."[2] He was greeted with either scorn or silence, a combination that would remain familiar throughout his life. It convinced Heyerdahl that his radical ideas on a South American origin for elements of Polynesia culture would not be taken seriously unless he could prove the seaworthiness of the pre-Incan balsa log raft.

Frustrated, Heyerdahl turned to an area of inquiry not even named when he turned to it: experimental archaeology. He traveled to Ecuador with drawings of native balsa log rafts drawn by the earliest European explorers of South America. He then managed to harvest nine enormous balsa logs and float them down the Palenque River to Guayaquil, and then on to the naval yard at Callao on the coast of Peru. There the logs were lashed together to form the deck of the raft he would soon christen *Kon-Tiki*. A deck, cabin, and bipod mast with square sail became the superstructure. With the raft complete, Heyerdahl and his companions drifted across the Pacific and into history.

Having proven that Polynesia lay within the range of at least one type of experimental craft from South America, Heyerdahl then found himself embroiled in a decades-long debate over the meaning of his experiment. As an experiment, the *Kon-Tiki* expedition, along with several other nautical replicas, was criticized because it was seemingly a mere one-time success, lacking the kinds of controls and recording that would permit replication of the experiment as a controlled comparison. At least on this score, however, even though Heyerdahl himself never re-created the entire experiment, several others did. Between 1947 and 1973 a baker's dozen of manned balsa or rubber rafts set out from Peru to cross the eastern Pacific to Polynesia, and all succeeded.

In his monumental compilation *American Indians in the Pacific*, and in subsequent publications, Heyerdahl commented extensively on his reasons for choosing to build a raft of balsa wood for his *Kon-Tiki* experiment. He simultaneously compiled a persuasive case that pre-Incan mariners on both Lake Titicaca and coastal Peru navigated large and sophisticated ships constructed from totora reeds, the same freshwater reeds discovered in the three Easter Island crater lakes of Rano Raraku, Rano Aroi, and Rano Kao. But at the time of his decision to build a balsa raft rather than a reed boat, Heyerdahl, who had rejected prevailing doubts about log rafts, accepted prevailing opinion that reed boats could never withstand transoceanic crossings. He thus built *Kon-Tiki* from balsa logs and not totora reeds.[3]

The experiment itself was as much one of enthnobotany as it was experimental vessel replication. Using historical sources, Heyerdahl linked several cultivated plants from America with islands of Polynesia. The most important was the South American sweet potato (*Ipomœa batatas*) or, in the local name, *kumara*, a plant name that, according to one ethnobotanist, "has stirred the imagination of scientists working in the Pacific like no other."[4]

Well established throughout Polynesia as both a cultivated plant and a name, the sweet potato spread throughout the Pacific islands by human agency. That agency is conclusively aboriginal, the cultigen observed in New Zealand by Cook on his first voyage and on Easter Island by Roggeveen in 1722, and described by traditional history as being located in Hawai'i as early as A.D. 1250. Even proponents of European introduction found it unlikely that the plant could have spread so far in the few decades separating the voyages of Cook and Roggeveen from those of the Spaniards Mendaña and Quirós in the 1560s. In any

case the kinds of long inter-island voyages necessary for the settlement of the expanse of Polynesia—and the introduction of *kumara* to
the islands—had stopped sometime after the close of the fourteenth
century.

Heyerdahl invoked traditional myths of Easter Islanders to support
his hypothesis of a Peruvian origin for the sweet potato, tobacco, and
chili peppers on the island and was quickly criticized by the anthropologist Alfred Métraux for using a native "myth to prove a thesis
and [then using] the thesis to test the veracity of the same myth."[5] To
isolate Heyerdahl further, recent research shows that of seventy-two
species tentatively classified as intentional introductions into Polynesia, only three, and perhaps only two, are seen as arriving in Polynesia from South America, and the evidence for chili peppers on Easter
Island is discounted because of an error in translation of an original
Spanish text. But the American origins of the sweet potato remain,
and current linguistic evidence points to the Cuna language spoken in
northern Colombia as the origin of the word *kumara*, which in its various transliterations followed the sweet potato across the Pacific. For
Heyerdahl, the natural way to introduce *kumara* to the Marquesas, or
Easter Island, was alive, in a pot, aboard a balsa log raft.

Easter Island, or Rapa Nui, has fascinated interested observers
since Roggeveen's landing there on Easter Sunday, 1722, both because
its extreme isolation means it is habitable only by species capable of
a journey of thousands of miles and, more famously, for its eternally
enigmatic statues. The island is the easternmost inhabited island of
Polynesia, 2,300 miles (3,700 km) from South America to the east and
over 1,200 miles (2,000 km) from Pitcairn Island in the west, its nearest inhabited Polynesian neighbor.

As a result of his expedition there in 1955 with the archaeologists
William Mulloy, Edwin Ferdon Jr., Arne Skjølsvold, Carlyle Smith, and
Gonzalo Figueroa, Heyerdahl concluded that the island was already inhabited by A.D. 386±100 years.[6] An Early Period culture constructed solar observatories oriented toward the equinoctial and summer solstice
before a Middle Period culture of stone carvers quarried the extinct
volcano of Rano Raraku to create the famous *moai* statues, which were
moved to ceremonial platforms, or *ahus*. When excavations suggested

the existence of a fire pit or ditch where the *moai* stone cutters, or "Long Ears," as Heyerdahl termed them, were annihilated by a race of "Short Ears" late in the seventeenth century, and with his comparison of *moai* statuary on Easter Island with the monoliths at Tiahuanaco near the shores of Lake Titicaca, Heyerdahl was quick to see a link, and the link was made of balsa logs.

As Heyerdahl saw it, the combination of balsa rafts, sweet potatoes, and megalithic industries, all in occurrence along the coast of Peru and Chile in a time prior to the first human movements into Polynesia, was at the very least interesting. When he observed a similar combination on proximate Easter Island in the first centuries A.D., his interest turned to a search for causal connections.

Kon-Tiki: The Passage Reassessed

After the many episodic drift voyages between 1947 and the 1970s, no further evidence was required to show the trend of balsa raft drift voyages originating from South America. The *Kon-Tiki* raft itself, brought to Heyerdahl's home country, remained afloat for over a year in Oslo fiord before it was hauled ashore into the museum where it is still exhibited today. The important point to keep in mind about these voyages in terms of the Easter Island and sweet potato question is that, while Heyerdahl made much of the fact that, for instance, *Kon-Tiki* drifted twice as far as would be necessary to reach Easter Island, none of these drifts came anywhere within a thousand miles of the elusive southeast corner of Polynesia.

The *Kon-Tiki* expedition set up an apposition in cultural diffusions that exists even today. As least as far as deep-water voyaging was concerned, the extraordinarily complex question of Polynesian cultural influences bogged down into two ruts: either dominant cultural components drifted in accidentally from the east, or they sailed in from the west on the brains of sophisticated and deliberate Polynesian navigators guiding voyaging canoes capable of proceeding to windward.

Major studies of native navigational abilities were conducted in part to show that native Polynesian navigation was no accident of unlucky mariners. David Lewis, for example, concerned himself with retrieving, as far as possible, ancient and in all likelihood very closely held deep-water land-finding procedures, in the hope that this might alter the dim notions of Indigenous sailing and navigating abilities put forth by, among others, Andrew Sharp.[7]

Computer simulations of the peopling of Polynesia provided mathematical models to show the relative probability of deliberate as well as drift voyages, primarily in western Polynesia, but offered no hope to those who sought statistical backing for connections to the Polynesian outliers.[8] And we could well expect that, since the settlement of Easter Island has all the appearances of a random event—albeit a random event that was likely repeated two or three times—any search for statistical pattern is bound to reveal nothing.

Belief in the deep-water capabilities of the Polynesian double-hulled voyaging canoe set anthropologist Ben Finney and his colleagues to organize the Polynesian Voyaging Society in the mid-1970s and undertake the construction of a replica vessel, for the experimental purposes of examining the canoe's sea-going capabilities around the islands of Oceania. Between 1976 and 1987 this double-hulled canoe, Hokule'a, traveled over 20,000 nautical miles (more than 32,000 km) of the Pacific, twice between Hawai'i and Tahiti and once on a roundtrip between Hawai'i and New Zealand, or Aotearoa. Finney used two legs of this last voyage—from Ofu in American Samoa to Raratonga and from Raratonga to Tahiti, and both concluded only with excruciating difficulty—to counter Heyerdahl's notion of "permanent trade winds" that act as an unalterable barrier to eastward canoe voyages.[9]

Even so, fighting these southeast winds and currents could not have been simple or easy for deep-water Polynesian ancients. And while difficult is not the same as impossible, David Lewis, for one, makes the point that none of the relatively small sailing canoes he is familiar with is sailed very close to the wind and adds that there "seems no reason to suppose that the larger craft of yesterday were handled any differently."[10]

All the foregoing considerations and comparisons are very interesting, but none bears directly upon the problem at hand, and which is one-half of the much larger question Heyerdahl originally sought to answer: the introduction of the sweet potato into Easter Island and the development of that island's megalithic industries. Heyerdahl presented opposition to his hypothesis primarily as opposition to the balsa log raft, but he could almost as easily have presented the opposition in terms of the totora reed boat. For while his experiment proved the sea-going capabilities of the balsa log raft as a potential culture- and cultigen-bearer from Peru to the Marquesas, it only confounded the Easter Island question, which remains in many ways as enigmatic today as in April 1947, before *Kon-Tiki* sailed from Callao.

Heyerdahl cannot be faulted for selecting a balsa log raft for his experiment in 1947, for it was not until 1970, after a nearly successful attempt a year earlier, that he himself proved the capabilities of the reed boat by sailing from Africa to the Caribbean in a craft of identical construction to those on Lake Titicaca. More recently, the Spanish explorer Kitín Muñoz successfully made the voyage from Callao to the Marquesas, along the old *Kon-Tiki* route, in the totora reed boat *Uru*. With these transoceanic capabilities now experimentally proven, it is a small leap to propose a series of nautical experiments, on several levels, that could bring new data to bear on the Easter Island problem.

As Heyerdahl noted, mythological scenes from Peruvian prehistory, before the highland Incas conquered the coastal region, depict not balsa log rafts but reed boats. The totora reed used to build boats on Lake Titicaca is the same species (*Scirpus riparius*) found in the crater lakes of Easter Island, nearly 2,000 miles (3,200 km) away. In 1828 the navigator J.-A. Moerenhout, sailing from Chile, made the first of two cruises that passed by Easter Island. Studying the currents around the island, Moerenhout was emphatic in his belief that any future voyagers to Easter Island start from northern Chile and utilize the free push of the southern branch of the Humboldt Current, which drifts almost directly to the island.

With both balsa raft and totora reed boat drift voyages from Callao experimentally demonstrated to miss Easter Island by over a thousand nautical miles, and with the point of the exercise to prove the introduction of a specific cultigen on that island, several experimental possibilities present themselves. At a minimum, experimental balsa raft and reed boat voyages need to be commenced in northern Chile, to take advantage of the southern branch of the Humboldt Current, and from all the geographic centers of maritime culture in pre-Incan Peru, while Polynesian canoe voyages should be attempted from the Marquesas to Easter Island.

Heyerdahl himself noted that the drift of the Humboldt Current bends southward and sweeps directly onto Easter Island during El Niño years. This would suggest that cultural injections into Polynesia could have occurred after El Niño events, a view supported by ethnohistory, which speaks of repeated El Niño disasters that brought floods, plagues, death and dislocation to the river valleys of pre-Incan Peru.

There is a final amplification required of experimental reed and balsa voyages. The study of episodic disasters like El Niño and the voyages of cultural dispersion they may have spawned needs to be statistically strengthened with the addition of dozens if not hundreds of oceanographic drift buoys, set into the Humboldt Current opposite the major centers of pre-Incan maritime cultures, and tracked in real time by satellite and recorded through a global geographic information system. This would help fill in the dynamic experimental picture of possible routes to Easter Island in relation to the cultural centers being advanced as sources for this remote and enigmatic Stone Age civilization. In this way, perhaps we can eventually offer some answers to questions asked by a young Norwegian explorer.

6

The Origins of the Raft

One of the great pleasures of archaeology is the opportunity to dive into the history and prehistory of an area you never imagined you would have the chance to visit. In the late 1990s a survey party in search of a historic aircraft sunk in a remote port in Irian Jaya invited me along. I enjoyed the luck of counting Bill Thomas, cultural anthropologist and explorer of interior New Guinea, as my closest colleague in anthropology. Still, with just a few weeks until departure, there was much to learn about a place seemingly as distant to the creeks of my youth as the far side of the moon.

Within a few weeks of writing the introduction to *Kon-Tiki*, another call invited me to participate in an expedition to New Guinea in search of an old Sikorsky flying boat lost in the 1930s. My history of this aircraft had just been published, and the expedition was a chance to search for a surviving example of this unique machine. Even more, it was an unexpected opportunity to see the great Pacific Ocean from another side, learn about the archaeology of the original Pacific navigators, and peek into the wide sweep of coastal cultures all the way to eastern Melanesia. As this expedition took shape, more letters arrived, from modern-day raft explorers John Haslett and Phil Buck, as both sought to explore the questions posed in the previous essay. For John it was prehistoric balsa raft contact between the culture areas of coastal Ecuador and those of Central America. For Phil it was in fact the very expedition posed by Moerenhout in 1828: an experimental voyage from northern Chile to Easter Island by reed boat. Was such a voyage even possible? No other drift voyage had yet come close.

Before one could see how these expeditions would fare, it was off to the Indonesian port of Manokwari in the Bird's Head Peninsula of Irian Jaya.

> The original Negritic immigrants to Greater Australia . . . reached the Sahul Shelf south of present-day New Guinea and so had equal access both to the high forested landmasses to the north and to the drier, more lightly wooded portions of the Shelf leading directly into present-day continental Australia. . . . [This begs a question] concerning the dynamics between an established continental population intermittently assailed by raft loads of incoming peoples of different populational character. It is easy to suppose that a second wave of immigrants across the islands to the Sahul Shelf would have been quickly and simply absorbed by those already in possession of Greater Australia. But the present distribution of peoples in New Guinea, as contrasted to Australia, indicates that it could not have happened that way.
>
> —Joseph B. Birdsell, "The Recalibration of a Paradigm for the First Peopling of Greater Australia" (1977)[1]

Although not a drift expedition, the voyage of the *Tai Ki* in 1974 revived long-standing speculation that the ancient civilizations of China had influenced—if not outright germinated—the great cultures of pre-Columbian Central America. An Austrian journalist named Kuno Knöbl and a team of explorers initiated a project to build a sailing vessel on the presumed model of a Chinese junk of around A.D. 100. The dating of such an expedition, of course, would have placed Chinese mariners in Central America just at the start of the greatest period of cultural development of the ancient Maya.[2]

Knöbl and his associates built a twenty-meter-long wooden junk and sailed in it from Hong Kong on June 18, 1974. By the middle of August various health problems forced Knöbl himself to abandon the ship. The rest of the crew continued as *Teredo navalis* worms attacked the vessel with the same viciousness with which they destroyed Eric de Bisschop's *Fou Po* forty years earlier. After sailing and drifting for another two months to a point about 700 nautical miles (more than 1,100 km) south of the Aleutian Islands—and still 2,000 miles (3,200 km) from North America, the *Tai Ki* was set adrift in October and the crew were rescued by a passing merchant ship.

The idea that Chinese mariners could have crossed the Pacific two thousand years ago leads one to consider the very origins of maritime travel. Could late Pleistocene-era bamboo rafts have drifted out from the low-lying settlements of continental Asia and across to the northern coast of New Guinea? Who were the first humans to take to the sea? What did their vessel look like? Where were they going? Did they know—could they see—where they were going? How would one explore this idea experimentally?

Thoughts of such remote prehistoric raft expeditions came forcefully during a week in Indonesia in 1997. Surveying the harbor at Manokwari, a small port situated in the Vogelkop (Bird's Head) sector of New Guinea, one could sense the almost crushing weight of the many layers of human history and exploration that have settled over the Southwest Pacific. The canoe we used for our bathymetric survey in search of a sunken American flying boat glided effortlessly over a harbor visited in the nineteenth century by Alfred Russel Wallace during his research into the evolution of beetles. The double-outriggers fashioned from thick bamboo logs barely kissed the water before their natural buoyancy lifted them back above the surface.

On our flight to the port city, one could look down upon an ocean of bamboo rafts and double-outriggers, like water bugs alight on a pane of glass. It was simple to imagine that our transport plane was really a time machine and we were instead flying over a prehistoric human colony from twenty-five millennia in the past. During evenings alone in my room I pored over histories of this swampy backwater of human history and prehistory, in search of its earliest human visitors.[3]

New Guinea, occupied by humans at least 10,000–20,000 years before the earliest human groups arrived in North America, went unseen by Westerners until 1606. When Magellan crossed and named the Pacific in 1519–20, his expedition missed seeing the Vogelkop by a hundred miles or so when it passed west of New Guinea en route home from the Philippines. Magellan's expedition, like dozens after it, sought in part an undefined *Terra Australis Incognita*, an Unknown Southern Land hypothesized since the time of the Pythagoreans, six centuries before Christ, as a counterbalance to the known landmasses of the northern hemisphere. Maps as early as 1529 purported to show the undiscovered country. The continent gripped the imagination of geographers and explorers alike for two hundred and fifty years until the meticulous Captain James Cook in the 1770s showed that the Southwest Pacific consisted of Australia, Antarctica, and hundreds of other islands of various sizes.

Between the eras of Magellan and Cook, Europeans largely ignored New Guinea and the Southwest Pacific. The Portuguese and Dutch fought over the Spice Islands of Banda and Ternate (which, with Western New Guinea, would later become parts of Indonesia). The Spanish gained control over the Philippines in 1565 and established a transpacific route home from Manila via Acapulco, overland to the Caribbean, and then across the Atlantic. British raiders such as Drake, Cavendish, and Hawkins pirated Spanish settlements and ships from Peru to the Indies and back again.

Although by far the largest island south of the equator, New Guinea existed in almost complete isolation from the outside world until well into the nineteenth century. With adjacent footholds in Batavia (now Jakarta), the Dutch and British seaborne empires competed for the wealth of all the Indonesian islands save New Guinea. With most of the riches to the west, neither colonial power made much of an attempt to explore or settle the vast island. Even today, in an age of maps created by satellites, detailed representations of the interior of New Guinea frequently carry the notation "unexplored." Previously unknown indigenous tribes were noted in the interior of New Guinea as late as 1969.

The Dutch asserted vague rights over western New Guinea as early as 1714 but did not formally claim this western sector until more than a century later, in 1828. If in fact a Dutch vessel from the 1830s rests at the bottom of Manokwari Harbor—as a local hinted during our 1997 survey—it represents a pivotal shipwreck in world history, existing at a boundary of Dutch control and British insurgency into the area. The British built a fort at Dore Bay near Manokwari as early as 1790, but starvation and beriberi killed so many that they abandoned the place within a few years.

By June 1885, after years of colonial anguish and wrangling over "interests," the island was divided between Dutch, British, and newly arrived Germans. Ten years later, with typical indifference to the natives, the Dutch had consolidated their claim to the parts of New Guinea west of the Fly River, while the British and Germans split the eastern half of the island. If the Europeans who claimed the regions knew little of the coast, the interior of New Guinea might as well have been on the back side of the moon. The natives of the interior mountain ranges were known as scattered, various, without common culture or appearance, and inviolately hostile to outsiders.

Such boundaries as Europeans might draw held little or no meaning to the native peoples. No European had more than a vague idea what lay in the interior. Such knowledge as existed consisted of occasional reports of Dutch naval vessels cruising along the coastal settlements, the odd scientist on an episodic investigation, the ubiquitous traders, and a few early missionaries. Protestants of the Utrecht Society established the first missionary settlement at Manokwari in 1855. There the wiry men of the Arfak Mountains, the tribes of the Moiray and Meach—and the Hattam we met at Minyambau during a flight into the interior—bore reputations as the fiercest headhunters in western New Guinea. They wore their ancestors' skulls as charms. By one account, armed with rifles dropped by Allied aircraft during World War II, these tribesmen fought and then ate the Japanese.

Three years after the arrival of the Protestant mission, Alfred Russel Wallace explored nearby Dore Bay for five months, collecting the birds and insects that became central to his understanding of biological evolution through natural selection. The interest of his fellow Englishmen in New Guinea pertained primarily to the southern coast, from a desire to ensure naval and commercial access to the Pacific through the Torres Strait. A Royal Navy captain by the name of John Moresby surveyed the southern coast in the 1870s, giving his family name to the best harbor on the southern shore. Germans approached the island from the north, trading in copra and trochus sea snails and tortoise shells.

Colonization plans abounded with notions of gold and spices imagined in the unknown interior. Pressure to colonize New Guinea from lawyers in London and speculators in Sydney derived from a seemingly timeless ability of Westerners to believe in the presence of tropical gold mines. Expeditions to the island returned with spectacular scientific collections but with otherwise little to stimulate an economic rush. Especially discouraging were the low-lying coastal swamps, the ever-presence of "fever" (malaria as such had not been identified), and the seeming impossibilities of penetrating into the presumably healthier interior.

The first true occupiers of New Guinea since the ice age of the late Pleistocene turned out not to be economic exploiters but religious fanatics. Traders had led the Zealots of the London Missionary Society to believe that New Guinea offered a fertile field for a modern crusade. These British missionaries were in equal parts spearhead of and witnesses to the British attempt to annex southern New Guinea.

Archaeologists have made several inroads into the culture history of the natives of New Guinea. By various reckonings, Indigenous humans arrived in New Guinea some 40,000 years ago, at a time when it was connected to Australia by an ice age land bridge, which accounts for racial similarities of some New Guinea tribes with those of the Aborigines of northern Australia. New Guinea and Australia were connected whenever worldwide sea levels dropped during periods of glaciation, to form a continent prehistorians call Sahul. For Stone Age tribes of the interior—as we could see for ourselves as we crossed the highlands of the Vogelkop—seemingly little has changed since Sahulian times. In fact, modern anthropologists have come to believe that these peoples resemble what all equatorial peoples looked like and how they lived 50,000 years ago.

The north coast of New Guinea 5,000 years ago was the periphery of a complex making pottery resembling that made in Asia, an indicator of the existence of Asian trade. By 3,600 years ago, a new pottery tradition known as Lapita erupted in New Guinea. This style of pottery spread as its makers colonized the western and central Pacific and then abruptly ceased with the arrival of specialist traders 2,000 years ago.

These traders worked within traditional kinship-based trade networks that exist to this day. Evidence for these trading networks is found in the arrival of Indonesian bronze and glass artifacts in New Guinea, trade items exchanged for bird of paradise skins and feathers. The desire to possess these feathers and skins drove the trading cycle with coastal settlements.

Around the year A.D. 300, one can trace a decline in interest in plumes and a rise in the spice and forest product trade. Local knowledge gained during the plume era allowed traders to exploit already established contacts. Although most of this trade occurred in what is now Indonesia, it drew traders from throughout Asia. Chinese traders reached the Spice Islands of Ternate and Banda in the thirteenth century and gradually expanded their influence over the next two hundred years. Traders extended their search to northern New Guinea by the fifteenth century.

It was this trade that drew the Europeans. The Portuguese in 1511 captured Melaka in an attempt to monopolize trade, and the Dutch later intervened in local conflicts, disrupting local economics and politics. As trade increased and locals began to sense an unequal share in the profits, fighting ensued. Bronze spearheads and daggers from the Jayapura region attest to confrontations with traders as early as two thousand years ago. In historical times Portuguese traders established a post in Ternate in 1522, only to be driven from the area by 1574. Bandanese traders were able to exclude Europeans until 1621, when a defeat by the Dutch established trade in this region.

As the prices for spices and forest products fell in the late 1600s, the Manchu invasion of Ming-controlled provinces of China in 1640 disrupted trade with New Guinea for more than forty years. In a small Manokwari shop, I found a Dutch East India Company coin, dated 1702, and evidence of a Dutch presence a century and a half before the founding of Manokwari itself. Soon after, whalers and others in search of resources decimated elsewhere began to arrive. The inevitable investors, settlers, and missionaries followed, but by 1900 industry had declined to a few copra plantations and local trading. Plume hunting ceased in 1926 due to a combination of a decline in the plume fashion craze and government prohibitions aimed at conserving remaining bird stocks. New Guinea returned to being a backwater of Pacific trading, the calm broken only by the occasional gold fevers and other mineral extraction expeditions. The same rugged mountains and swamps that had isolated the interior since the last ice age had also hidden the real richness of the islands until modern methods of travel and extraction made mining the interior profitable, operations that continue with all the heavy industrial technologies of the twenty-first century.

These European arrivals and influences in New Guinea can be traced fairly exactly. The timing and effects of prehistoric landings in New Guinea are other matters altogether. It is thought that there was no great mass migration of early humans into Indonesia. Rather, Indigenous peoples arrived in fits and starts throughout this enormous archipelago over the course of forty millennia. Through recent archaeological excavations, *Homo erectus*, long thought to have been extinct nearly half a million years ago, may have been alive as recently as 25,000 years ago on Java. If so, they likely competed for space and resources with modern humans. It seems clear that Java was one of the earliest areas in which a variety of humans sought to live, at a time when the island was part of the Asian landmass and most of Europe was covered by continental sheets of ice.[4]

The fossil skull of Java Man (*Homo erectus*) was first found in Trinil in Central Java in 1891. Charred remains of bones seem to attest to the controlled use of fire. Beginning about 40,000 years ago, *Homo sapiens* began a movement from Australia into New Guinea and the Lesser Sunda Islands. Others arrived in western Indonesia from southern China some 30,000 years ago. Deep in the jungles of Irian Jaya one can find the genetic descendants of the Negritos, pygmy-like humans who also spread through Indonesia beginning 30,000 years ago. Skulls found at Wajak in East Java are evidence of the first ancestors of the present-day Indonesians, the *Homo sapiens* who populated the area 10–12,000 years ago. A still more problematic discovery was that of *Homo floriensis*, likened to a dwarf *erectus* or even earlier *Homo habilis* species, discovered on the island of Flores in 2003 and the subject of intense debate ever since.

How these early peoples voyaged over long stretches of coastal and inter-island waters is a matter of intense interest to archaeologists. J. B. Birdsell identified five different routes from the ancient Southeast Asian continent of Sunda to the combined Australian–New Guinea continent of Sahul. It seemed probable to Birdsell that "the watercraft used in the late Pleistocene were superior to those found in recent times in Australia and Tasmania. It is highly probable that there was a constant if somewhat straggling trickle of small groups of human beings over all or most of the routes. The size of the watercraft likely to have been used suggests that the groups consisted of small biological families."[5]

Birdsell identified thirty-five different species of bamboo along these routes, indicating both the possible raw materials that prehistoric mariners may have used to construct rafts and the paths for which they were set adrift. Such varieties of both routes and raw materials provided scores of testable hypotheses. As Birdsell noted, assuming these many species of bamboo existed during ice age times of lower sea levels, they offer "a useful role for experimental archaeology."[6] One could readily imagine a fleet of different bamboo rafts exploring dozens of possible routes for early humans from Asia to Sahul.

During an archaeological expedition to the Indian Ocean archipelago of the Maldives Islands in the mid-1980s, Thor Heyerdahl spotted a large, abandoned bamboo raft in a lagoon at the island of Viringili. This particular type of raft was foreign to the Maldives, and a group of children were playing on it. The locals told Heyerdahl that fishermen had discovered the raft the day before, on the outer reef off the east coast of the island. Because it carried no crew, the fishermen were suspicious and tried to burn it.

Obviously it was no use to try to keep Thor Heyerdahl away from exploring a raft that had just drifted from some distant shore. He arrived at the bamboo vessel just as the boys were tearing it apart to sell the pieces at a local auction. The children jumped overboard as the adults arrived to inspect the apparition.

It was a raft indeed: large, and built from giant bamboo. I had never seen bamboo as thick as this. Thick as telegraph poles and tied together in three layers under eight cross beams of wood with another layer of thick bamboo as a deck well above the water . . . Twelve meters long and three wide (39 feet by 10 feet, approximately) with a freeboard of 40 centimeters (16 inches), the whole structure recalled the balsa raft *Kon-Tiki* which had been large enough to carry me and five companions across the Pacific.[7]

Seventy-year-old Heyerdahl then boarded the raft, which did not rock or move under his feet and, almost immediately, felt himself transported forty years into the past. Though badly burned, the bamboo cabin reminded him of the small space he had shared in 1947 with Danielsson and Haugland, Raaby and Watzinger and Hesselberg. The cabin floor was some eight inches above the main bamboo deck, and a baked clay cooking area occupied one corner. A watertight layer of coconut palm thatch covered the cabin roof.

Making his way down the length of the raft, Heyerdahl encountered a few dried fish, which he thought had probably leapt on board as the raft drifted on the open ocean. The only clues as to the origins of the raft were two paper labels that he later identified as Burmese candy wrappers. The raft had most likely therefore floated nearly 2,000 nautical miles (3,200 km) from Burma, through the Bay of Bengal, and into the Indian Ocean to the Maldives. From his own rafting experience, Heyerdahl looked at the barnacles growing on the bamboo and estimated that the vessel had been at sea about two months, pushed ahead of the Northeast Monsoon.

After his lifetime of drifting on Indigenous rafts, the sight of this Buddhist raft in the Maldives triggered much interesting speculation. Heyerdahl concluded that the teachings of Buddha had likely made a similar drift to the Maldives—a thousand years before Moslems settled in the islands—traveling from Nepal down the Ganges to the Bay of Bengal, to Burma, and across the Indian Ocean. But what of the ultimate question? Had the cradle of civilization been constructed by farmers or fishers? If the latter, was it made from reeds, balsa, or bamboo?

7

Thor Heyerdahl and the Theory of the Archaeological Raft

Any form of competent research inquiry relies on a solid design. A good research design is a good roadmap, without which you will very likely find yourself lost. The motivations behind the many raft expeditions that followed in the wake of Thor Heyerdahl's *Kon-Tiki* can be ascribed to four distinct categories: science, pseudo-science, adventure, and survival. The expeditions identified as having a core of scientific intent were largely those that most closely identified their method with Heyerdahl's examples in his *Kon-Tiki* and *Ra II* expeditions.

By the time of the publication of *Sea Drift* in 2001, John Haslett's final balsa raft expeditions had ended on the rocks near the Costa Rican village of Golfito. But he had accomplished his mission to link by raft the central and south American coasts. In the year 2000 Phil Buck sailed his reed ship *Viracocha* from Chile to Easter Island in little more than six weeks, a brilliant performance that answered once and for all whether a reed ship were capable of making such a journey. Excellent accounts appeared on both expeditions: John's luminous *Voyage of the Manteño* in 2006 (recently rereleased as *The Lost Raft*) and Nick Thorpe's excellent *8 Men and a Duck* in 2003. Thor Heyerdahl, the progenitor of these expeditions, passed away at the age of eighty-seven in April 2002, almost fifty-five years to the day since his *Kon-Tiki* drifted to sea from the Peruvian harbor at Callao.

Soon after, another Norwegian explorer sought to follow *Kon-Tiki*. On a bright early summer morning in June 2004 Torgeir Sæverud Higraff and I sat on the wall near the Akerhus Fortress that overlooks Oslo Harbor. He had read *Sea Drift* in its original English and asked if we could meet when I came to Oslo that summer to study, write poetry, and enjoy a slow wander around the city I love more than any other. Torgeir wanted to re-create a balsa raft expedition in the Pacific and wanted a scientific rationale for doing so.

Torgeir was in many ways typical of the Norwegians met in many years of traveling in and around Norway, from Oslo to arctic Svalbard. He lived a strenuous outdoors, adventurous life. Tall, rugged, good-looking, he had been a river guide in western Norway but now sought much wider horizons. He was impatient not to advance further into adulthood without a major expeditionary accomplishment behind his name. This became 2006's *Tangaroa*, named after the Polynesian god of the sea, and the only major balsa expedition between 2000 and 2010.

As we talked of the history of raft expeditions, it became clear that the time was long overdue to categorize these expeditions by their aims and outcomes. This in turn led to the following essay in *EXARC*, *the journal of experimental archaeology*, in 2012. It divided the motivations of these expeditions into four major categories, examined more closely the expeditions based on serious scientific hypotheses, and established criteria for ranking the eleven expeditions deemed to have produced archaeologically significant results.

In the aftermath of Thor Heyerdahl's *Kon-Tiki* expedition in the summer of 1947, thirty-seven similar expeditions sought to employ Heyerdahl's method of re-created maritime technology in order to reach widely varying goals. Of the two survival expeditions, one used a rubber boat and the other was created by salvaging water barrels carried on a previous raft. Of the nine expeditions for which motivation was exclusively adventure, five used balsa rafts, and all these operated in the Pacific. Of the six expeditions for which motivation can be seen as wholly pseudo-scientific, one used Chilean cedar, while four employed modern plywood, and one even more modern fiberglass.

Science as Motivation; Heyerdahl as Method

The *Kon-Tiki* expedition transformed the oceans of the world into a kind of gigantic archaeological laboratory. The repeated target of critics both inside and outside the academy who rely on cursory readings of the popular account of the expedition, *Kon-Tiki: Across the Pacific by Raft* (1950), and not the scholarly theoretical discourse *American Indians in the Pacific: The Theory behind the Kon-Tiki Expedition* (1952), the expedition laid the foundation for modern experimental archaeology in re-created watercraft.

A year in the Marquesas in the 1930s had led Heyerdahl to a radical hypothesis concerning the peopling of Polynesia. In 1941 he advanced the idea of a dual migration into Polynesia from the Americas. The method he chose to demonstrate his belief in his hypothesis, a living experiment on a transoceanic raft in which he subjected himself and several crew members to a mission some considered suicidal, removed diffusion studies from the purely theoretical and from 1947 onward made them dependent upon the experimental.

The three significant expeditions led by Heyerdahl—*Kon-Tiki, Ra II*, and *Tigris*—made increasingly sophisticated experiments based on finer and finer variables. *Kon-Tiki* sought largely to demonstrate that a balsa raft could cross an ocean, a fairly simple and straightforward proposition. *Ra II*, undertaken twenty-three years after *Kon-Tiki*, sought to do the same for papyrus reed vessels but also sought to test refined reed ship construction and navigation methods learned from the failure of the first *Ra* expedition.

Tigris, in 1977–78, confronted a whole series of variables. These included the nature of berdi reed harvesting; long-term buoyancy; the efficacy of the circumferential rope in holding the reeds together; rudder design efficiency; keel design and use; river, estuary, and ocean navigation; and the nature of ancient world maritime and trading relationships. The performance of the *Tigris* led Heyerdahl to conclude that a reed ship could carry a cargo of as much as fifty tons. Later reed boats expeditions, like those of *Mata Rangi* and *Viracocha*, would use Heyerdahl's experience to both detriment and profit.

The 1997 *Mata Rangi* expedition used Heyerdahl's belief that a ship carving on the breast of Moai No. 263 on Easter Island (Rapa Nui) represented a three-masted reed ship. Heyerdahl had learned that to form an effective reed ship the reeds themselves must be harvested at a specific time in their growth cycle (for the berdi reeds of southern Iraq that time was late summer) in order to preserve their buoyancy. *Mata Rangi*, an enormous reed ship some 120 feet long, was constructed entirely of reeds harvested in the crater lake of the extinct volcano of Maunga Terevaka on Rapa Nui. It remained on a Rapa Nui beach for so long that these reeds very likely became brittle and rotted, losing both their flexibility and their natural buoyancy.

The very size of the vessel also seemed to contradict the lessons learned by Heyerdahl and his crews in the design, construction, and sailing of the *Ra* ships and the *Tigris*. Reed ships bigger than sixty feet seemed to work themselves apart and lose buoyancy quickly. The lack of a rope wrapped around the length of the reed bundles—a so-called circumferential rope—allowed the reed bundles to work apart longitudinally. Heyerdahl employed such a rope on all three of his reed ships and not one of them worked apart longitudinally. *Mata Rangi* lasted less than three weeks at sea before the ship broke apart and forced a rescue of the crew.

Viracocha, on the other hand, used a smaller, *Ra II*-like design as well as a tightly bound circumferential rope to hold the reed hulls together. The ship left Arica, Chile, on February 25, 2000, and with steady trade winds from the south and southeast averaged about two knots an hour. Over the course of the next forty-four days the reed boat continued to average about fifty nautical miles a day. It reached Rapa Nui on the afternoon of April 9 and anchored at Hanga Piko. *Viracocha*, by following the experience of the *Tigris* expedition, had sailed over 2,000 miles (more than 3,200 km) and was still in excellent condition. The cumulative effect of Heyerdahl's experience, then, reveals the potential global

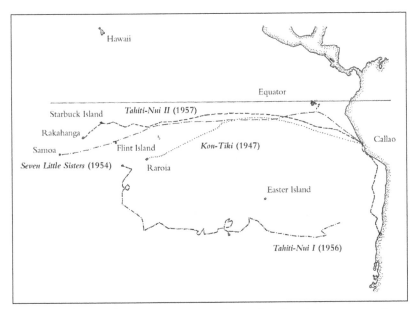

Pathways of the early transoceanic experimental archaeology voyages. Courtesy C.L. Devlin.

reach of the reed ship when the reeds are both properly harvested and properly employed in raft construction.

Like Heyerdahl, Eric de Bisschop, who organized the *Tahiti Nui* expedition in 1957 in opposition to the results of *Kon-Tiki*, had little patience for academics with no practical maritime experience upon which to base their theories of Polynesian origins and migrations. De Bisschop was equally at odds with prevailing views of maritime geography as essentially static, railing against anthropologists who "blandly assume that the geographical features of the Pacific and Indian Oceans, with all the lands which emerge from them or border them, have not budged an inch for thousands of years—an assumption based on nothing except perhaps man's subconscious reluctance to admit that he inhabits an unstable and ever-changing crust."[1]

Bisschop saw a Polynesian sphere of influence extending from Easter Island and perhaps the shores of South America in the east, to Madagascar off the coast of Africa in the west, a span more than half the distance around the world. To study this enormous problem of cultural geography, de Bisschop envisioned a new field of maritime ethnology, where scholars would use re-created voyaging technologies in order to study ancient diffusions.

Like Heyerdahl before the *Kon-Tiki* expedition, de Bisschop came to believe that no attention would be offered to his ideas unless he took them to sea, on an actual transoceanic voyage. While Bisschop's bamboo raft *Tahiti Nui*, like Tim Severin's later bamboo junk *Hsu Fu*, demonstrated that a bamboo craft possessed the range to bridge almost an entire ocean, both craft broke apart and sank before they reached their objectives. In an attempt to follow up this initial observation a year later, Bisschop would lose his life, remarkably the only death during such experiments over the course of six decades.

A series of scientifically meaningful balsa raft expeditions over the past thirty-five years have all patterned themselves after *Kon-Tiki*. Two of these—the *La Balsa* expedition of Vital Alsar and the *La Manteño* expedition of John Haslett—designed their balsa rafts after the prehistoric cultural model of the Huancavilca Indians of Ecuador. Alsar cited the work of the Argentine anthropologist Juan Moricz in supporting his belief that the prehistoric Ecuadorian mariners were no strangers to the islands of the Pacific.

> [Moricz] points out that the Huancavilcas thought of the ocean as "a forest of rivers," with predictable currents to and from the Polynesian islands. They also knew about "friendly and unfriendly" winds and the use of astronomy in navigation. Commenting on the presence of South American cocoa trees, *quecha kuka*, in the far-off Mexican highlands, Moricz concludes that the Ecuadorian natives had sailed all the way to Mexico long before the conquest of Montezuma by Hernán Cortés.[2]

The third scientifically meaningful balsa expedition, the *Tangaroa* experiment of Torgeir Higraff in 2006, outperformed *Kon-Tiki* on several levels. After experimenting with the correct placement of the centerboard *guaras*—which were too long and had to be cut down to maintain the raft's sailing balance—the Norwegian crew settled on a course of 270° that took them more or less directly toward the west. Compensating for the northward drift of the Humboldt Current, the raft was kept on a northwesterly course but in a flatter, more southerly arc than that taken by *Kon-Tiki*.

Tangaroa reached the islands of eastern Polynesia a month faster than *Kon-Tiki* in 1947. In the end it drifted farther and faster than *Kon-Tiki*, and landed at Polynesia's ancient cultural center of Raiatea, demonstrating that an improved sail rig and active use of the *guara* centerboards allowed a balsa raft to be steered on a direct and rapid course from Peru to Polynesia. *Tangaroa*, along with *Viracocha*, stand as the logical scientific outcomes of the experiments in re-created maritime technology begun by Thor Heyerdahl with *Kon-Tiki* in 1947 and continued with *Ra II* in 1970 and *Tigris* in 1977.

Pseudo-science as Motivation: The Essentially Non-Scientific

After the sinking of the bamboo raft *Tahiti Nui*, Eric de Bisschop intended to build a copy from the same materials for a return voyage to Tahiti. But with no bamboo available in Chile, where Bombard was rescued, he instead had a new raft built from buoyant Chilean cypress wood. There was no experimental reason for this choice. It was made simply because there was no other suitable wood available.

For this reason, despite the success of *Tahiti Nui* as a drift experiment from Tahiti to the offshore waters of South America, the *Tahiti Nui II* expedition can be seen as one of half a dozen raft expeditions based not on science but on absurd notions that were at best pseudo-scientific. Bisschop could at least claim a long and detailed interest in the problems of Polynesian diffusion. The other pseudo-scientific expeditions could claim no such distinction.

In 1954 a drift expedition across the Pacific was used by a devout Mormon by the name of Devere Baker to turn Thor Heyerdahl's thesis of a bearded white god bearing the gifts of civilization into the second coming of Jesus Christ. Incongruously, Baker built a plywood raft in San Francisco in order to test an idea from *The Book of Mormon* that a "great, fair, highly cultured race of people [had] sailed from the Old World to the New World on 'caves of wood.'"[3]

Rather than set himself adrift from the Old World to the New, Baker instead sought to drift from California to Hawai'i, for no apparent reason other than convenience. The raft, called *Lehi*, was abandoned just a week after its launch from San Francisco. The second *Lehi* expedition, like the first, was also abandoned soon after its launch from San Francisco.

Baker's *Lehi III* raft succeeded in making a voyage from San Francisco down the California coast to Los Angeles. Finally, on July 14, 1958, Baker launched *Lehi IV* from Redondo Beach, California, and reached Maui two months later on September 20, 1958. Feeling himself vindicated, Baker announced plans for a new drift expedition from the Red Sea to the Central American birthplace of the ancient Olmecs via the Indian Ocean and the Japan Current. The expedition never materialized, but with his antics, Baker contributed almost single-handedly to decades of academic dismissals of even well-designed archaeological experiments.

The final expedition to take to the ocean for dubious reasons of presumed scholarly research was that of Santiago Genovés, a Mexican social scientist who had been a crew member on board Heyerdahl's *Ra I* and *Ra II* expeditions. In 1973 Genovés, with four other men and six women, set out to test human compatibility on a raft voyage across the Atlantic. Genovés envisioned his raft as a kind of "floating laboratory, a real sea adventure in which volunteers agreed to participate with the consequent risks, to obtain firsthand data about aggression, conflict, misunderstandings, and possibilities for harmony in a world of violence."[4] The scientific nature of the experiment, however, was undermined from the start, when Genovés decided that he himself would be one of the humans trapped on the raft.

The raft, made of fiberglass and nearly forty feet long and twenty-one feet wide, was named *Acali*. It drifted away from the Canary Islands in May 1973. In late July the experiment was brought to a halt in the Caribbean. By then Genovés himself seemed at a loss to explain the meaning of his audacious experiment. What exactly had he explored? What kinds of data had he really produced? Given the ill-conceived nature of the "experiment," it is not surprising that it has never been replicated except for its modern reincarnation as *Survivor*-type television programming.

Adventure as Motivation: The Non-Scientifically Essential

One can trace the basic motivation of a good adventure to at least nine of the expeditions that followed *Kon-Tiki*. Of the expeditions for which motivation can be described as essentially adventurous—that is, with little or no serious scientific component—seven took place in the Pacific Ocean. Of these seven, five used some version of a balsa raft.

These adventures were typified by William Willis's solo balsa raft voyage on *Seven Sisters* in 1954. Willis was certainly interested in the effects of prolonged isolation on a raft on the endurance of his body and mind. But during the 115 days it took him to drift from central Peru to Samoa, the sixty-one-year-old American was mostly interested in re-creating the feelings of being young, alive, and healthy; in other words, of reliving the sensation of childhood adventure, only on a massive trans-Pacific scale.

It was a similar motivation Willis used again in 1963, when he again set sail alone, at the age of seventy-one, to "prove that age is no barrier to physically challenging tasks."[5] The corollary to this notion, of course, is that youth is a natural inducement to take on such challenges. Over two years in 1963–64 Willis sailed his makeshift aluminum raft from Peru to Australia, a distance of 9,800 miles (nearly 16,000 km) in an elapsed time of 200 days. A spiritual as well as physical adventurer, Willis spent a considerable amount of time just prior to leaving Peru trying to convince his wife that they would be able to communicate telepathically while the raft drifted thousands of miles at sea ("distance means nothing in electricity and in thought even less.")[6]

Five other expeditions in the Pacific can trace their motivation almost exclusively to the desire for adventure. If William Willis was the most introverted and thoughtful of the adventurous raft expedition leaders, Eduardo Ingris was certainly the most colorful and cut the most carefree profile. Ingris was described as "a cheerful curly-haired Czech."[7] In 1955 Ingris built a balsa raft named *La Cantuta* and drifted from northern Peru toward the Galapagos Islands. Ingris had assembled a crew that consisted of men from Argentina, Holland, and Peru, as well as a woman from Lake Titicaca, the high altitude lake and home

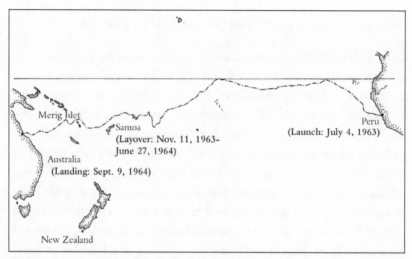

Transoceanic pathway of William Willis's raft *Age Unlimited.* Courtesy C.L. Devlin.

of master reed boat builders. When the raft approached the Galapagos, it was snagged for three months in the Equatorial Counter Current. Unable to proceed east or west, Ingris and his crew had to be rescued.

Three years later, when Eric de Bisschop's raft *Tahiti Nui II* landed at the Peruvian port of Callao in March 1958, Ingris begged to be included in de Bisschop's crew for its planned drift to Polynesia. "Despite the unfortunate result of [his 1955 expedition], Ingris was so eager to begin again that he came back every day and tried by new and ingenious arguments to persuade us to take him with us."[8] When de Bisschop decided against taking Ingris in his crew, the Czech built another balsa raft for himself.

In 1959 *La Cantuta II* carried Ingris and a new crew from Callao all the way to Matahiva in central Polynesia. Along the way Ingris occupied himself making a movie of the expedition and writing the theme music for it.

Motivation—Survival: Deliberate and Accidental Death and Near-Death

Given the nature of transoceanic raft expeditions, with their inherent danger and long-term challenges to physical and psychological survival, it is perhaps surprising that only two of the nearly forty such efforts can be regarded as essentially experiments in survival. And only one of these two was planned specifically as such.

In the spring of 1951 a young French doctor by the name of Alain Bombard combined a series of laboratory experiments in the comparative compositions of seawater and the water squeezed from various species of fish with historical research into the psychological and physical state of shipwreck survivors. With these data he observed that 90 percent of shipwreck survivors died within three days, even though a human being could survive far longer than that even if completely deprived of food and water. He concluded that if one could overcome initial despair and eventual thirst—the latter by drinking water squeezed from fish flesh and supplemented with a pint and a half of seawater per day—the major factors causing death amongst shipwreck survivors could be reduced.

Four years after *Kon-Tiki*, Bombard deliberately set out use Heyerdahl's global ocean as a scientific laboratory. "If my theory was to be something more than a hypothesis, if it was to serve some real purpose, it was essential to reduce the experiment to human terms in an actual sea voyage. I had to find some way of isolating myself on the ocean for a period of between one and three months."[9]

As with *Kon-Tiki*, word of Bombard's plans caused most experts to say that an inflatable boat could never remain afloat on the open ocean more than ten days, which in the event would not matter because Bombard would likely be dead by then anyway.

After a false start in the Mediterranean, Bombard started from the Moroccan port city of Tangier in midsummer 1952. Reaching Casablanca on August 20, he set out four days later on a drift toward the Canary Islands to the southwest. In early September he landed near Las Palmas in the Canaries. On Sunday, October 19, 1952, Bombard was towed to sea and cast adrift. The raft set into the current and its small sail began to catch the northeast trade winds that would push it toward the Caribbean.

In the end, Bombard and his raft landed on the island of Barbados on December 22, 1952. He had demonstrated that a castaway could in fact survive on the most meager of diets from the sea, could in fact survive death by thirst by drinking small quantities of seawater each day. He had lost fifty-five pounds and become anæmic, but he was alive—and lived on until his death at the age of eighty in 2005.

The second raft expedition to experience a similar, though unplanned, survival experiment was that of the *Tahiti Nui III*. In the summer of 1958 Eric de Bisschop's *Tahiti Nui II* experiment—the pseudo-scientific follow-up to his moderately successful *Tahiti Nui* voyage of 1957, was drifting into the central Pacific and toward disaster. The raft, ill-conceived and constructed from cedar wood, was thoroughly water-logged as it passed the Marquesas Islands. The increasingly disturbed crew had taken to living together on the top of the cabin of the sinking hulk.

On August 6, when the raft was within 250 miles of Starbuck Island, the crew decided it was time to forsake the large raft and build an escape raft out of a series of aluminum water tanks. Large tanks served as a main hull, while ten smaller ten-gallon tanks were divided equally to serve as the port and starboard outriggers.

The crew abandoned the *Tahiti Nui II* and set it adrift in mid-August, but the escape raft *Tahiti Nui III* missed Starbuck Island by twenty-nine miles. After a series of mutinies by the crew during the remainder of August, the windward reef at the island of Rakahanga came into view on August 30.

When the raft was caught by the surf that evening the entire crew was thrown into the ocean. The crew found de Bisschop bobbing in the waves, having suffered a severe trauma to the back of his head and a broken neck. *Tahiti Nui III* had washed ashore on an island with a population of only one hundred souls. But the raft crew was only four people and their leader was dead—hardly the most auspicious way to enter a potentially treacherous New World.

Analysis: Establishing the Archaeologically Significant Expedition

Of the total number of drift expeditions in re-created maritime technology that began with *Kon-Tiki*, eleven can be seen as producing significant results for studies of experimental archaeology and cultural diffusion. Of these eleven, only two—*Ra II* and *Tigris*—were conducted somewhere other than the Pacific Ocean.

Each of these eleven expeditions contributed to the evaluation of unique variables in prehistoric voyaging by watercraft essentially aligned with the prevailing winds and currents of the planet. The first three, *Kon-Tiki*, *Tahiti Nui*, and *Ra II*, demonstrated the durability of long-distance watercraft constructed from three materials—balsa, bamboo, and [papyrus] reed—previously thought incapable of such range and endurance. The next three expeditions, *La Balsa*, *Tigris*, and *Hsu Fu*, more than doubled the range of the first three expeditions and thereby demonstrated that these same materials—balsa, [berdi] reed, and bamboo—possess enough durability that they would have allowed prehistoric mariners to encircle the globe.

The next three expeditions, *Mata Rangi*, *Illa-Tiki*, and *La Manteña*, were expeditionary failures but experimental successes. The massive reed ship *Mata Rangi* broke apart soon after its launch from Rapa Nui, providing evidence to believe that reed ships of prehistory must have been built more within the parameters of *Tigris*. It also provided support for Norwegian archaeologist Arne Skjølsvold's belief that the unique Rapa Nui *moai* statue known as No. 263 and used as the basis for *Mata Rangi* probably represents not a prehistoric Rapa Nui ship but a historic European sailing vessel.[10]

The *Illa-Tiki* and *La Manteña* expeditions of John Haslett demonstrated the very great struggle to navigate a balsa raft successfully northward along the coasts of South America to Mexico.[11] This route, speculated as an avenue for the transmission of the knowledge of metal working in prehistory, is fraught with dangers.[12] These include oceanographic dangers such as the spiral of currents near Panama known as the Gyre as well as the evident risk to balsa wood from the marine invertebrate *Teredo navalis*.

The final two expeditions of experimental significance—the 2000 reed ship *Viracocha* and the 2006 balsa raft *Tangaroa*—extended our knowledge of the speed with which prehistoric mariners could have traveled across vast distances. *Viracocha* showed that a reed ship launched from the west coast of South America could reach Rapa Nui in as little as six weeks. This suggests the possibility of frequent round trips between the megalithic cultures of Rapa Nui and the reed-ship-building cultures of Lake Titicaca in Bolivia. Similarly, *Tangaroa* made the journey from Peru to Polynesia a full month faster than did *Kon-Tiki* in 1947.

The imitative focus on the Heyerdahl-inspired balsa and reed ships has almost entirely obscured other, potentially more valuable vessel types and natural materials from the body of experimental nautical archaeology. Only two transoceanic bamboo voyages have been undertaken, and both had the object of reaching the Americas. The idea that Asian mariners could have crossed the Pacific two thousand years ago naturally leads one to consider the very origins of maritime travel, as we touched upon in the previous chapter. Could late (or, if *Homo floriensis* is some direct descendant of *Homo habilis*, even earlier!) Pleistocene-era bamboo rafts have sailed or drifted out from the low-lying settlements of continental Asia and across to the northern coast of New Guinea?

A model for such voyages already exists. In January 2000 a dozen men led by Robert G. Bednarik paddled a forty-foot bamboo raft called *Nale Tasih 4* from the east coast of the Indonesian island of Bali across eighteen miles (30 km) of open ocean to the neighboring island of Lombok.[13] This expedition continued Bednarik's experimental attempts to support a theory that *Homo erectus* and not *Homo sapiens* was the first hominid species to possess both the tools and maritime technology to cross the Wallace Line, some 800,000 years ago. In 1998, in a fifty-eight-foot-long bamboo raft, Bednarik and crew sailed from Timor to Australia, 600 miles (965 km) in thirteen days. Bednarik's experimental nautical archaeology suggested that an optimal length for a bamboo raft was—as was the bamboo raft found in the Maldives by Heyerdahl—about forty feet. This fascinating series of experiments connecting Indonesia to Australia should lead scholars of prehistoric population movements to a focus on underrepresented yet equally significant maritime domains such as the Bay of Bengal and the Andaman Sea.

Conclusions

More than half of the expeditions in re-created maritime technology following Heyerdahl's 1947 *Kon-Tiki* experiment traced both their motivation and their method to that expedition or to the pioneering work done by Heyerdahl in the re-creation of reed boat technology in the late 1960s. In these twenty expeditions, the motivation was the perceived application of the scientific method to problems of prehistoric technology; to prehistoric maritime drift or sailing routes; and to questions of cultural diffusion.

Fourteen of these twenty expeditions took place across or in the coastal areas of the Pacific Ocean, by far the most popular arena for experimental maritime archaeology studies. Of these fourteen, six used balsa rafts and six used reed ships for their experiments. The remaining two used bamboo, and one of those—the *Tahiti Nui* expedition— was carried out in direct scientific opposition to *Kon-Tiki*. *Kon-Tiki*, then, along with the *Ra* expeditions, can be seen both as establishing the method by which experimental archaeology expeditions would be carried out and as influencing nearly every experimental archaeology expedition that followed.

Taken as an experimental whole, the eleven expeditions seen as producing significant experimental results have offered a convincing case that the ancient Pacific Ocean could very well have been an arena of dynamic and rapid exchanges of people, technology, and culture. Future experiments should shift to a fuller examination of the nature and development of the bamboo raft and its role in the coastal movements of prehistoric populations along the complex and under-studied maritime domains from the Bay of Bengal to the Andaman Sea.

8

Eric de Bisschop and
the Response to *Kon-Tiki*

The core of a good research design is a testable hypothesis. The scientific method relies on nothing less. If a concept cannot be subject to testing it cannot be evaluated scientifically. One can believe anything one likes, but if you want to think it, that thought needs to be testable.

In 2014 Torgeir Higraff proposed a second balsa raft expedition: this would complement the 2000 expedition of Phil Buck's reed ship *Viracocha* and demonstrate that a balsa raft could also sail to and from Easter Island. Torgeir's vision and imagination led to the creation of not one but two giant balsa rafts in the port of Callao in the spring of 2015. Sailing more or less in tandem, the two vessels reached Easter Island in just forty-three days. No other balsa raft had reached this remote island in modern times.

At this point, however, the expedition took a turn that would have been very familiar to Eric de Bisschop. As he sought to make a roundtrip voyage to South America, Torgeir and the two rafts faced the same dilemma as had de Bisschop on board his *Tahiti Nui* in 1957. One could try to reach South America more or less directly east from

Easter Island and face adverse winds all the way, or sail south toward the prevailing and very dangerous Westerlies of the Roaring Forties latitudes. Either way, a return journey from Easter Island to South America would prove a very difficult task indeed. The near-impossible conditions forced Torgeir to abandon his incredible voyage after more than seventy days, about halfway between Easter Island and South America, and set the abandoned rafts adrift. The remarkable de Bisschop would not have been surprised.

What on earth was that queer craft lying there right in front of the Post Office, in just the same place where our one and only Kon-Tiki raft had found sanctuary nine years before? . . . When I looked more closely I saw . . . that the raft at the quay differed from ours in several respects, most notably in being built of bamboo and having two double masts. Bursting with curiosity, I asked my friend the harbor-master whence this new raft came. He gave me a searching look and replied: "She doesn't come from anywhere, for she was built here. Are you pulling my leg, or do you really mean to say that you have not yet heard of Eric de Bisschop's new expedition? He's going to sail to Chile in that tub—Tahiti Nui he calls her—at the beginning of next month, with four other lunatics."

—Bengt Danielsson, *From Raft to Raft* (1960)

Every boat that arrives in Papeete brings stupid individuals who think they have come to the islands of their dreams, where they can live off trees groaning with coconuts, on bananas and fish, and live among 'primitive natives' who will be only too happy to provide them with lodging and food, not forgetting the youngest of their daughters. One can understand why the French authorities cast an unfavorable eye on the pitiable victims of [romantic Pacific] literature, human flotsam they will soon be obliged to deport back to their own countries bitter and deceived.

—Eric de Bisschop, *Tahiti Nui* (1959)

Thor Heyerdahl's idea of a bearded white god-man bringing civilization to Polynesia from the direction of the rising sun did not sit well with many Pacific islanders. Yet the first direct and sustained Polynesian drifter's challenge to the Norwegian came from a French baron living in Tahiti. By his own admission, Eric de Bisschop had invested the better part of thirty years in a study of Polynesian navigation and anthropology prior to his 1956 voyage in a bamboo raft. But de Bisschop was far more than an armchair explorer prior to his raft expedition. A case can be made that only James Cook himself had sailed more of the Pacific Ocean in search of scientific truth than had Eric de Bisschop.

Like another late life raft explorer, William Willis, Eric de Bisschop was in his sixties and had already spent much of his life at sea before living the last years of his life on rafts. In the 1930s, after four years in China, de Bisschop had saved enough to purchase an old Chinese junk, the *Fou-Po*. When a cyclone wrecked this ship off the coast of Taiwan he built a second, the *Fou-Po II*. On board this second junk, after wrecks in Australia and New Guinea and attacks by wood-eating marine *Teredo navalis* worms, de Bisschop explored whether the 9,000-mile (14,500 km) equatorial counter-current could have served as a prehistoric seaway between Asia and America.

Just before the Second World War de Bisschop built a Polynesian double-hulled canoe he named *Kaimiloa* and sailed it from Hawai'i to France. *Kaimiloa* raced from Honolulu to the Wallis Islands in little over a month, and then crossed the 6,000 miles (9,600 km) of the Indian Ocean in less than two. These were extraordinary reaches and convinced de Bisschop that watercraft of Polynesian design were the equal of any ocean distance anywhere.

Settling in Tahiti after the war, de Bisschop was called back to the sea by the success of *Kon-Tiki*. Two aspects of Heyerdahl's voyage in particular bothered him mightily. First, Heyerdahl's raft, presumably a copy of the pre-Columbian sailing raft, was built with fixed centerboards. De Bisschop was adamant that this was not the case: such centerboards had been designed to be moved up and down according to the navigational needs of the raft, a fact Heyerdahl himself learned in 1952, five years after his first raft trip. Similar centerboards control the movements of bamboo rafts of ancient design in both Taiwan and the coasts of China and Viet Nam.

These centerboards, or *guara*, allowed one to tack and cross a raft into the wind like a European sailing vessel. As Heyerdahl wrote in 1994 to John Haslett, then planning the first of his three balsa raft voyages, "balsa rafts of from 3 to 5 balsa logs are still used in several fishing ports in both Ecuador and north Peru, and they go out at night and come back to the same beach by noon." Long before Heyerdahl's experiments with *guara*, Eric de Bisschop met *Kon-Tiki* crew member and anthropologist Bengt Danielsson in Tahiti after the expedition and Danielsson had to admit that the centerboards had likely not been employed properly.

Much more central than this esoteric question of raft design, however, was the suggestion that Polynesians could not have reached the shores of South America because the prevailing winds and currents would effectively have prevented such a passage. This de Bisschop refused to accept. He himself had tacked Chinese junks and double-hulled canoes against prevailing winds for much of his life and saw no reason why prehistoric Polynesians could not have accomplished the same thing. What was startling, however, was the technology de Bisschop chose to employ in an attempt to refute the *Kon-Tiki* theory.

When Bengt Danielsson arrived in Tahiti for the fifth time in the fall of 1956, he saw a raft moored along the docks of Papeete, in the same spot where he and the rest of Heyerdahl's crew had stepped off *Kon-Tiki* almost ten years earlier. But this was a raft of a very different sort. Again, like William Willis before him, de Bisschop had distilled a lifetime of sea-going experiences into the design of a transoceanic raft. In de Bisschop's case, his raft reflected his experiences in Polynesia and China as well as his knowledge of Chinese and Peruvian centerboards.

The raft was built of bamboo, equipped with the Peruvian *guara*, and rigged like a double-masted Chinese junk. Remarkably, rather than use all his accumulated experience to demonstrate that a true Polynesian double-hulled voyaging canoe could manage a journey from Tahiti to South America, de Bisschop proposed that his polyglot bamboo raft

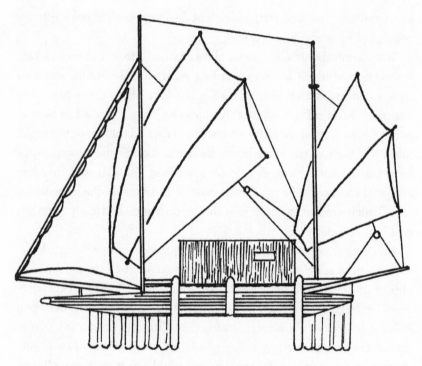

Eric de Bisschop's raft *Tahiti-Nui*. Courtesy C.L. Devlin.

could make the same voyage against 5,000 nautical miles (more than 8,000 km) of prevailing winds and currents. He advanced this proposal to general disbelief. When he announced that he would set his course far to the south, to take advantage of the shifting westerly winds and currents that prevail around 40° south, most sailors thought the expedition a suicide. Any raft caught in the cold and Roaring Forties, they argued, would be quickly torn to pieces.

To de Bisschop's credit, he was merely taking anthropological hypothesizing to a logical conclusion. Like prevailing winds, the prevailing anthropological view was one of an ultimate Southeast Asian origin for Polynesian culture. De Bisschop, on the other hand, considered the "Polynesian problem," as many called it, far from solved. Like Heyerdahl, he had no time for academics with no practical maritime experience upon which to base their ideas of Polynesian origins and migrations. Heyerdahl had had the courage to put his raft where his theory was. For this reason, and this reason alone, de Bisschop told Bengt Danielsson that he had more respect for Thor Heyerdahl than for all his other opponents put together.

In this, as in other notable aspects, de Bisschop was far ahead of his time. In de Bisschop's view, if anthropologists wanted to understand the essentially maritime culture of the Polynesians, they had better start to understand the nature of the maritime world. That meant a vast expansion of scholarly geographic horizons and a total abandonment of the idea (still subconsciously prevalent in many academic discussions) that the geography of the Pacific has remained unchanged since time immemorial.

For de Bisschop, no outsiders had taught Polynesians to sail; rather it was the Polynesians themselves who, by spreading their sea-going knowledge from Indonesia and India and then all the way to Madagascar, had accomplished quite the reverse. He imagined the Polynesians visiting South America before the time of Christ, to return with plants common to both places—and this nearly two thousand years before Europeans made tentative voyages with the currents and winds from Spain to the Caribbean. With such a tradition, de Bisschop proposed rewriting the maritime history of the world, with the Polynesians in their rightful place at the center of that history.

To study this enormous problem, de Bisschop envisioned as well a new field of maritime ethnology where scholars would use re-created voyaging technologies in order to study ancient diffusions. Taken together, the fact that genetic evidence now points to the likelihood of transoceanic migrations to Madagascar originating in the Pacific, and the fact that experiments in long-distance voyages by re-created Polynesia canoes are now integral facets of maritime anthropology, only reinforce de Bisschop's pioneering and little appreciated role in Pacific studies. Like Heyerdahl before him, de Bisschop believed that no one would pay him any attention unless his took his ideas to sea on an actual transoceanic voyage. His bamboo raft would be the instrument of his attack on academic convention.

Like Danielsson, many others wondered why de Bisschop would choose a raft for his experiment, rather than the double-hulled and double-outrigger canoes with which he was so familiar. This repeated criticism clearly stung de Bisschop. He countered that in his studies of Polynesian navigation, a maritime culture as sophisticated as that of the Polynesians surely would have possessed different vessels for different missions. He imagined that single outrigger canoes were appropriate for skimming over shoals and reefs; much larger double-hulled and double-outrigger canoes would have been used for quick hit-and-run raids on neighboring islands or voyages to known destinations.

But for long-distance voyages of exploration and colonization, with their essential cargoes of people and provisions, only large rafts would suffice. As de Bisschop saw it, when equipped with the moveable *guara* centerboards, these rafts became sailing vessels capable of true navigation. "It was by no means a floating contraption at the mercy of winds and currents."[1] Furthermore, the slow speed of a raft voyage, de Bisschop imagined, was no hindrance for a Polynesia people with a fundamentally different view of time.

To test whether Tahitian bamboo could remain buoyant for the duration of a long ocean voyage, de Bisschop had a diving platform constructed from bamboo and moored near a friend's house for a year. While *Teredo navalis* did attack some of the bamboo, the platform was still afloat after a year. As for whether Polynesians ever used bamboo rafts, de Bisschop was unequivocal. He cited several voyages on bamboo rafts navigated by prehistoric Marquesans fleeing tribal wars. Some of these bamboo rafts, constructed with five layers of bamboo logs, ventured as far as Tahiti and even Hawai'i.

In building the raft, de Bisschop had little to go on in the way of local knowledge. If bamboo rafts had ever navigated Polynesia, they had long since become distant memories. So he relied instead on his knowledge of sailing, on the assumption that, confronted with similar building materials on the same ocean, ancient Polynesians would have come to the similar nautical design conclusions. Retreating to the solitude of the island of Rurutu, where he had a home and a wife, de

Bisschop built a one-tenth scale model of the actual raft he hoped to build in Tahiti.

> What a joy it was to come back to the pleasant *fare* (home) which I had built facing the sea, to my sweet *vahiné*, and above all to the peace and silence of the nights, broken only by the muffled booming of the surf pounding on the reef—a peace so light that you could feel it floating everywhere, only waiting for the slightest opening of a door to insinuate itself into the most secret fibers of your heart and soul.[2]

Returning to Tahiti with his model, de Bisschop set up a quarantined area at the naval dockyard where he could build his raft and at the same time "keep out the inquisitive and the inevitable 'advisors.'"[3] Among those visitors curiously peering over the fence at de Bisschop's raft workshop were two of the world's greatest explorers, one already famous and one whose fame was still twenty years away. Thor Heyerdahl, returning home after his intensive and pioneering stratigraphic archaeological Easter Island excavations, "shook his head seriously and solemnly declared that he would never dare entrust his life to such a fantastic craft."[4]

The second visitor, a fascinated graduate student by the name of Ben R. Finney, hesitated to disturb the work going on behind the secured naval compound and so lost his only chance to meet de Bisschop personally. But Finney would later revolutionize the world's thinking about the sea-going capacity of the Polynesian double-hull canoe. With Heyerdahl, Bengt Danielsson, Finney, and de Bisschop and his crew, all on Tahiti at the same time, was a young American sailor by the name of Norman Baker, who later in life would become the navigator and second-in-command of Heyerdahl's three reed boat expeditions. Never before had there been and likely never again would there be assembled in one place so many explorers who already possessed or would later amass such an overwhelming amount of experience in drifting and sailing prehistoric rafts and canoes.

Those who did dare venture through the gates of de Bisschop's compound were the usual assortment of would-be adventure-seekers and potential crew members. As Bombard had so sharply discovered, and de Bisschop himself sarcastically noted, these drifters were individuals who were "keen enough at first, but who, as the hour of actual departure approaches, gradually deflate like a tire with a slow leak."[5]

When the bamboo was ready it was lashed together with coconut fiber rope. De Bisschop plaited sails from vegetable fibers. Once finished, he christened the whole creation *Tahiti Nui*, Great Tahiti. The one concession to the twentieth century was a cabin made of double walls of plywood, to house an echo sounder, radio, darkroom, and dry sleeping area for the crew. Unlike Alain Bombard, whose voyage de Bisschop cited, he had no desire to conduct a human endurance test, "to be made to swallow plankton and other revolting stuff of that sort, to drink sea water or the juice squeezed out of raw fish."[6] De Bisschop was sixty-five years old and debilitated by bronchitis and emphysema. In no uncertain terms his doctor told him that he would not survive the journey, a knowledge that bothered de Bisschop not at all. He knew his time was close. He felt death "like a patient, comfortable, smiling friend, near at hand, only waiting your pleasure to fall into step with him to make the long journey toward the Unknown."[7]

By de Bisschop's reckoning, the last great voyages by a Polynesian fleet had taken place some seven hundred years earlier, during the fourteenth century. On November 8, 1956, he prepared to follow that fleet to sea, on a strange polyglot raft at the start of an even stranger scientific experiment. Provisions were stowed for five: "beer and lemonade . . . a dozen enormous stems of bananas, numerous sacks of potatoes, kumara, onions, taporo, gourds, not to mention mountains of coconuts both green and dried."[8] De Bisschop reckoned that the voyage to South America would take between three and four months. Any longer than that on a raft and de Bisschop feared the consequences. "It is not only bamboo that begins to degenerate after seven months at sea," he wrote laconically.[9]

Like all previous raft expeditions, the voyage of *Tahiti Nui* began with a tow by a diesel-powered ship to its place of departure. Fifty outrigger canoes escorted the raft from Papeete harbor, perhaps unconsciously suggesting a method by which prehistoric rafts were maneuvered off the beach and into position to take advantage of wind, tide, and current. Chased by a friend's yacht, the crew enjoyed one last view of Tahiti in the form of a beautifully tanned young woman who, as de Bisschop related warmly, "lifted a corner of her bikini toward us (I cannot say more!) in a charmingly simple gesture of adieu. I turned to my crew and said, "Take a good look, my boys—it will be many moons before you see anything like that again!"[10]

In the event, only four moons passed. Even before clearing Tahiti, de Bisschop became concerned with the raft's buoyancy and decided to put ashore to lay in additional bamboo for the long voyage ahead. The same gunboat that had towed them out now returned to tow them back in. To Alain Brun, de Bisschop's second-in-command, the gunboat saved them all from embarrassment when it "mercifully took us to a remote creek on the south coast of Tahiti."[11] Thus reinforced, the raft started south toward the Austral islands of Rurutu, Raivavae, Tubuai, Rimatara, and Rapa, making three and a half to four knots of speed on a following wind that lasted for a week.

At this early stage of the experiment, the raft surprised even de Bisschop by its ability to use its *guara* centerboards to make a passage toward the southeast. Before the voyage, de Bisschop thought the best the raft might do was approach his own Austral island of Rurutu. Now he found himself approaching the seas that separated Raivavae and Tubuai, more than two hundred nautical miles *east* of Rurutu.

Heyerdahl had just called at many of these islands after his work on Easter Island. His colleague archaeologist William Mulloy had carried out extensive archeological excavations at the spectacular aerie at Morongo Uta, one of twelve entirely unexplored mountaintop fortresses on Rapa Iti. Arne Skjølsvold, the Norwegian archaeologist who had discovered the inscrutable "kneeling statue" of Easter Island, spent several weeks mapping the ceremonial *marae* platforms of Raivavae. Contrary winds now blew the *Tahiti Nui* in a complete circle around Raivavae. A few weeks later the raft passed the latitude of Rapa Iti, and so moved beyond the limits of French Polynesia. As 1956 turned to 1957, 5,000 nautical miles (8,000 km) of cold open sea lay between the raft and its destination in Chile.

Beyond Rapa, at about 33° south, the raft picked up shifting west winds, and de Bisschop set his course directly eastward to South

America. For two months *Tahiti Nui* careened furtively eastward in tolerable temperatures that hovered around 68°–77° F. On February 23, 1957, the raft passed the longitude of 117° west, the halfway point on its voyage. But the mark brought little consolation. The experiment was now three and a half months old, at a point when de Bisschop had believed they would be safely ashore in Chile. Instead, the bamboo, put in the water in September, had been afloat now for more than five months. It was approaching the limits of its buoyancy with still more than 2,500 nautical miles (4,000 km) to go. The crew, to the contrary, thought the worst was over, that the remaining miles would speed by.

Instead, they were met almost immediately by a dreadful fortnight of winds blowing from the east. De Bisschop had told Bengt Danielsson that he intended to sail down to 40° south, where he would be assured of steady winds and currents from the west. But now he hesitated, staying in an area of wavering winds around 35° south. Even here the seas were rough, and de Bisschop was convinced *Tahiti Nui* would lose its two masts if he tried to sail any farther south.

Ben Finney, for one, believes it was the only decision de Bisschop could have made. At 40° south, mountainous seas would have torn the raft apart. If prehistoric Polynesians had voyaged along this route to the east, they did so only at great risk to themselves and their expeditions. Even at 35° south, heavy winds forced de Bisschop to take in most of the raft's sail to prevent it from being carried away.

When the raft began show signs of breaking up in late February, de Bisschop put down a minor mutiny by the three other crew members. All were half de Bisschop's age and cared little for the scientific substance of his experiment. They advocated instead an audacious retreat as far as 50° south in an attempt to speed their passage. Daily radio interruptions suggesting steady winds farther south—and thereby further enticing the demoralized crew in that deadly direction—nearly drove de Bisschop to pitch the set overboard. When the raft circumscribed a complete circle on March 11, returning the crew to a point they had passed seventeen days earlier, morale sank even further.

One unexpected advantage of de Bisschop's more northerly course was a near miss of Easter Island during the first week of March. The sea-going raft wandered to within 350 miles (563 km) of anthropology's most enigmatic island on March 7, 1957, demonstrating a plausible access route from the west to this most remote corner of Polynesia. De Bisschop in fact began to spin a theory that the island had originally been colonized by a raft caught in the same contrary winds his raft now endured. His crew wished he would follow his own hypothesis and make for a landing at Easter Island, at the very least so that they could make repairs to the raft.

Had de Bisschop done so, it is likely that the voyage of *Tahiti Nui* would have taken a rightful place alongside *Kon-Tiki* as one of the great Pacific drift voyages—and ironically increased its value to maritime anthropology. *Tahiti Nui* had linked the Austral islands of Rapa Iti and Raivavae, with their stone fortifications and ceremonial *marae* platforms, with the stone *ahu* platforms and carvings of Easter Island. The raft had voyaged almost as far as *Kon-Tiki*, and remained afloat for more than six months, four of them on the high seas. By continuing eastward to certain destruction, de Bisschop weakened the plausible case he had already made for the efficiency of the long-distance seagoing bamboo raft in prehistoric Pacific expeditions.

That destruction now arrived in slow and painful measures. The raft drifted through April as the crew suffered through a near-total lack of fresh water. The month of May brought with it fresh winds from the west but the raft was still 1,000 miles (1,600 km) from Chile. A week later, still 800 miles (1,285 km) from the coast, the big four-inch main bamboo logs began to break away in fifty-knot winds. The situation became desperate, with the raft listing heavily. To worsen matters, de Bisschop found his bamboo hull "riddled with tunnels the size of your little finger, each one with its fat white [*Teredo navalis*] worm.

> They have wicked heads with two hard curved plates at the business end, only too well designed for the dastardly work of boring and destroying.
>
> I have seen natives, especially in Melanesia, reveling in these large white worms, which they eat raw. Here, now, is a field of survey which has been ignored by the specialists—something to add to the menu of those who cast away at sea. I myself had never thought of it. I wish I had; it might have been most useful when,

on *Fou Po II*, I went for nearly three weeks [without food]. But
how I could have harvested the little beasts into the frying pan
when they were snug below the waterline in the very planks of
the hull which kept the boat afloat, I don't know.[12]

By the middle of May, after six months at sea, even de Bisschop was
tired of the cold southern seas and began to long for the warm and
light blue waters of Polynesia. When a severe storm forced the crew to
abandon the idea of a landing at the Juan Fernandez Islands off the
coast of Chile, where Alexander Selkirk had found himself marooned
in 1703, de Bisschop at last signaled for a tow. Over their radio they
listened to spurious reports that the raft had been dismasted, that the
crew was injured by the attack of a giant fish, that giant mollusks had
attached themselves to the raft and were dragging it down. The expedition had taken on a distinctly Vernian tone.

The raft plowed on to its farthest point east: 87° 54'W. Winds then
forced it back more than a degree to the west, where a Chilean naval
vessel caught up with it on May 22, 1957. The unsuccessful tow resulted
in the final break-up and abandoning of the raft on May 26. As the crew
salvaged a tiki figure carved by a Marquesan artist, de Bisschop heard
the final sickening splintering of the bamboo. On board the Chilean
ship, he took to a bunk and lamented his failure to prove his theory.

Once ashore in Chile, de Bisschop began writing up his experiences
on board the *Tahiti Nui*. Now, at the age of sixty-six, he was more
determined than ever to complete a full-circle voyage from Tahiti to
South America and back. On February 15, 1958, he christened a new
raft *Tahiti Nui II* and prepared to drift from South America to Polynesia, along the track pioneered by the balsa rafts of Thor Heyerdahl and
William Willis. It would prove to be the final expedition in the long,
adventurous life of Eric de Bisschop.

I've had my fill of knocking about the world and the oceans, and
I can only thank the gods for having made life so wonderful for
me—so colored, so varied. I could depart this life today happily
and with no regrets, and what better way for a sailor to die than
by making a hole in the sea?—though I would have preferred

a somewhat gayer setting for my last plunge, a bluer sky and a more inviting, more warmly embracing sea.

—Eric de Bisschop, *Tahiti Nui* (1959)

Drifting toward his death in the mid-Pacific in 1958, Eric de Bisschop made one last call upon the Polynesian god of the sea. He had always believed that he would die somewhere in the Marquesas archipelago, where latitude 10° south meets longitude 140° west, and now it seemed as if his prophecy was a true one. He had always been drawn to the Marquesas, a chain of islands settled by Polynesians around the time of Christ.

The Spaniard Mendaña landed in the islands in 1595. James Cook explored the area for a few days in 1774, as did Thor Heyerdahl in 1956. The *Essex*, a U.S. Navy vessel under the command of David Porter, launched a seven-week war against the native Taipi in 1813, one of the very first American actions against native peoples outside North America. It is not an easy place to fight a naval action, with its 1,000-foot-high cliffs.

The famous captain Edmund Fanning arrived at Nuku Hiva in the Marquesas in May 1798 on one of his five circumnavigations of the globe. Commencing the usual trade with the natives, he observed "something wrapped up in palm leaves, on board one of [the canoes], the native in which did not offer it for barter." Fanning examined the item, finding to his surprise that it was "a piece of human flesh, baked." The individual explained that it was a part of one of his enemies, and so of course very good to eat, and that "whenever he was hungry, he was going to eat it."[13]

The crew of twenty on board a Nantucket whaleship also called *Essex* could have sailed south to the Marquesas were they unafraid of cannibals, or northwest to Hawai'i were it not for storms. Operating in the Pacific on November 20, 1820, the whaler was rammed twice and sunk by its supposed prey, an eighty-five-foot sperm whale. There began one of the most agonizing sagas of the sea, the basis of Melville's *Moby-Dick*, and a story so bizarre that even Melville left out the gruesome details when he wrote the greatest of all sea novels. Rather than make for the cannibals of the Marquesas, Captain Pollard of the

Essex headed his surviving boats southeast, even though they were over 3,000 nautical miles (4,800 km) from the nearest land in that direction, and against wind and current for good measure.

The boats from the *Essex* arrived on Henderson Island in December, where three crew members decided to remain and try their luck at survival on the minute island. Captain Pollard himself insisted on South America, so the remaining crew sailed dutifully on, to endure storms, sharks, starvation, thirst, madness and, ironically, cannibalism. Three crew members were lost when one of the boats disappeared in December. Two others died and were buried at sea. By February 1821, with the men starving after two and a half months in open boats, the Nantucketers were forced into the kinds of flesh eating that so repulsed them when practiced by Marquesan natives. As the Nantucketers died, they were eaten.

First mate Owen Chase wrote later of the fate of one of the dead men: "We separated his limbs from his body, and cut all the flesh from the bones, after which, we opened up the body [and] took out the heart . . . which we eagerly devoured." On board Captain Pollard's boat, cabin boy Owen Coffin was not so fortunate. The four survivors drew lots to choose who among them would die so that the rest might live. When Coffin drew the morose assignment, Captain Pollard remarked as gently as possible given the circumstances, "My lad, if you don't like your lot, I'll shoot the first man that touches you." To which the cabin boy replied, "I like it as well as any other."[14] Whereupon his starving mates quickly dispatched and devoured him. Only five *Essex* survivors were rescued from the sea to testify to what quickly became a Pacific legend.

Native Marquesan navigators, with their specialized local knowledge, sailed from the northwestern islands to their southeastern neighbors during November and December, when the dominant winds from the east slackened somewhat, a technique rediscovered by anthropologists centuries later. Their business concluded, they would then wait for the prevailing west winds to blow them home. But now, as Eric de Bisschop's raft built of Chilean cypress sank inexorably toward the abyss, those same prevailing winds and currents pushed *Tahiti Nui II* north of the northernmost island in the Marquesan chain. As a mariner who had circled most of the earth in a long life of adventure, de Bisschop knew what this meant all too well. His raft expedition might drift into the wastes of the central Pacific, where islands were as scarce as water on the moon. He and his four companions would die miserably, of thirst or madness. It would be the *Essex* all over again.

Thirst had already driven one of de Bisschop's crewmen crazy. He had begun literally sawing the raft apart, in order apparently to build himself a private escape pod. De Bisschop, rather than exhibit the caustic temperament he showed to many during his life of adventure, treated the wretch with a gentleness most had never seen him display in far less strenuous circumstances.

After the sinking of the bamboo raft *Tahiti Nui*, de Bisschop intended to build a copy from the same materials. After all, the original had floated for almost nine months, and even though it missed the Chilean coast by 800 miles (1,287 km), this was a creditable showing after a voyage of more than 4,000 miles (6,437 km) from Polynesia. But no bamboo was available in Chile's cold climate, nor did balsa trees grow in the countryside.

When a collection of shipyards in the port of Constitucion offered to replace his bamboo raft with a small cutter—and attempt to drum up some Polynesia cutter business into the bargain—de Bisschop protested that he required a raft to continue his ethnological studies. The shipyard owners replied that their only experience in rafts involved a large oak car ferry ordered by the government, which had promptly sunk upon launch. A compromise was reached in the fall of 1957 wherein the shipyards would build a raft of approximately the same dimensions of *Tahiti Nui* from buoyant Chilean cypress wood. De Bisschop then retreated to a friend's home to write a book of his experiences on the voyage from Tahiti, and left the work of building what would become *Tahiti Nui II* to crew member Alain Brun.

Unable to lash the cypress logs together, Brun fastened them instead with hardwood pegs. The principle of navigation would be similar, however, as Brun rigged the raft in the Chinese junk style of the first raft, and added several *guara* centerboards as well. When de Bisschop arrived back in Constitucion in January 1958, with his manuscript complete, his raft was ready as well. A month later, with four young crew members including Alain Brun, the raft put to sea. De Biss-chop chose to cut across the Humboldt Current and sail offshore as far as Callao in Peru, 1,500 miles (2,400 km) to the north, where the raft would be pointed toward Polynesia. He adapted himself immediately to a renewal of his drifter's life:

> [Eric] simply hung up his briefcase on a nail over his bunk and took out his beloved papers and books: then he felt at home at once. This matchless power of adapting himself was of course due mainly to the fact that he lived entirely in a private world of his own and seldom noticed where he was and what was going on round him.[15]

The raft proved extremely simple to handle, but not so the human re-lationships on board. Almost immediately the two newcomers to the crew skirmished with de Bisschop—a difficult personality at the best of times—and a pattern of shifting alliances began that would ulti-mately doom the expedition.

The first half of the coastwise journey to Callao took three weeks, at an average of forty miles per day. At this speed—about the pace of a leisurely walk—*Tahiti Nui II* slowly drifted past many of archaeol-ogy's most intensely interesting prehistoric coastal sites. On March 21, 1958, the raft maneuvered along a "steep stony beach, inside which a desolate sand desert stretched as far as we could see in every di-rection."[16] The expedition had reached the land of the ancient Nazca. These people, creators of the famous "geoglyphs" that ornament this coastal desert, populated the southern coast of Peru from about the time of Christ to the middle of the sixth century. It is the same ap-proximate time horizon as the Moche people of Peru's north coast, the likeliest candidates for the balsa raft navigators that Thor Heyerdahl believes drifted into the eastern Pacific sometime around A.D. 500.

Three days later the raft passed the prehistoric burial grounds of Paracas, a site discovered and excavated by the first great native Pe-ruvian archaeologist, Julio C. Tello. The burial grounds were in use during the five centuries or so prior to the Nazca and Moche periods of Peruvian coastal prehistory and contained both cavern-type and ma-sonry vault–type crypts. These crypts, with their mummified human

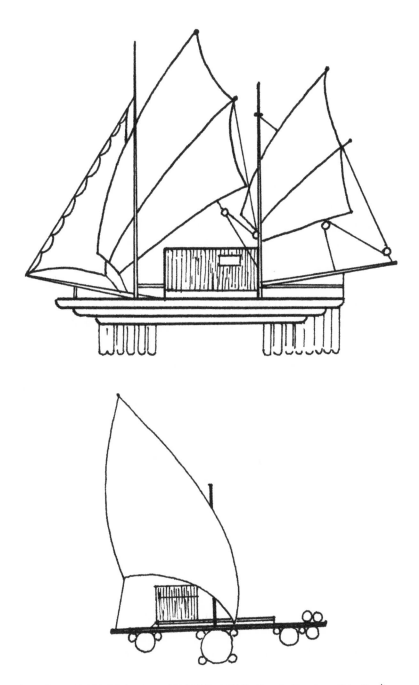

The rafts *Tahiti Nui II* (*top*) and *Tahiti Nui III* (*bottom*). Courtesy C.L. Devlin.

remains, attest to a belief dating to least 4,000 B.C. in Peruvian pre-history that human remains should be salted and preserved, for only a physically intact corpse could "enter the afterlife and join the realm of the ancestors."[17]

Thor Heyerdahl noted that several hardwood *guara* centerboards had also been excavated from this area and dated to the same period as the Paracas burials. The ocean just offshore from this necropolis was an area of shifting currents and forced the raft's crew to keep constant watch, as Alain Brun noted, for they "had no desire to end our days in this burial ground, however famous it might be."[18]

On March 26, the raft was taken in tow by a Peruvian naval vessel and pulled the final ten miles of the distance to Callao. This was accomplished with such skill that Brun laconically surmised that "Peruvian patrol boats were accustomed to towing rafts of prehistoric model."[19] An inspection of the raft revealed no *teredo* infestation of the cypress logs, which appeared still to possess about 90 percent of their original buoyancy. Even so, de Bisschop thought it prudent to reinforce the raft with a dozen balsa logs obtained free from local benefactors as well as fourteen aluminum water tanks bought from a Belgian chemist living in Lima. Unbeknownst to the crew at the time, these tanks would later form the basis of *Tahiti Nui III*, the rescue raft that would save all but one of their lives.

During their stop in Callao, Eduardo Ingris, captain of a balsa raft during a misbegotten voyage from northern Peru to the Galapagos in 1955, begged de Bisschop to be allowed to join his crew. Even with the early splits in his expedition, de Bisschop resisted Ingris's appeals and, with his original crew, was towed from Callao into the Humboldt Current on Sunday morning, April 13, 1958. It was eleven years since *Kon-Tiki* had drifted away from the same port and into history.

To avoid Ingris's fate on the *La Cantuta* drift, de Bisschop steered a course to the west, across the currents that would sweep them toward Panama if the raft were allowed to drift uncontrolled. One week out from Callao the raft, like a train switching tracks, left the north-setting Humboldt Current and picked up the South Equatorial Current, which set the raft on a course for the mid-Pacific. The voyage at this point was so easy that Brun occupied watch after watch discussing navigation and anthropology with de Bisschop. Another of the crew took to comparing the daily speeds and distances of *Tahiti Nui II* with *Kon-Tiki*, having brought a copy of the German edition of Heyerdahl's classic book on board the raft. As Brun considered this most "original race with eleven years' difference in time," *Tahiti Nui II* was holding her own against her balsa raft predecessor.

> As everyone knows, the *Kon-Tiki* men wanted to prove that it was possible to sail from South America to Polynesia on a balsa raft, but it really made no difference to them at which of the many Polynesian islands they ended their voyage. We, on the other hand, were firmly resolved to reach Tahiti, and therefore kept a rather more northerly course than our predecessors to avoid the insidious coral reefs of the Tuamotu group. But this did not prevent us from comparing their daily runs with our own. We soon found to our satisfaction that we were keeping up at least as good a speed as the *Kon-Tiki* raft, i.e., thirty-five to fifty miles a day.[20]

The ease of the first few weeks dissipated as Brun found that the crew had trouble with the many steering *guara*—six forward and eight aft—directing the movement of the raft. There simply were not enough crew members to shift the *guara* rapidly enough when the situation called for such maneuvers. Yet they accomplished the first half of the expedition to Tahiti in just six weeks, and on June 2, 1958, the crew found that the raft had drifted eighty nautical miles (128 km) during the previous twenty-four hours, their best run yet.

When the rudderpost snapped, three of the forward *guara* were pulled up and nailed together to form a new and larger rudder. When the new rudder required more muscle to keep in trim, the crew pulled up even more *guara* to build a platform for the helmsman to stand upon to avoid being washed overboard. The men needed the larger rudder immediately. The more northerly course de Bisschop had steered coming from Peru now began to backfire, as the raft stubbornly refused to turn southwest toward Tahiti. They had assumed that like *Kon-Tiki*, their raft would begin its southerly arc toward Polynesia when it passed 120° west. Yet as the raft passed that longitude it continued to drift west at around 4° south, and as they all knew, Tahiti lay at 17° south. To make matters worse, they discovered that *Tahiti Nui II* was slowly sinking out from under them. In their repeated comparisons with *Kon-Tiki*, the crew now found the *Tahiti Nui II* wanting in both trajectory and buoyancy.

By the middle of June, eight inches of water were sloshing over the decks and filling the cabin. The crew moved their sleeping bags onto the flat roof of the cabin, as de Bisschop himself began to grow weaker and feel the chill of the night winds even more than the younger men. By June 20, it became clear that the trajectory of the expedition was taking them away from their Tahitian destination. A landing in the Marquesas, 400 nautical miles (643 km) away to the west, was still possible if they were favored with sustained northerly winds. But perversely, as soon as they wished for them, the wind veered over to the southeast, blowing the raft farther north, away from the Marquesas.

During the midnight watch on the evening of June 26–27, Brun watched the raft suddenly lose its buoyancy and sink three feet. He left the rest of the crew to their sleep during the emergency, but in the morning they examined the cypress logs to find them riddled through by *Teredo navalis* worms. Brun cut a piece of one log and threw it into the sea. It sank immediately. With the raft awash and increasingly difficult to steer, most of the crew wondered what the point was of keeping continued watches. Unable to make steerageway, the raft had become a derelict drifting at the caprice of wind and current.

To Brun's surprise, de Bisschop now agreed with the crew, telling the men to save their strength and let the raft drift where it liked. As the raft floated far north of the Marquesas on July 1, 1958, a helpless hulk, de Bisschop called upon Taaroa, the Polynesian god of the sea, to look after them. Brun, refusing to submit to the fates, insisted that the men maintain some semblance of naval discipline or risk drifting benumbed into the wastes of the central Pacific. De Bisschop, telling the men that he was too "old, tired and ill" to force his will upon them, turned command of the raft over the Brun and retired to his sleeping box on the roof of the cabin.[21] De Bisschop was no doubt thirsty as well. Only fifteen gallons of water remained of the one hundred with which the raft had started. Worse, since leaving Peru, they had experienced not a drop of rain. The daily ration of fresh water was now mixed with increasing quantities of seawater.

When two of the crew wanted to build a small boat and try to row back to the Marquesas, Brun and de Bisschop managed to dissuade them. Instead, the main masts were cut away and replaced by a smaller mast carrying a tiny storm sail. Yet the raft continued to drift farther to the west-northwest, into the most desolate area of the Pacific. Morale diminished further in mid-July when then crew sighted a cargo ship and the vessel passed within three miles of the raft without seeing it.

As July turned to August, the crew was in outright mutiny, openly laying plans to build an escape raft. Brun squelched this uprising by pointing out that they were 300 nautical miles from Caroline Island and were drifting to the north of it. Only if the *Tahiti Nui II* managed to drift within close proximity of the windward side of an island would they take the very great risk of constructing an escape raft and attempting a landing over a coral reef. At this point, Eric de Bisschop made it clear that he was not leaving the raft under any circumstances. This did nothing to quiet the malcontents, one of whom had evidently gone mad from thirst and hopelessness. When de Bisschop tried to calm the man, the captain was threatened with an axe. De Bisschop and the rest of the crew then held a ship's council, at the conclusion of which they swore out a document allowing the madman to build his escape raft, provision it with his share of stores, and sail away.

The night following the mutiny, the first rain since the raft left Peru began to fall, and the spirits of the crew rose a bit. The crew member building his escape pod regained his senses, and the expedition members gloried in both a renewed supply of freshwater and a bottle of brandy. Yet the same rain that saved the humans now made the cypress raft even more top-heavy. With their options rapidly running out, the crew tried to steer toward one of the copra islands of Vostok or Flint, where William Willis had passed so closely on his balsa raft four years earlier, in far better health and spirits. But unlike Willis's beautifully designed sailing raft, the *Tahiti Nui II* was now a useless derelict, rolling heavily with each storm. The life of the crew was reduced to a ten-foot by thirteen-foot cabin roof.

On July 29, 1958, Brun took a sun sight that placed the raft of a course to miss all of the copra islands by a wide margin. They still had a chance of reaching Starbuck Island, a small, uninhabited atoll. But even Starbuck was 400 nautical miles (643 km) away, and the raft by now was completely unmanageable, listing along at a meager twenty-five miles (40 km) a day. By August 6, still 250 miles (400 km) from Starbuck, the crew had taken to throwing all extraneous weight overboard, including all of the scientific water samples one of the crew had made all the way from Callao. That night the crew decided it was time to build their escape raft. If they approached Starbuck or any other island, they would make a break for shore and salvation. Unbeknownst to the men, the only things that would meet them at Starbuck would be a thousand-yard-wide (900 m) coral reef, the ruins of a British guano mine from the 1880s, and a complete absence of any fresh water.

The *Tahiti Nui III* took shape over the course of the next four days, as the crew frantically tried to ready their rescue raft before the *Tahiti Nui II* drifted past their rendezvous with Starbuck Island. They were like astronauts gauging their reentry into earth's atmosphere, and the slightest miscalculation would send them back into a hopeless void of ocean. The aluminum water tanks they had almost scorned in Callao, now came back to save their lives. Yet it was no small feat to create a small escape raft from the hulk of another, larger, sinking raft, with both bobbing in the waves, one threatening to sink at any moment while the other sought to sail away.

Under de Bisschop's guidance the crew built a main framework balanced by a double-outrigger. The ten smaller ten-gallon tanks were divided equally to serve as the port and starboard outriggers. This accomplished, Brun built a box on the deck of *Tahiti Nui II* that would serve as de Bisschop's sleeping area, and the explorer was moved into it on the afternoon of August 10. The larger of the water tanks, the five forty-gallon tanks, were then cut away from *Tahiti Nui II* and pressed into service as the main hull of no. *III*.

On Monday, August 11, 1958, Brun and his crew completed the deck, mast, steering oar, and additional crossbeams of the rescue raft. Only 70 nautical miles (120 km) from Starbuck Island, and after 180 days at sea on board the raft since its launch in Chile, the crew abandoned *Tahiti Nui II* and set it adrift. The expedition had gone from its original conception as a voyage of science to one of obvious pseudo-science and now had devolved to a struggle to survive.

But it was too late to reach Starbuck. On August 16, after fighting vainly against contrary winds, the *Tahiti Nui III* passed just 29 miles (46 km) south of the island and drifted on toward the central Pacific. They were now drifting too far north even to reach Tongareva, or Penrhyn as it was also called, and instead were looking at another 1,000 miles (1,600 km) of open ocean between themselves and Samoa.

When the raft missed Tongareva by 40 nautical miles (64 km) on August 21, another mutiny broke out, this time over food rations. The raft drifted along at about 9° south, and Brun knew that the Samoan islands lay between 13° and 16° south. De Bisschop, now semi-conscious, began to pray for death to take him. As Brun tightened the raft's lashings after a two-day storm, the other crew members listlessly ignored him. When the wind suddenly shifted around from southeast to northeast, Brun set course for the northern Cook Islands of Manahiki and Rakahanga.

On August 30 the reef at Rakahanga was only 30 miles (48 km) away. Almost incredibly, Brun now proposed disassembling *Tahiti Nui III* to build a smaller, fourth raft, to try to get the men safely over the coral. By four o'clock the next afternoon, the reef lay only 10 nautical miles (16 km) off, and Brun was confronted with three choices: lay off the reef until they could attempt a landing in daylight; make for Manahiki, which de Bisschop believed was inhabited; or try to run ashore at Rakahanga at night. When the current, inexorably pulling the raft between the two islands, decided the issue, the men made ready to try to land over the reef at night.

They sighted Rakahanga around 5:15 in the afternoon. As darkness fell and the moon rose, the raft lay only a mile off the reef. As Brun vainly sought a passage between the coral, he knew they were engaged in the very "dangerous adventure [of] stranding on the weather side of a coral island."[22] Just before 9:00 p.m. the raft suddenly struck the reef, pitched into the surf, and the entire crew was thrown into the ocean. Alain Brun came to the surface and found de Bisschop bobbing in the surf, unresponsive. The other crew members managed to get the explorer ashore, and his third and final raft washed ashore as well around midnight. De Bisschop never regained consciousness. Despite the crew's attempts to revive him, his limbs began to stiffen around four in the morning. A medical examination would later reveal a severe trauma to the back of his head and a broken neck.

His last expedition and his life of adventure both at an end, the harrowing second leg of de Bisschop's radical experiment in drifting led to little serious discussion. Attention is most often focused instead on his failed bamboo drift on *Tahiti Nui I*, an expedition Ben Finney would correctly appraise years later as "valiant, if anthropologically misguided."[23]

Yet by setting himself adrift on a too-high trajectory into the Pacific from South America, de Bisschop had perhaps unwittingly showed the possible impact of accidental voyagers on an alien island. Why, it has been asked, if they had truly reached the Polynesian islands in prehistoric times, did South Americans never transmit familiar cultural elements like stirrup-spouted ceramics or any other forms of pottery? De Bisschop showed that a raft crew, *in extremis* and attempting merely to survive, will lighten their load and increase their raft's buoyancy by throwing overboard anything they can.

Second, the culture-bearers among the voyagers—like de Bisschop with his vast knowledge of the sea and navigation—may have died en route. This would have the effect of leaving the survivors little in the way of a cognitive tool-kit with which to attempt to create a new and stable society. Even if the voyagers still possessed the knowledge to create pottery or voyaging boats, the raw materials for such works may have been unavailable on their newly gained islands. Lastly, voyagers landing on a remote and sparsely populated island at the end of such a horrendous voyage would be lucky to be alive. They would have been unlikely in such a state to exert a profound effect upon a well-established population, other than to be quickly assimilated or eliminated. *Tahiti Nui III* had washed ashore on an island with a population of about one hundred souls. The arrival created a great stir at the time, but it would be interesting to learn whether knowledge of it survives in any form today.

Searching along the shoreline in the days following the burial of de Bisschop, the natives discovered the metal jar in which Brun had stowed all the expedition's charts, films, and diaries prior the wreck. All were intact. Soon after, a telegram arrived from Tahiti. The French authorities there had decreed that de Bisschop was to be exhumed, disinterred, and transported back to Papeete for burial. Taaroa would see him home after all.

III

Aeronautical Archaeology

9

The Airship Hangar
at the Top of the World

While "collecting data to support good research design" might seem a positively dreadful activity, it becomes a superior use of time when called what it is in archaeology: fieldwork. Fieldwork is a period of time often spent in a tent in a place you never imagined you would find yourself, engaged in gathering evidence to support a well-grounded hypothesis. Or, as Francis Bacon described it four centuries ago in his *Instauratio Magna*: "Men have sought to make a world from their own conception and to draw from their own minds all the material which they employed, but if, instead of doing so, they had consulted experience and observation, they would have had the facts and not opinions to reason about, and might have ultimately arrived at the knowledge of the laws which govern the material world."

Soon after my return from the High North in 1993, a request arrived from *Air & Space Smithsonian* magazine to contribute an essay on the archaeological research into Walter Wellman's polar airship base camp. This was the first chance to present something like a notion of aeronautical archaeology to a national audience. One can find the beginnings of many of the themes that would guide this work in the two decades to follow: the history of exploration, what it means to be an explorer, the archaeology of remote shorelines, and the intersections of sea, air, and space.

Loose scree scudded down the steep slope each time I grappled my way higher up a narrow ridge on an uninhabited arctic island called Danskøya. Few archaeologists conduct research this far north, and none have ever done aviation archaeology at this latitude. Norwegian for "Dane's Island," Danskøya is only 700 windswept miles from the North Pole. The nearest telephone was 100 miles away; the nearest town, almost 200. Oslo, the capital of Norway, was well over 1,000 miles to my south. I was suddenly struck by what was for me a major irony. Too skinny and nearsighted to be the astronaut of my boyhood dreams, I was exploring the closest thing our planet has to the cold surface of Mars.

Finally reaching the top of the ridge, I gained the view I had worked ten years to see: the desolate shoreline of Virgo Harbor (Virgohamna), where in 1906 the American journalist and explorer Walter Wellman established a base camp. From this small and historic arctic harbor on the northeast corner of Danskøya, Wellman launched two airship expeditions in search of the geographic North Pole.

Now, in the short arctic summer of 1993, I surveyed the ruins of Wellman's hangar, collapsed on the rocky shore like the remains of some prehistoric beast. Clouds of kittiwakes buzzed my ridge, shrieking as if in laughter at the evidence of the human folly below. It was a majestic sight, one I longed to capture, but my camera lay at bottom of the harbor, where I had dropped it my first day on the island, watching it sink with something akin to grief.

Why did I journey five thousand miles to study aeronautical artifacts in such a bleak place? Couldn't I have gleaned enough details of Wellman's expeditions from books or from visits to an air museum? Several cruising yachts visited Danskøya while I was there, and that was the question each group asked me. Yes, certain details can be dug out of books and other documents, but Wellman, like many interesting characters from history, left behind no plans, no diary, and comparatively few photographs. And no museum had preserved either of his arctic airships.

The only place, then, to discover the details of how a polar airship was put together in 1906 is on Danskøya. Only three hangars were ever designed specifically to house polar airships, and all three were built in the Spitsbergen archipelago; the remains of two of them lay on the shore at Virgo Harbor. As these aeronautical base camps had never before been mapped, one of my major goals was to use a laser rangefinder to create a plan of the site.

Aviation archaeology is often regarded by academic professionals as the province of amateur groups seeking Amelia Earhart's Electra or some other famous wreck. Little archaeological work has been done with the aim of elucidating particular events and general trends in aeronautical history. Neither has aviation archaeology been applied to a far more complex process for which it is especially suited: that of offering general propositions about human behaviors, such as the urge to explore. As technology opens ever more avenues for exploration, such research can only increase in importance.

So, in addition to the technological details of his expeditions, what I sought was some direct connection with Walter Wellman and his world. The newspaperman had launched two sledging expeditions in search of the North Pole, one from Spitsbergen in 1894 and one from neighboring Franz Josef Land in 1899. The 1894 voyage reached 81 degrees north latitude faster than any other known expedition before Wellman's ship was trapped by ice and sunk, creating one of the world's northernmost shipwrecks.

In his 1899 voyage Wellman pushed another degree north, only to break his leg. With every painful retreating step, he grew more determined than ever to reach the North Pole. He was now convinced that the only true route to the pole was through the air. He would wrest the exploration from the nineteenth-century technology of sails and sledges and bring it into, as he billed it, "the Aerial Age."

A Swedish explorer, S. A. Andrée, had sought the Pole in 1897 by floating from Danskøya in the *Eagle*, a balloon controlled by drag ropes of limited utility, only to vanish with two companions. Wellman thought

Wellman's airship hangar on the shore at Virgo Harbor in 1909. (From Walter Welman, *The Aerial Age* [New York: Keller and Company, 1911]).

he had a better idea: a powered airship, capable of being steered and of fighting headwinds—unlike Andrée's *Eagle*—could reach the pole from Andrée's launch point in about twenty-four hours. A flight in 1907 covered about twenty miles, and another went twice that far in 1909. But later that year Wellman learned that Robert Peary and Frederick Cook had both claimed to have reached the pole. He abandoned his northern base camp, never to return.

As efforts to reach the North Pole, Wellman's expeditions were failures (one newspaper opined, "[Wellman] has always been daring in his conceptions, but rather backward in his performances"), but they did blaze a technological trail that other explorers, notably Roald Amundsen, Lincoln Ellsworth, and Umberto Nobile, would soon follow. Wellman himself enjoyed pointing out that when the Pole was finally and unquestionably attained by Amundsen's airship Norge in 1926, it was done with the aeronautical methods of Wellman, not the sledging tortures of Peary. Wellman lived to see the day when the Norge lifted off from a hangar just south of Danskøya, reached the pole, and continued across the top of the world to Alaska.

While surveying Wellman's base camp, I discovered the wrecks of the two airships used on his polar flights. The original ballast bags, still filled with rocks, lay underneath his collapsed hangar. Behind the hangar I drank from a wooden funnel that still channels icy water from a spring toward Wellman's hut, as if, after ninety years' absence, the old aeronaut himself would somehow reappear and take a drink.

While the details of these and other artifacts begin to reveal something of Wellman's world, they also open up whole new avenues of inquiry. For one, there's the construction of the framework of the airship's nacelle. Photographs taken after the last flight show that the frame buckled at several points. On Danskøya I was able to trace these failures to a vital metal joint at which the wooden frame was joined. It was an inherently weak structure. Did Wellman know this? Did he ignore it? Does such construction tell us anything about his seriousness or that of the Frenchman who designed it? Or was such construction standard on French dirigibles of the day, and if so, what was the basis for believing it could survive in the Arctic?

And what of the can with "Chicago, U.S.A." printed on it, which my guide, Lucy Gilbert, discovered, or the bottle fragments I found with "Lambert Pharmacal Company" molded across it? I have since learned that Lambert Pharmacal was located in St. Louis and that their only

The ruins of Wellman's hangar as they appeared in the summer of 1993.

product at the time of Wellman's flights was the ubiquitous Lister-ine. Were these simply items Wellman packed for himself? Or were midwestern corporations donating supplies to Wellman's expeditions, and did they have ties to his employer, the Chicago Record-Herald? If so, what advertising advantage did Lambert hope to gain by hav-ing its mouthwash reach the North Pole? (Today the phrase "First on the North Pole" appears on cans of the popular Norwegian beer Mack Øl. Perhaps Lambert thought such a slogan would be more romantic than "Even your best friends won't tell you.") Wellman's expeditions were repeatedly criticized as little more than stunts aimed at raising the circulation of his newspaper, and these artifacts could buttress an analysis of such criticism.

Even though Danskøya is as remote as any Polynesian atoll, sev-eral kayakers from Oslo on their own dangerous adventure paddled in to our shoreline camp one night, and I am greatly indebted to one of them, an architect named Wilhelm Munthe-Kaas, for lending me his camera to photograph the site. The next day, once again, I scaled my ridge, and once again the kittiwakes laughed. But the last laugh was mine, for I got my picture of the airship hangar at the top of the world.

The night before the Norwegian vessel *Polarsyssel* returned to take my guide and me off Danskøya, we tore down the wire perimeter rigged with explosive charges that served as our alarm against polar bears. For three weeks we had seen only reindeer and a solitary arctic fox, and for three weeks I had hiked around large sections of the is-land armed with nothing more than an antique flare pistol. But at 5:00 a.m. that morning we were awakened by a barely perceptible noise just outside our tent. Through the tent flap grommets I saw an enormous white back, less than ten feet away, stalking around the tent. I cocked my flare pistol, Lucy cocked her rifle, and we crept to the flap of the tent. There, in the cold, in our underwear, we waited, momentarily paralyzed.

When we didn't hear another sound we finally escaped from the tent and saw that the bear had gone, as quietly as it had come. With the alarm down, we had been completely surprised. We checked our weapons. I fired the flare pistol: it worked. The rifle—our only real defense—was hopelessly jammed. Had the bear charged the tent we would have been as good as lost. Shaken, we cleared the rifle, fired it twice, and cautiously explored the surrounding hillocks and ridges. We found no trace of the fearsome intruder.

We did, however, find a friendly lone French kayaker, a visitor to our camp several days earlier, whom we thought had left the island. Bad weather had pinned him down. He said our shots had awakened him and, sitting up in front of his tent, camera at the ready, he had casually snapped photographs of the bear as it wandered by his camp. "The camera might have shaken a little bit," he said, adding with a slightly strained insouciance, "probably because my hands were cold." We invited him back to our camp, where we sat, our guns laid on the table as if in some Wild West saloon, silently drinking cup after cup of hot chocolate.

Just as Walter Wellman never made it to the North Pole, it's unlikely I will ever persuade NASA to send me to Mars to practice archaeology on those mysterious "pyramids." But studying the artifacts Wellman left behind on Danskøya brought me a little closer to an understanding of what drives us to reach for such places and gave me an appreciation of the cost. For despite the shoddy workmanship and the possible commercial tie-ins, despite naysayers and stay-at-homes, in the final analysis there is always the human: vulnerable, naked, the noble explorer and the courageous fool, at once blessed and cursed by a tormenting vision, straining to roll back the frontiers of ignorance with an open heart—and fresh breath.

10

Buried Treasure

Because archaeology is in many respects grounded, as it were, in the Baconian scientific method, it is usually antithetical to the concerns of those who attempt to salvage artifacts for commercial or personal gain. While some of the early processes such as project formulation might be similar (background research, feasibility studies, permit applications, funding pleas, logistics and administration), most of the later phases of research (data processing, analysis, interpretation) are not.

This brief essay appeared in late 1996 in *Air & Space Smithsonian* magazine just as several high-profile aircraft salvage cases were in the news. Some of these were dramatic successes, such as the recovery of a Second World War Lockheed P-38 fighter from under nearly 270 feet of ice in Greenland. Others ended in disaster, such as an attempt to fly a stranded post-war United States Army Air Forces Boeing B-29 Superfortress off the Greenland ice cap in 1994. Having just defended the first doctoral dissertation in aerospace archaeology, I thought it seemed a good moment to weigh in on the situation from an archaeological point of view. Two decades later, it is clear how self-conscious one was to construct a "scientific kinship" between archaeological research in more traditional areas and this new arena of aerospace archaeology.

Consider the intrepid salvager of historic aircraft, trudging through the ice and snow of Greenland or flippering in the frigid waters of Lake Michigan. After months or years of struggle, he has come upon the stuff of dreams: an intact Grumman F6F Hellcat, say, or a perfectly preserved Lockheed P-38G Lightning. All that remains is to haul the thing off the ice or pluck it from the lake, truck it to the nearest salivating Hellcat or P-38 owner-wannabe, and make piles of dough. With a bit more luck, the future might hold articles, books, even a glorifying spot in a television documentary.

All things considered, such a mini-epic seems the very model of productive adventuring and pluck and, on the whole, rather harmless entertainment. However, to people studying such wreck sites for what they can tell us about the progression of earthbound humans into the dimensions of air and space, or the ways in which our technological society wages war, such salvage adventures often harvest whole bargefuls of unintended negative consequences, none of them very obvious at the time.

It seems as though everywhere we turn these days someone is off retrieving another historic aircraft for restoration or sale or both. These expeditions are often organized, mounted, and patronized as "aviation archaeology." But is there such a thing? If so, what is it? And does it have any scientific kinship to pursuits such as, say, the excavation of the famous prehistoric mounds of the Ohio Valley or the block-by-block clearing of the buried Roman cities of Pompeii or Herculaneum?

These questions are being asked more and more frequently as aircraft salvage operations meet with either great success or disastrous failure. More often than not, it seems aircraft salvagers destroy the very thing they seek. In 1986 salvagers discovered a Handley Page Hampden bomber in 600 feet of water near Vancouver, British Columbia, the sole intact survivor of 160 produced in Canada during the Second World War. Items that could have revealed details of bomber training in the war were recovered without their positions being recorded. What handheld and cockpit instruments had been in use, for example? What were their settings? And had they been working? Far worse, during the salvage the aircraft was itself torn to pieces.

After half a century undersea, a Consolidated Vultee B-24 Liberator was plucked from the bottom of the Mediterranean with the remains of three crew members still on board. No one seems to have been concerned that the recovery was undertaken before even a rudimentary recording of the position and condition of the aircraft or the human remains inside had been completed.

A hundred years ago, Heinrich Schliemann furiously dug to the bottom of the great mound at Hissarlik in Turkey, seeking the lowest level of human occupation, where he was certain lay the site of his beloved Homeric Troy. But in his haste he dug too deep and destroyed the very place he had dedicated his life to finding. The difference between recent aircraft salvage efforts and Schliemann's excavations is that Schliemann did not have a century of archaeological survey and exploration methods to drawn upon. The modern salvagers of aircraft have no such excuse.

To understand what these methods are and how they are used, one must first understand what it is archaeologists do. Archaeologists study things people make and the ways in which these things can change our behavior by making our bodies and our brains more adaptable to our world. To simplify things, it is enough to say that archaeologists study the evolution of the human body by finding clues to how humans have come to dominate their environment so completely. They study the evolution of the human brain by looking at the material things the brain conceives, the objects of culture that lie all around us. (Culture is a loaded word; I like to define it as what most of the people are doing most of the time.) Whether it's a Roman waterworks, a stone statue on Easter Island, or a British shipwreck in Bermuda, an archaeological artifact can tell us what it was like to be a participant in a particular society at a particular time.

The way such sites yield information is by our studying them in terms of the two most important concepts in archaeology: "context" and "association." These are code words for the relationship of objects in time and space. You can think of context as a vertical or chronological idea: what happened before, during, and after those objects. The undersea wrecks of the U.S. Navy airships *Akron* and *Macon*, for example, testify to the context of the military's fear in the 1930s that a carrier-based attack would be mounted from the western Pacific (and in this case, of course, the fear was entirely justified).

The challenge for archaeologists who want to study aircraft is a large one. Thousands of sites exist where operational aircraft have been brought to earth by accident or design. When this happens, the aircraft leaves the realm of history and enters that of archaeology. It has been taken from the air and made a part of the land or the sea. It has found, to use that all-important word in archaeology, a new context.

Association is more of a horizontal or spatial term: the spread of the sweet potato across the Pacific islands, for example, or the array of radar installations along the British coast that helped turn back the Luftwaffe in 1940. By placing aircraft wreck sites in association with one another, we can contribute to historical debates regarding, say, the success or failure of British radar against the He 111; or the He 111 versus the Ju 88; or, even more complex, the extent to which a society under the stress of total war salvages and recycles the weapons hurled against it.

These sites, if examined with a view toward what their context and association can tell us, can speak to us directly from the past. The wrecks of the great naval airships fairly shout of the ways our grandparents and great-grandparents sought to provide a defensive screen for their culture (and for us, their biological and cultural heirs), even amid a crushing financial depression. Such sites can enrich our understanding of ourselves and our culture, a far greater reward, I believe, than what the salvage of them whole or in pieces might provide to a few individuals monetarily or materially.

Aircraft and spacecraft are a vital part of our modern technological culture. Many of us fly more or less frequently in commercial jets, and while only a few of us fly in spacecraft, we all pay taxes so that the government can take those risks for us. Our aircraft wreck sites therefore represent a large piece of who we were at the time of the wreck. They are also now a part of the landscape where they came to rest. In these contexts and associations, they have much to tell us about who we are and where we might be going.

No one can eradicate aircraft salvage. And I don't want to. But salvage without documentation is destruction. In any case, there will

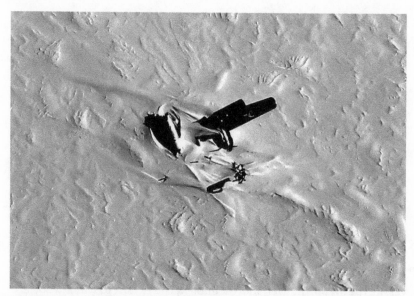

The *Kee Bird*, a wrecked B-29 Superfortress that made an emergency landing on a northwest Greenland ice sheet in 1947. Image acquired May 1, 2014, by the Digital Mapping System (DMS) attached to NASA's P-3 Orion airplane for the Operation IceBridge campaign. Courtesy of NASA.

never be enough professional archaeologists to sort through the thousands of aircraft wreck sites around the world. There is, however, a long and generally honorable tradition of amateur assistance to archaeological endeavors, so there is no reason why the irreplaceable amateur cannot be trained in the rudiments of historical research and archaeological analysis to examine and catalogue the sites before the salvager takes over.

These sites need to be read like the books they are, without first tearing the pages out, or selling them off piecemeal at a fire sale, or consigning them to a bonfire. Through the digital abilities of regional and global geographic information systems, archaeology now has the tools to register every cultural resource on the planet. If all aircraft wreck sites were accorded this rudimentary recording in a central repository, no matter what their final disposition, they would be registered in this database as part of the natural landscape forever.

But where does all this lofty intellectualizing leave our intrepid aircraft salvager? No doubt burning with resentment at academics trying to keep all the neat toys to themselves, and hotter than the fire started when an attempt to refurbish and fly a B-29 off the Greenland ice cap led to its complete destruction and abandonment by those who sought to retrieve it. And therein lies the difference between aviation archaeologists and aviation salvagers who call themselves archaeologists. One group studies aeronautical wrecks; the other creates them.

11

A Rock in the Fuselage

Large and popular artifacts such as aircraft and spacecraft involve a whole host of research and ethical considerations, beginning with the issue of potential human remains still on board, and extending to the condition and transformation of the artifact over time, the timing and competence of its recovery, and the skill and knowledge of a restoration team. And an artifact often decides to tell its tale in its own way in its own time. As I wrote in my doctoral dissertation: "The historical record cannot be accepted as 'the final word,' and instead must be tested, or filtered, through 'screens' constructed by the material remains left behind by the aeronauts and explorers themselves. Then (and only then), can new avenues of investigations be opened, investigations 'triggered' in many instances by individual artifacts that bear on particular historical or culturally general questions." Just such a case occurred when curators at the National Air and Space Museum restored a jet bomber from the Second World War.

Soon after writing the preceding essay I returned to Suitland, Maryland, and a visit to the former site of the Smithsonian Institution's Paul Garber Restoration Facility. I was there to revisit the Sikorsky S-43 flying boat, my favorite aircraft in the entire collection. It had been my great pleasure to meet Garber himself very late in his long life. In the late 1980s he was in his own late eighties and occupying a semi-retirement office at the National Air and Space Museum in Washington, D.C. Born in 1899, Garber was the first head of what was originally called the National Air Museum, and he related vivid memories of being an eleven-year-old boy in Atlantic City, New Jersey, in the fall of 1910 when Walter Wellman attempted to fly his dirigible *America* across the Atlantic Ocean. Garber was making a nuisance of himself when Wellman lifted him up and placed him out of the way on top of a crate. Garber went to work for the Smithsonian in 1920 and over the next seventy-two years until his death worked to assemble the greatest collection of aircraft in the world. Many of these are lone surviving examples, like the Arado Blitz in this essay. At the facility named for Garber, a team of restoration professionals had set the Sikorsky aside for a planned restoration they estimated would take place some fifty years in the future. The Sikorsky was in relatively good shape, and other projects took precedence, like the somewhat strange episode of the Arado. This brief essay touches on some of the issues that confront aircraft restoration teams in a professional museum setting.

To restore an aircraft to something approaching its original state of grace is a prospect both daunting and exhilarating; a process as frustrating as it is rewarding. The survey and mapping by archaeologists of aerospace launch sites and crash sites can seem elementary when compared to the problems faced by those who attempt to restore an aircraft to the way it looked at a certain time, in a certain place.

Karl Heinzel knows. When I met him some years ago at the Smithsonian's Paul Garber Restoration Facility in Suitland, Maryland, he had already been an integral part of aircraft restoration teams for more than twenty years. And like archaeological detectives, he and his colleagues have uncovered dozens of odd items embedded in the airframes of their restoration projects. These small, seemingly disconnected artifacts often reveal whole universes of humanity within their anonymous aluminum hosts. Take the case of the rock in the fuselage of a Second World War German Arado 234B-2 Blitz restored by Heinzel and his colleagues.

The Nazis constructed 274 of these remarkable twin-jet bombers, and the only example that survives today fell into American hands at the close of the war. The sleek and unique Blitz could blaze along at 460 miles per hour with a 1,000-pound bomb under its belly. (The Boeing B-17 Flying Fortress, by comparison, lumbered along at less than 200 miles per hour.) The price of such speed was endurance, as the Blitz's twin Junkers Jumo 004 axial jet engines were rated for little better than twenty-five hours of use.

Almost by design, it was an aircraft destined to spend the over-whelming majority of its existence in a museum. As such, this early jet bomber provided an excellent example of what one can learn as an aircraft goes to war, survives, is coveted, recovered, moved, hangared, studied, forgotten, pulled apart, moved again, and finally restored.

The Arado had a brief operational career. In the summer of 1944 one model flew, undetected, 30,000 feet above the Allied beachhead at Normandy, snapping pictures that showed a million and half men assembling against the German Reich. The Allies discovered the Smith-sonian's model alongside a runway in Norway. Along with several other advanced German aircraft, it was shipped to the United States.

When the U.S. military wanted to test fly the bomber at Wright-Patterson Air Force Base in the late forties, the German oxygen system and radios were replaced with American models they wanted to evalu-ate. Then, since U.S. Army Air Force General Henry "Hap" Arnold had ordered that a type specimen of every aircraft from the war be saved, the Arado was set aside at an Illinois storage facility until the start of the Korean War, when the air force told the Smithsonian to move the Arado or lose it.

It wound up in a wood and fiberboard box in Suitland, where like much of the World War II collection it sat outside for twenty years at the then primitive facility until a Smithsonian restoration team was ready to tackle it. When Heinzel and his colleagues began to restore the hangar-rusted Arado in the 1980s, they simultaneously began to rewrite its history, based on the strange modifications they found in-side the aircraft as they took it apart.

Of course, finding strange little quirks hidden inside supposedly uniform assembly-line aircraft is nothing new at Suitland. A Hawker Hurricane had produced a medallion with a British Lion and the still-undeciphered letters "PHAL" on it, along with Juicy Fruit and Kit Kat wrappers from 1943. An Aichi M6A1 Seiran seaplane undergoing restoration had produced a mini-museum display of extraneous artifacts: a custom-made bucket bar for setting rivets, a spool of safety wire, both found in the fuselage; another bucket bar lost—innocently or deliberately—inside the port wing; papers and forms stuffed inexplicably into the starboard forward fuel tank. Another Japanese aircraft was found to contain penciled inscriptions inside the fuselage ranging from the banal to the profane to the romantic.

But the Arado topped them all. "When we finally got around to it," said Heinzel, "most of the damage to the aircraft had been done by time and weather, not by the war. It was suffering from a severe case of 'hangar rash.'" Heinzel noted the hundreds of dings, dents, and scratches an airframe endures by being moved around increasingly cramped sheds over the years, as more and more historic aircraft crowded into Suitland's limited storage spaces. But it was when they began to take apart this machine of a million pieces that unusual "design modifications" began to appear.

"First we noticed that someone had put rivets in the fuselage but hadn't bucked [seated] them," recalled Heinzel. "Then, when we removed the main fuel lines, we found file marks on their undersides, that is, the side facing the fuselage. The file marks had been made where no ordinary pre-flight inspection would have noticed them."

It began to seem as if someone had been less than enthusiastic to see the Arado take to the air. When it was learned that the bomber had been assembled originally by forced laborers working for the Nazi regime at the Arado plant in Eastern Europe, a motive emerged: sabotage. Then they found the rock.

Because it flew with jet engines, the Arado landed at high speed. On runways designed for prop aircraft, this was a problem. The Germans addressed it in part by mounting a drogue parachute near the tail of the aircraft. Upon landing, the pilot pulled a lever that activated a small door covering the chute. The drogue—similar to the one that helped slow the space shuttle—would then deploy and brake the force of the jet bomber's landing. Apparently, among the enslaved workers assembling the aircraft, there was at least one who sought to make it the last time the drogue stopped an Arado jet.

The Arado 234B-2 Blitz, now fully restored (minus the rock) and on display at the National Air and Space Museum's Steven F. Udvar-Hazy Center near Washington Dulles International Airport.

Near the mechanical release by which the drogue would have been deployed, someone had neatly fitted a rock. Presumably, if a Nazi pilot had attempted to stop his Arado on a short field by deploying the chute, the hope was that the rock would have jammed the mechanism, preventing the chute from billowing behind the Blitz, whereupon the pilot would have overshot the runway and crashed.

Given the certain punishment that would have followed the discovery of the rock in the fuselage, it had taken an act of enormous resistance and courage to place it there. Of great irony is the possibility that one or all three acts of deliberate sabotage directed against the Germans could have killed a post-war test pilot from one of the countries that liberated the prisoners of the Nazis. "When the U.S. Air Force tested the Arado, they may or may not have tried to deploy the drogue," said Heinzel. "But they never discovered what we found."

For Heinzel and the other restorers, such thoughts were interesting sideshows among the million pieces of the Arado that they had to

restore and put back together. Unlike the other 999,999 pieces, however, the rock presented them with a problem: what to do with it. Obviously it was never meant to be a part of the original bomber. And once
the restoration was complete, the drogue cover would be bolted back
in place. No one would ever see the rock. So why put it back?

It became one more item in what Heinzel called the "negotiation"
that goes on between an aircraft and its restoration team. For example,
a First World War Nieuport N28C-1, "restored" as a model from the
94th Aero Pursuit Squadron, was completed with wing panels from no
less than four different Nieuports, along with a different fuselage.

At times, the negotiations with the Arado broke down. After it was
repainted, old photographs were found showing Suitland's Arado on
the Norwegian runway at the end of the war. To their dismay, the restorers discovered that they had applied the wrong registration number to their Blitz. But new paint technologies used since the restoration made it prohibitively expensive to attempt to resurface large areas
of the aircraft. So the mis-numbering remained, and can be seen at
the Arado's permanent home at the National Air and Space Museum's
Steven F. Udvar-Hazy Center near Washington Dulles International
Airport.

And what of the dramatic evidence of sabotage? What was the out-
come of those negotiations? Like a moon rock, was it mounted on a
pedestal where it could stand as a direct physical reminder of a solitary
brave act of defiance to tyranny? Or, unsuccessful in war, undiscovered
during test flights, and unwanted by a restoration team, was it after all
merely a singularly unlucky stone?

"It bounced around the shop for a while," recalled Heinzel. "But then
it was lost." In the years since the restoration, the view of the rock
and artifacts like it has changed. "Now, we would most certainly have
documented it, photographed it, and depending on what was deemed
the best idea, either displayed the rock with the story of the sabotage
or put it back in the door where it belonged. I have no idea what finally
became of it, but it may still be living somewhere on the grounds of the
Garber facility in anonymity."

12

The Tupolev TB-3 on Rudolf Island

The secret history of an aircraft, such as that revealed in the Arado's poignant rock, can also come to the surface as the result of archival research conducted after an aircraft is surveyed in the field. In the following case of perhaps the world's northernmost aircraft wreck, a briefly noted serial number led to a secret history from the archives of the former Soviet Union. It is a good example of how library and archives research works hand in hand with fieldwork to produce a more complete construction of the human past.

As tools fashioned by humans, aircraft are unique in that they are the first and only artifacts that can literally be found anywhere on the planet. Most artifacts can be found in tight windows in time and space, but an aircraft, depending on the model, can rise from either land or water and then land anywhere, including as far north and south as the ice of both poles. By anywhere, of course, we mean that they can land—deliberately or accidentally—or crash, or otherwise be discarded, at any point on Earth. In 1990 my Norwegian colleague Susan Barr participated in a pioneering joint Norwegian-Soviet expedition to Franz Josef Land. It was the first Western glimpse of several historic sites in this remote archipelago in the Arctic, only discovered in the 1870s and which later served as a dramatic arena in the search for the geographic North Pole. On the northernmost land in the archipelago

Dr. Barr photographed an unusual aircraft wreck. Using these data, in the summer of 2006 I set out to rediscover, survey, and identify this wreck, which would mark the northernmost wreck of an aircraft in the world.

In 1936 Otto Schmidt, Russian Arctic explorer and leader of the doomed *Chelyuskin* expedition of 1933–34, and Mikhail Vodopianov, one of the pilots who rescued the *Chelyuskin* survivors, combined to draw up a plan for further research in the polar basin.[1] This research would gather data on the nature of drift ice, ocean currents, and marine life in the polar basin, all in support of the navigational requirements of Russian ships working the Northern Sea Route. In addition to the emplacement of a drift station near the North Pole, the plan included flights across the pole to the United States.[2]

This comprehensive plan required the location and construction of bases to service, launch, and provide weather reports for arctic aircraft. The flights to search for and establish these bases were carried out by many of the same pilots, such as Vodopianov, who had been involved in the rescue of the *Chelyuskin* survivors. Franz Josef Land was the logical place for these bases so, in the spring of 1936, Vodopianov and V. M. Makhotin made a series of "exceptionally difficult and complicated" flights throughout the islands.[3] They identified the ice dome of the archipelago's northernmost land, Rudolf Island—just 600 miles (965 km) from the North Pole—as suitable for the construction of an airstrip and support base.[4]

Soon after Vodopianov's aerial survey flights of the island, the ships *Rusanov* and *Gertsen* delivered the supplies and staff necessary for the construction of an airstrip on the island's ice dome, some 750 feet above Teplitz Bay. Twenty-four personnel over-wintered in 1936–37, and in the spring of 1937 four Tupolev TB-3 heavy bombers with registration numbers CCCP-H-169 to 172 arrived at the airstrip.

The TB-3, built by Andrei Nikolaevich Tupolev, was "one of the outstanding aircraft in aviation history in that it was the world's first four-engine cantilever monoplane bomber."[5] The heavy bomber (*tyazholy bombardirovshchik*, hence "TB") had a seventy-five-foot-long rectangular fuselage crowned with a curved top deck. Several of these massive aircraft were specially converted for arctic exploration and re-designated as ANT-6 4AM-34R. These special modifications included enclosed pilot cabins, a covered top observation deck, cold-weather engines, skis, and a braking parachute like that on the Arado Blitz discussed in chapter 11. The arctic variant was painted bright orange for visibility in case the aircraft was forced down on the ice.[6]

On April 18 four of these heavy aircraft, registered to the Independent Arctic Directorate of Aeroflot (Polyarnaya aviatsiya/Aviaarktika), lifted off for the north. Landing within twenty miles of the North Pole, the TB-3s remained on the ice for sixteen days and successfully deposited I. D. Papanin and his polar drift-ice station. All four aircraft returned safely to Rudolf Island, and by the end of June 1937 all had returned to Moscow except for N-169, which "remained at Rudolf Island to assist the researchers left on the ice at the North Pole."[7]

At this point, competition became intense over which Soviet aviator would claim the honor of the first flight over the pole.[8] Valery Chkalov was the first to try. On June 18, 1937, Chkalov and his crew piloted a Tupolev ANT-25 from Moscow over the pole and then on to Vancouver. A second flight in another ANT-25 by Mikhail Gromov flew from Moscow to California in mid-July. As polar aviation fever gripped both the Soviet Union and the international popular press in the summer of 1937, another hero of the *Chelyuskin* rescue prepared for another journey.

In mid-August Sigismund Levanevsky chose a TB-3, No. 209, for an attempt to break the record set by Gromov. Somewhere in the vicinity of the pole Levanevsky lost radio contact with the North Pole 1 station and disappeared. A massive international search effort, one that included Australian polar explorer Sir Hubert Wilkins, found no trace of the lost aircraft.

After the successes of the ANT-25 flights and the NP-1 station, the loss of Levanevsky's TB-3 came as a shock to the Soviet aviation community. Instantly, according to John McCannon's excellent history, "the fault-finding began."[9] The radio man at the Rudolf Island station was accused of falling asleep during crucial weather report transmissions between N-209 and NP-1. The death sentence originally given for this alleged lapse was later commuted to twenty years at hard labor.

A study of the image of the wrecked aircraft recorded by Susan Barr

Norwegian ethnologist Dr. Susan Barr took this intriguing image of the remains of a wrecked aircraft during a joint Soviet-Norwegian expedition in 1990.
This image led directly to our request to visit the site in 2006 to try to identify
the exact model of this northernmost aircraft. Courtesy Susan Barr.

suggested that the wreck might be one of the specially modified arctic
TB-3s, perhaps even one of the four that landed at the North Pole in
1937.[10] This supposition was sufficient to persuade the captain of the
Russian icebreaker *Yamal* to allow us to investigate the site during one
of two cruises from Murmansk to the North Pole and back in August
of 2006.

Dr. Barr's photograph seemed to indicate that the wreckage was on
its side, with the remains of wings, engines, and landing gear scattered
nearby. It seemed possible that the wreckage may have been reused as
a kind of runway shelter, since the photograph appeared to indicate
that the top observation deck was now a side window, possibly even
decorated with curtains.

Unfortunately, the only indication of a location was that the wreckage was somewhere near the Rudolf Island ice cap airstrip. After much
international communication prior to our polar cruises on board
the *Yamal*, it became apparent that the aircraft wreckage was within

walking distance of the Teplitz Bay station and probably to the north of it. As the *Yamal* cruised near the island around midnight on August 21, 2006, one of its helicopters lifted from its deck and carried a small search party toward Teplitz Bay.

We spotted the giant wreck almost immediately, resting in a rocky swale approximately a mile east of the former Soviet meteorological research station. Even from the air, and although it was nearly buried in fresh snow, it was clear that the aircraft had not merely been discarded. It lay downhill from the ice dome, having apparently crashed on its way either on or off the ice dome airfield. During this operation it had broken into several huge pieces.

Once on the ground, with our survey time limited to less than an hour before we had to return to the ship, we got to work quickly on a rapid series of measurements. The central surviving segment of fuselage was fifty-two feet long. In cross section it was rectangular, with a curved top decking. One of the large blisters was covered, just as in the special ANT-6 arctic variant expedition aircraft. The forward section of the fuselage, which would have housed the covered pilot's cockpit and forward observer's cabin, was missing. The neatness of the break between the surviving fuselage and the missing cockpit area suggests that this section was removed after the wreck, perhaps for use on another TB-3, perhaps as part of an accident investigation, or maybe for some other reuse at the station or elsewhere. If this be the case, it suggests that the aircraft was not moving at a very high speed when it suffered its calamity.

There was little question as we examined the wreck that it was a TB-3. No other Soviet aircraft so large and used in the Arctic existed in the 1930s. An attempt was made to locate evidence of a serial number, but the large fuselage number on one side had been scoured away by wind. On the other side, where one might find surviving paint, the number was buried under much new snow and old ice. With little time available, a quick and improvised excavation was all that was possible.

Digging through the loose snow by hand, I managed to crawl inside the fuselage and found it remarkably well preserved. Once inside the fuselage, I quickly uncovered two diagnostic elements. The first was

The author (*center left*) measuring the remains of the Tupolev's starboard wing. Very large Russians with automatic weapons stand lookout for polar bears. In the upper right are the remains of the Teplitz Bay science station. Somewhere in the bay beyond lay the remains of the steamship *America*, sunk during the 1903–5 Ziegler polar expedition under Anthony Fiala. Courtesy Gordon Kilgore.

a section of twisted fuselage metal coated with bright orange paint, a clear indication of a Soviet Arctic aircraft. The other was scrawled writing with the number 210 and the Russian letters P-K. This was the only identifying marking found on the entire fuselage.

Subsequent to our survey, we located a reference indicating that both TB-3 No. 210 and No. 211 had been damaged and left behind in Franz Josef Land in the spring of 1938.[11] The location of the painted number 210 during the survey supports this documentary evidence insofar as it relates to TB-3 No. 210. Other documentary evidence, however, suggests this is incorrect with regard to No. 211 and that that aircraft had been previously destroyed.

Identifying the wreckage as TB-3 (ANT-6) No. 210 was significant. While it was not one of the famous four North Pole aircraft, it was involved in a notorious episode in Soviet polar aviation: the loss of, and search for, the missing flight of S. A. Levanevsky in the autumn of 1937 and spring of 1938. As such, it represents the only surviving wreckage of the main aircraft used by the Soviet Union in its attempts to explore the region around the North Pole by air in the 1930s.

The series of incidents were both aeronautical disasters and tremendous embarrassments for the Russian Northern Maritime Route (Glavsevmorput) bureaucracy. On March 14, 1938, four TB-3s—Nos. 210, 211, 212, and 213—left Archangel'sk intent upon continuing the search for Levanevsky. Over the White Sea two of the aircraft collided. One of them, No. 211 piloted by Mikhail Babushkin, crashed and exploded, killing all on board.[12] The pilot of the other aircraft, Yakov Moshkovsky, was prosecuted for the incident. Belov recounts this disaster differently, with Moshkovsky's aircraft going down on the way south to Moscow after a take-off from the airfield at Arkhangel'sk.[13] In this version Babushkin and three others on board Moshkovsky's TB-3 were killed.

But the aviator who came in for the harshest treatment was the overall commander of the four-aircraft flight element, Boris Chukhnovsky, pilot of TB-3 No. 210, whose aircraft crash-landed at Rudolf Island on March 17. Chukhnovsky was accused of being too old to pilot his TB-3 and therefore incompetent to assume the additional burden of command. Fellow pilots such as Vodopianov signed a letter to director Otto Schmidt that castigated Chukhnovsky both as a failed leader and either reckless or a homosexual, the latter an especially notorious denunciation during the Stalinist purges.[14]

Another report sent to Schmidt, this one uncovered by author G. Weston DeWalt, went further, claiming that Chukhnovsky had earlier been told by the leadership of Glavsevmorput that he was not to land or take off in the N-210 and suggesting that several observers on the ground had been injured in the crash. "The N-210 had onboard commander Chukhnovsky, copilot Lisitsyn, navigator Shelygavnov, radio operator Makarov, mechanics Petrukhin, Gursky and Kulikov. The plane crashed at Rudolf Airfield after returning to Rudolf from Tikhaia [Bay, another Russian research station in Franz Josef Land]. Injured seriously in the crash were Babushkin, mechanics Nelidov and Kulikov. Lisitsyn, Shelyganov, weather forecaster Klemin and worker Griaznov were wounded slightly. Mechanic Gursky, Chukhnovsky and an engineer Rudniy received serious bruises. The plane is a total loss. Investigations indicate that the crash occurred because Chukhnovsky interfered when Lisitsyn landed the plane."[15]

The wreckage of the crash shows little pitting or corrosion, although the original paint had long been scoured by wind and snow, and the side of the fuselage that faces the sky shows extensive tearing. This latter damage could have been caused by polar bears; by any initial attempts to rescue the crew from the wreck; or by the subsequent partial salvage of the aircraft (see note 15). Whatever the case—and with the dramatic increase in arctic tourism experienced in recent years on the islands of Franz Josef Land—Russian polar authorities should demarcate the site, place it under a protective regime, and add a wayside panel near the site, in several languages, to explain the history of the Soviet polar program of 1937–38 and the importance of the site in preserving the material culture of that period.

The TB-3 wreckage at Teplitz Bay is a well-preserved archaeological site. Further study and a more complete excavation would certainly reveal a myriad of design, construction, and performance details of this aircraft and its role in polar aviation. An exploration on the ice dome of Rudolf Island itself might reveal the location of the 1930s airstrip and perhaps other archaeological data. If the Teplitz Bay wreckage *is* TB-3 No. 210, as our preliminary examination indicates, then it constitutes the archaeological remains of both the triumphs and tragedies of the daring Soviet aeronautical explorations of the North Pole in 1937–38 and, at 81°47.5'N, the northernmost aircraft wreck yet identified.

IV

Aerospace Archaeology

13

Space

The Final (Archaeological) Frontier

While the pyramids of Egypt and the moai of Easter Island will always and rightly represent a popular view of archaeology and the times studied by archaeologists, in fact anything made, modified, and discarded or abandoned by humans is archaeological. This includes artifacts too recent to tell us anything about ourselves that we do not already know. The case of archaeology in space shows just how wrong that view is.

During my doctoral work in archaeology, it was a great privilege to correspond with the renowned anthropologist Dr. Ben Finney at the University of Hawai'i. Dr. Finney had pioneered the reconstruction of the technology and techniques used by Polynesians to settle the Pacific Ocean, so his work had obvious applications to my interests in diffusion and exploration. When I mentioned a potential combination of the exploration of space with the field of archaeology, he suggested the construction of a catalogue of the archaeology of aerospace sites on the Moon and Mars, "the remains or imprint of Russian and American space ventures there."

From this suggestion I began to collect such data in the early 1990s, some of which found its way into my dissertation at Rutgers University. I was grateful that preeminent archaeologists of early hominids and human behavior at Rutgers such as J.W.K. Harris and

Rob Blumenschine, who worked on archaeological sites millions of years in the past, allowed me the intellectual freedom to follow these data into archaeologically meaningful implications for human evolution. Finney, Harris, and Blumenschine, as well as Richard Gould of Brown University and Scott L. H. Madry, then of the Remote Sensing Center at Rutgers, all encouraged me to expand my archaeological horizons. From their own work at the poles and the equator, colleagues like Susan Barr of Riksantikvaren in Oslo, and Bill Thomas, now director of the New Jersey School of Conservation at Montclair State, provided intellectual templates for my own thinking.

At the turn of the new century my future friend and colleague Beth O'Leary in New Mexico had begun the remote survey of the remains of the *Apollo 11* camp on the Moon. Beth then led a discussion of the subject at the Fifth World Archaeological Congress in Washington, D.C., in 2003. Almost simultaneously, a session on "Space Heritage and the Potential for Exoarchaeology in the Solar System: National and International Perspectives" was organized by John B. Campbell of James Cook University in Queensland, Australia. The following essays reflects how far the idea of archaeology in space had come, from a very brief and cautious mention in my 1996 doctorate to a featured essay in a 2004 issue of *Archaeology* magazine. Even so, as you can read, it was still necessary to introduce this "far out" subject with an interpolation of a science fiction tale.

Summer 2205

During a preliminary survey of late twenty-first-century mining outposts in the asteroid belt, Dr. Gan Shishu, director of the Institute for Space Archaeology at the China National Space Administration, recognized a unique opportunity. Leaving her field team as they continued to document the massive Halliburton gantry on asteroid Q36, she piloted her team's one-person archaeoprobe *L.S.B. Leakey* toward a strange-looking artifact nearby that had been drifting in heliocentric orbit for more than two centuries.

* * *

Science fiction? Not any longer. The notion of archaeological research and heritage management in space is an idea whose time has already arrived.

It has been more than twenty years since Brown University anthropologist Richard Gould proposed that aircraft wrecks might yield important data—laying the foundation for systematic archaeological studies of sites from the history of human flight. Then, in 1993, University of Hawai'i anthropologist Ben Finney, who for much of his career has explored the technology and techniques used by Polynesians to colonize islands in the Pacific, suggested that it would not be premature to begin thinking about the archaeology of aerospace sites on the Moon and Mars. Finney pointed out that just as today's scholars use the archaeological record to investigate how Polynesians diverged culturally as they explored the Pacific, archaeologists will someday study off-Earth sites to trace the development of humans in space. He was certainly clear-eyed about the improbability of anyone being able to conduct fieldwork any time soon, but he was equally convinced that one day such work would be done.

There is a growing awareness, however, that it won't be long before both corporate adventurers and space tourists reach the Moon and Mars. The Russians already carry very-high-paying tourists to the International Space Station, and the recent launch by the private company Scaled Composites of the three-passenger SpaceShipOne has shown that corporate space travel will soon be feasible. We have a wealth of important archaeological sites from the history of space exploration on the Moon and Mars, and protective cultural heritage regimes need to be in place before these people get there. Otherwise we must be prepared to see pieces of *Apollo 11* listed for sale on eBay someday.

In 1999 a company called Lunacorp proposed a robotic lunar rover mission beginning at the site of Tranquility Base and rumbling across the Moon from one archaeological site to another, from the wreck of the *Ranger 8* probe and a *Surveyor* spacecraft to *Apollo 17*'s landing site and a lost Soviet *Lunakhod* rover. The mission, which would leave more than 600 miles (965 km) of tread marks at some of the most famous sites from the history of exploration, was promoted as a form of theme-park entertainment. In addition to the threat from profit-seeking corporations, scholars cite other potentially destructive forces, such as wanton souvenir hunting as well as uncontrolled or unmonitored scientific sampling, like that which has occurred in explorations of remote polar regions.

According to the vaguely worded United Nations Outer Space Treaty of 1967, what it terms "space junk" remains the property of the country that sent the craft or probe into space. But the treaty doesn't explicitly address protection of sites like Tranquility Base, and equating the remains of human exploration of the heavens with "space junk" leaves them vulnerable to scavengers. Another problem arises through other treaties proclaiming that land in space cannot be owned by any country or individual. This presents some interesting dilemmas for the aspiring manager of extraterrestrial cultural resources. If the United States owns the archaeological remains of *Apollo 11* but not the ground underneath it, how do we protect the former without disturbing the latter? Does America own Neil Armstrong's famous first footprints on the Moon but not the lunar dust in which they were recorded? Surely those footprints are as important in the story of human development as those left by hominids at Laetoli, Tanzania. But unlike the Laetoli prints, which have survived for 3.5 million years encased in cementlike ash, those at Tranquility Base could be swept away with a casual brush of a space tourist's hand.

In what may be the first instance of funded space archaeology research, a team led by Beth O'Leary, a New Mexico State University archaeologist, is studying legal ownership of artifacts and structures in space and how one might go about documenting and preserving them. O'Leary's group argues that even though the United States cannot, by treaty, own the land on which the lunar module *Eagle*'s descent stage rests, U.S. federal preservation laws and regulations nonetheless apply to the objects left there. They see the base as a natural candidate for the National Register of Historic Places, as a National Historic Landmark, and potentially as the first extraterrestrial site on UNESCO's World Heritage List.

*   *   *

Dr. Gan's doctoral work on the rise and fall of the American Empire had taken her to several aerospace museums around the world. But museums, she knew, were of limited use to the archaeologist, since they frequently reinforced an established order while, consciously or not, shifting the attention of museum visitors away from manifest failures in the technological and social history of that established order. Now, as the *Leakey*'s robot arm reached out and snared the slowly tumbling artifact, Gan viewed the only surviving lunar module of the American Apollo program, the first (and ultimately only) successful attempt to put humans on the moon prior to the permanent Chinese colonization in 2043. Of the eight lunar modules sent into space, only one survived destruction—and Gan was about to climb on board.

*   *   *

Unless procedures and protocols are developed for evaluating and registering sites and artifacts, "there will be uncontrolled sampling and even outright treasure hunting," says John Campbell, an archaeologist at James Cook University in Queensland, Australia, who has been responsible for organizing recent international seminars on the subject of preserving space heritage. Federal cultural resource management legislation, he notes, has the potential to lift aerospace archaeology away from the profiteers and souvenir hunters and into its proper bailiwick within the discipline of historical archaeology.

As a first step in that direction and with funding from the New Mexico Space Grant Consortium, O'Leary's group of archaeologists, curators, and physicists have researched and documented an archaeological assemblage of dozens of artifacts and features at Tranquility Base alone. Using these data, they have drawn up a preliminary site plan, one that, thanks to the Moon's lack of atmosphere, will doubtless remain unchanged for centuries, provided looters leave the site untouched.

The challenges of surveying and preserving old spacecraft discarded on the surface of Mars will be greater. Dust storms could damage landers or even bury them beneath the red Martian soil. And since Mars has no protective ozone layer, ultraviolet energy from the Sun could damage the spacecraft. It may be necessary to deploy shields over such sites to protect them from the continual abrasion and decay caused by extreme temperatures, radiation, wind, and dust.

Eventually the *Viking* landers (1976), the Mars *Pathfinder* (1997), and the *Spirit* and *Opportunity* rovers (2004) might need to be moved indoors to protect them from the Martian environment that they helped explore. And, of course, field survey teams—human or robotic—will need to be dispatched to Mars's North Pole to answer the mystery of what became of NASA's lost 1997 *Polar Lander*, and to the Isidis Planitia basin in search of the European Space Agency's ill-fated *Beagle II* (2003).

Yet it is one thing for a few archaeologists to realize the almost unlimited potential of archaeological studies in space, and quite another to do something about it. When O'Leary and her team approached various federal agencies responsible, such as NASA, to discuss legal issues related to space and national historic place designations, they were rebuffed by terse bureaucratese: "Placing Tranquility Base under protection might imply that the U.S. intended to exert sovereignty over the Moon." "Our office does not have jurisdiction." "Our office does not have the inclination." Similar problems cropped up with regard to the use of UNESCO's World Heritage List, since Tranquility Base can be seen as not so much a global cultural achievement as another battle in the Cold War.

O'Leary believes it may be time to look to new kinds of worldwide treaties for the preservation of old structures on the new frontier that would bypass the cultural baggage associated with UNESCO's World Heritage List and the vague, contradictory possession clauses of the UN's space treaty. She points out that an archaeologist on Earth needs a permit from a relevant authority prior to conducting any intrusive research. If no authority can own property in space, what authority would issue such permits for the extraterrestrial archaeologist? The problem requires the creation of new international administrative structures unlike anything archaeologists have to contend with on Earth.

*   *   *

As she crossed from the *Leakey* to the primitive lunar module, Gan recognized the faded red, white, and blue symbol that represented the classic fifty-state alliance at the height of its global preeminence, a time of technological triumph, social unrest, and dietary disaster. She noted the fine coating of dust that covered the lunar module ascent stage and took great pains not to disturb it, except for one small patch. There, she wiped clear a small area to reveal the image of a stylized dog with a long snout. Above the dog was the word "Snoopy."

Gan was the first human to touch the command module since it was abandoned by pilot Eugene A. Cernan and mission commander Thomas P. Stafford on May 24, 1969, 236 years earlier. Having studied it for this mission, she and her team had developed a field tool that now enabled her to loosen the hatch cover that once connected *Snoopy*, the lunar module, to the command module, *Charlie Brown*. As it swung free, Gan squeezed through the narrow passage, leaving the year 2205 and entering a chamber of technology, language, and culture untouched for more than two centuries.

*   *   *

The Cold War, which provided so much of the backdrop to the race for the Moon, is replete with failures that may never be examined until archaeology takes them up. The site where the Soviet *Luna 5* probe crash-landed onto the surface of the Moon on May 9, 1965, may one day provide excellent archaeological opportunities for the study of the secretive *Luna* series of unmanned probes launched in an era of intense superpower competition for priority on the Moon. The questions that could be asked of such a site are almost limitless. Does its location correspond with archival records of its guidance and trajectory? Does the composition of the craft match its specifications? Is there any instrumentation or technology on board—Cold War or otherwise—that was never announced, recorded, or used on Earth?

Dozens of sites exist on the Moon where operational spacecraft have been discarded, whether by mission requirements, accident, or obsolescence. The Apollo program alone left six lunar module descent stages fixed at base camps, and another six ascent stages were deliberately discarded and impacted on the lunar surface after they had delivered their crews back to the mission's command module. (The exact impact sites of two of these wrecks, *Apollo 11*'s *Eagle* and *Apollo 16*'s *Orion*, have never been located.)

If one accepts the idea of archaeological research on sites from the history of human exploration in space, it is hardly a giant leap to consider the search for extraterrestrial intelligence (SETI) and the potential for archaeological fieldwork on the evidence of extraterrestrial civilizations. The late biochemist and science fiction writer Isaac Asimov once speculated that the galaxy may contain 325 million planets with traces of civilizations in ruins. Perhaps our astronomers and their SETI stations are hearing only static through their radio telescopes because they are, in effect, listening for a message from the extraterrestrial equivalent of the ancient Maya or the Sumerians—dead civilizations that can speak to us now only through archaeology. Constructing a catalogue of visual signatures of advanced civilizations will someday be within the province of aerospace archaeology. And with a potential cultural resource database of 325 million planets with civilizations in ruins, there sure is a lot of fieldwork to do "out there."

*   *   *

For two hours Gan recorded the instrument settings and the arrangement of discarded clipboards with their innumerable checklists, marveling at how many functions the humans had had to attend to manually back in 1969—functions long since given over to the computers of the Central Bureau. Then, as she prepared to leave *Snoopy* and return to *Leakey*, she uncovered a small bag that held a minuscule amount of bright orange residue. She removed a tiny sample and placed it in her portable gas chromatograph mass spectrometer. The results were confusing. Though she read the English words on the bag as "Breakfast Drink, Orange," all the mass spec revealed was sugar, fructose, titanium dioxide (which apparently accounted for the bright orange color), xanthum gum, cellulose gum, and two chemicals she knew had been listed as poisons for over a century—Yellow 5 and Yellow 6.

*   *   *

The Moon, with its wealth of sites, will surely be the first destination of archaeologists trained to work in space. But any young scholars hoping to claim the mantle of history's first lunar archaeologist will be disappointed. That distinction is already taken.

On November 19, 1969, astronauts Charles "Pete" Conrad Jr. and Alan L. Bean made a difficult manual landing of the *Apollo 12* lunar module in the Moon's Ocean of Storms, just a few hundred feet from an unmanned probe, *Surveyor 3*, that had soft-landed in a crater on April 19, 1967. Unrecognized at the time, this was an important moment in the history of science. Bean and Conrad were about to conduct the first archaeological studies on the Moon.

After the obligatory planting of the American flag and some geological sampling, Conrad and Bean made their way to the artifact made accessible by their brilliant piloting. They observed that *Surveyor 3* had bounced after touchdown and carefully photographed the impressions made by its footpads. Conrad noted the artifact's brownish tint, and learned from Mission Control engineers in Houston that the probe had been white when it was launched. The photographic system's mirror was warped and the whole spacecraft covered in dust, perhaps kicked up by the landing.

Conrad and Bean used a cutting tool to remove the probe's television camera, remote sampling arm, and pieces of tubing. The astronaut-archaeologists bagged and labeled these artifacts, stowed them on board their lunar module, and returned them to Earth. The Johnson Space Center in Houston, Texas, and the Hughes Air and Space Corporation in El Segundo, California, later analyzed the changes in these aerospace artifacts left on the Moon for more than two years.

Published by NASA in 1972 as *Analysis of* Surveyor 3 *Material and Photographs Returned by* Apollo 12 (NASA SP-284, 1972), this sophisticated multidisciplinary investigation of the *Surveyor 3* artifacts focused on the ways the retrieved components had been changed by the craft's voyage through the vacuum of space. As such, the mission of *Apollo 12* provided the first example of aerospace archaeology, extraterrestrial archaeology, and—perhaps more significant for the history of the discipline—formational archaeology, the study of environmental and cultural forces upon the life history of human artifacts in space.

On April 17, 1967, NASA's *Surveyor 3* spacecraft launched from Cape Canaveral Air Force Station, Florida, on a mission to the lunar surface. A little more than two years after it landed on the moon with the goal of paving the way for a future human mission, the *Surveyor 3* spacecraft was visited by *Apollo 12* Commander Charles Conrad Jr. and astronaut Alan L. Bean, who snapped this photo on November 20, 1969. Courtesy of NASA.

A piece of the television camera, subjected to a microbiological examination, revealed evidence of the bacteria *Streptococcus mitis*. For a moment it was thought Conrad and Bean had discovered evidence for life on the Moon. As all other competing hypotheses were systematically eliminated, the origin of the seemingly extraterrestrial life became apparent. While the camera was being readied for launch, someone had sneezed on it. The resulting virus had traveled to the Moon, remained in an alternating freezing/boiling vacuum for two and a half years, and returned promptly to life upon reaching the safety of a petri dish back on Earth.

Lunar archaeology had made its first great discovery: not even the vastness of space can stop humans from spreading a sore throat.

*   *   *

Sealing the hatch of *Snoopy*, Gan returned to her own research vessel, backed it away, and set the ancient space artifact adrift once again on its orbit around the sun. As it floated out of sight, she entered the results of the mass spec analysis into the *Leakey*'s computer. She discovered that the orange substance she had tested was known in 1969 vernacular culture as "Tang." As she navigated her way back to her field team on Q36, she suddenly remembered from her food history that it was another half century before Americans realized—too late—that such sugar- and corn syrup–based foods had led their nation into cultural and physical obesity. In her mind, she was already spinning a new hypothesis. The same processed foods that had led America to the moon had led to its downfall. She would present at the next Interplanetary Archaeology Congress. She would call it her "NAPA" hypothesis: North America Pre-Atkins.

14

Surveying Fermi's Paradox, Mapping Dyson's Sphere

It can be difficult to separate the archaeology of spacefaring humans from more speculative considerations of what artifacts other forms of intelligence in the universe might exhibit in their own museum and exhibition halls or as traces of their prehistoric cultures and dead civilizations. As a lifelong fan of science fiction novels and movies alike, I finally gave up trying, and penned a chapter that lays out just what the as yet unborn archaeologists of the future might search for "out there."

The development of a formal aerospace archaeology, with its attendant methods for cultural resource management, forms the methodological and theoretical basis for the survey, study, and stabilization of sites of human exploration throughout the solar system. On a far larger scale, it also allows one to consider the archaeological possibilities inherent in the search for potential signatures of intelligent life throughout the universe. A massive, pioneering 2009 work, the *Handbook of Space Engineering, Archaeology, and Heritage*, edited by my colleagues Ann Garrison Darrin and Beth Laura O'Leary, allowed me a chapter in which to examine this larger theme, one derived directly from my earlier considerations of the study and preservation of planetary sites from the history of aerospace exploration. Such sweeping considerations encompass the potential for intelligent life elsewhere in the universe, the possible archaeological signatures of such life, and the parameters by which such signatures might be recognized and might have archaeological surveys conducted on them on several levels: galactic, planetary, area, and site.

"Where is everybody?" asked Enrico Fermi over lunch at Los Alamos Laboratory in the summer of 1950.[1] Fermi's three colleagues at lunch— Herbert York, Emil Konopinski, and Edward Teller—understood right away what he was referring to. If popular estimates of thousands of extraterrestrial civilizations are accurate, why don't we see evidence of such alien civilizations in the form of communications, spacecraft, and other alien artifacts, or even visits to Earth?

A decade after Fermi formed what became known as his universal paradox, astronomer Frank Drake created an equation to estimate the number of technological civilizations that reside in our galaxy.[2] The functional aspects of such a construct are no doubt sound. If it holds a conceit, it is perhaps the assumption that if intelligent life has developed something similar to *Homo sapiens*'s civilization, such a civilization exists now, in real time, somewhere in the galaxy, in a mode capable of contacting Earth.

It was Isaac Asimov who first explored this notion as it might relate directly to aerospace archaeology.[3] Asimov used a more reasonable approximation of the lengths of the stages of technological development in human civilization to calculate the probability that similar such civilizations exist in our own galaxy.

As in all such constructs, one makes a few dramatic assumptions. For Asimov, writing in the Cold War era of the 1970s, it was that a civilization such as that of *Homo sapiens* destroys itself within, at most, several generations of developing nuclear power. Asimov further assumed that every habitable planet with a life-bearing span of 12 billion years developed an intelligent species after 4.6 billion years, which then developed an increasingly sophisticated and lethal civilization over the ensuing 600,000 years.

He continued:

Since 600,000 is 1/20,000 of 12 billion, we can divide the 650 million habitable planets in our Galaxy by 20,000 and find that only 32,500 of them would be in that 600,000-year period in which a species the intellectual equivalent of *Homo sapiens* is expanding in power.

Judging by the length of time human beings have spent at different stages in their development and taking that as an average, we could suppose that 540 habitable planets bear an intelligent species that, at least in the more advanced parts of the planet, are practicing agriculture and living in cities.

In 270 planets in our Galaxy, intelligent species have developed writing; in 20 planets modern science has developed; in 10 the equivalent of the industrial revolution has taken place; and in 2 nuclear energy has been developed, and those 2 civilizations are, of course, near extinction.

Since our 600,000 years of humanity occur near the middle of the sun's lifetime, and since we are taking the human experience as average, then all but 1/20,000 of the habitable planets fall outside that period, half earlier and half later. That means that on about 325 million such planets no intelligent species has as yet appeared, and on 325 million planets there are signs of civilizations in ruins. And nowhere is there a planet with a civilization not only alive but substantially farther advanced than we are.

If all this is so, then even though . . . hundreds of millions of civilizations [may have arisen] in our Galaxy . . . it is no wonder that we haven't heard from them.

Asimov's analysis may be dispiriting to exobiologists hoping to make contact with an intelligent form of extraterrestrial life. For archaeologists, however, the calculation that "on 325 million planets there are signs of civilizations in ruins" is a notion to stagger the imagination. Not even the National Historic Preservation Act of 1969 could have envisioned a requirement for 325 million cultural resource professionals, much less the need to equip each of them with survey and transport technologies the equivalent of the Apollo program.

To this potential planetary database, we need to add two additional considerations. The first is obvious: on Earth, there is evidence not just of one civilization in ruins but of many. Therefore, while we might speak of 325 million planets with signs of civilization in ruins, such a reality would translate to actual ruins numbering in the billions.

Second, we need to consider the possible forms such ruined civilizations might take if they managed to achieve, prior to their destruction, a level of technological development far beyond anything contemplated in the near-term cultural evolution of *Homo sapiens*. Freeman Dyson suggested the possibility that potentially massive engineering works might exist in the universe when he proposed a galactic search for sources of infrared radiation as a necessary corollary to the search for radio communications.[4] Dyson assumed that given the enormous scales of time and distance in the universe, any technological civilization observable from Earth would have been in existence for many millions of years longer than comparable civilizations on Earth. (Dyson was—again—assuming a living civilization, but the argument holds perhaps even more closely for a civilization that survives only as an archaeological entity.) Such an advanced civilization—if our own are any kind of galactic model—would long ago have outstripped its planetary resources. In response, it might conceivably have developed solar system–scale technological structures to provide for its post-Malthusian energy requirements and, as Dyson wrote, its *lebensraum*.

Dyson proposed such an artifact in the form of a shell or sphere that would surround a solar system's star, effectively capturing all its radiant energy and enabling the mining of the material resources of all the planetary and asteroid bodies in the system. Using our solar system as a model, Dyson conceived of an industrial operation that, over the course of 800 years, would disassemble the planet Jupiter and reassemble its mass as a 2–3m-thick shell at a distance of twice the distance of the Earth from the sun. People occupying the inside surface of this sphere would have access to the entire output of the sun's energy. Presumably, given this enormous energy source, this entire inside surface would resemble a tropical rain forest.

In terms of a galactic archaeological survey, such a notion would require archaeologists to search not just for those places most visible to radio telescopes but for those dark areas where the light of an entire solar system is being harnessed for occupants living on the inside edge of a Dyson sphere. In terms of cultural anthropology, the magnitude of such an effort, in both technology and time (800 years by Dyson's lights), would require the concentrated efforts of an entire planet over the course of forty generations or more.

There are no international Earth corollaries to such an effort, although national and nationalist structures such as the Egyptian pyramids or the Great Wall of China perhaps come closest to predicting what a planetary-scale effort would require. The former, a response to a spiritual requirement, and the latter, a response to security threats, would suggest the difficulty of predicting the precise rationale for an undertaking of this magnitude.

In the end, the implication of Asimov's calculations and, to a lesser extent, Dyson's conjecture, is evident. SETI stations are hearing only static through their radio telescopes because they are, in effect, listening for a message from the interplanetary equivalent of the Mayans, or the Sumerians, or any of dozens of dead civilizations who can speak to us now only through their archaeology.

Given the time spans and likely cultural resistance (and/or résistance) that such an effort as a Dyson sphere would generate, it is more likely that a long-term project in extraterrestrial cultural survival would result in a loose federation of hundreds of smaller outposts. And this, of course, is assuming that such an advanced technological society, upon completing such a structure, would then retreat to a band-level tropical rain forest existence that its forebears presumably walked away from millions of years earlier. Each of these scattered outposts, given the time and distances involved even in solar system–level travel, would within several generations have developed a variety of distinctive cultural adaptations and the different dialects or distinct languages that evolve with them.

An Earth corollary to such a planetary scenario would be the Norse colonization of the North Atlantic.[5] A mother culture for a variety of reasons spun perhaps 10 percent of its population away from the fjords of Norway, with some of the voyagers settling Iceland. Once this area became too crowded, 10 percent of this Icelandic population eventually settled even farther to the west, in Greenland. Explorers from this population pushed on to a place they called Vínland, Wine Land, but were just as quickly pushed back when Native Americans opposed the new colonization. A combination of factors then beset the Greenland colony over the course of several hundred years, until it was finally cut off from its originating cultures of Norway and then Iceland. Eventually the Greenland colony vanished, leaving the barest trace of written records, none of which testified to its fate. With written records absent or indecipherable, as in the Norse Greenland colony or the civilization of Mohenjo Daro, the archaeological record then became the primary means to study the vanished civilization.

The "scientific politics" of discussing the notion of archaeological evidence of extraterrestrial intelligence is evident from an article by a professor of physics who described the *Mars Pathfinder* probe as it was being readied to explore for fossil life on Mars.[6] Faculty and graduate students in the Department of Geophysical Sciences at the University of Chicago gathered to discuss the more speculative aspects of the mission. Like Enrico Fermi, they felt comfortable bringing the subject up only outside the formal parameters of a scheduled seminar. Questions of life on Mars were brought into the open only after the scientists had consumed large quantities of beer—and this even though their multimillion-dollar mission was already an accomplished fact.

Such fears are increasingly unfounded. Carl Sagan suggested that the search for evidence of intelligent life in the universe had to begin first by verifying the criteria for intelligent life with corollaries on Earth.[7] Without access to fine-resolution imagery, one would fall back on basic requirements for life in general: water and oxygen. To this, add carbon dioxide to warm the planet and the presence of methane as an indicator of life. Chlorophyll or some other mechanism for absorbing solar radiation and transmuting it into a form necessary to both sustain life and produce oxygen would also be present.

The search for intelligent life on Earth begins with the search for radio wave transmissions that are sequential and irregular and travel along predictable frequencies. With space-borne imagery of less than 100-meter resolution, one would begin to see a planetary penchant for geometric shapes and linear settlements and pathways. Perhaps one would mistake modes and means of transportation as intelligent life rather than its by-product.

For archaeologists this raises the question that if structures similar to the Jonglei Canal or the Aswan High Dam exist on Alpha Centauri, would we be able to recognize them as artifacts of intelligence? If in fact what we will find in space is not life but the traces of past life, not civilization but the traces of past civilization, it makes sense for us to start discussing what forms such life and such remains might take based on existing terrestrial analogues. As noted, this process is well along in the biological sciences but has been all but ignored in archaeology.

At a minimum, existing satellite imagery of Earth could be used to create analogues for the kinds of artifacts and structures that might be encountered on future exploratory space missions, analogues that could begin by drawing upon examples of similar work already accomplished.[8] Constructing such a database of structural analogues for potential signatures of advanced civilizations is well within the province of aerospace archaeology.

It seems appropriate—not least given its unique place amid discussions of extraterrestrial visits to Earth—to apply here a cautionary note from Easter Island (Rapa Nui). During his 1955–56 archaeological expedition to the island, the Norwegian explorer Thor Heyerdahl discovered a subculture of Rapa Nui culture that had gone underground, living a cave-like existence.[9] A society under the stress of resource depletion, external security threats, climate change, overpopulation, pollution, or any combination of these might well radically reduce its planetary archaeological footprint to a level problematic for external space-based sensors. In such a case, the absence of a planetary surface archaeological signature does not rule out a cultural adaptation that exists (or existed) on the outer edges of our theoretical constructs and is all but invisible to much of the current methodology and technology of our remote sensing.

Given the limitations on direct human exploration of the universe, archaeological expeditions to search, survey, and study interplanetary or intergalactic sites will of necessity be conducted through the techniques and technologies of remote sensing. Given the requirements of

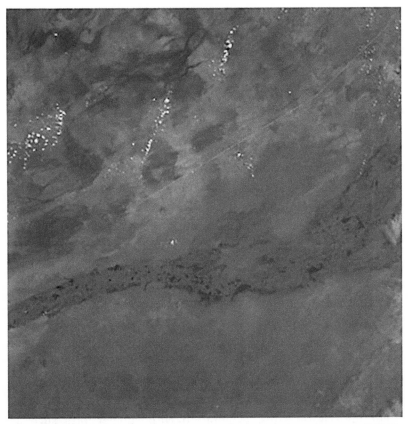

Jonglei Canal, seen from space. The canal is the straight line. Courtesy of NASA.

water and oceans as essential to life, and current models, such as the planning of the mission to Europa, these remote sensing techniques will owe as much to the history of underwater archaeology as to aerial archaeology.

The shift toward remote sensing of archaeological sites began in the 1970s as one method to elevate archaeology from its reliance on "the limited observational capacity of the human senses."[10] It took on greater momentum in the latter part of the twentieth century not only from the accelerating refinement of survey technology but also because of encroaching political considerations that threaten to overwhelm traditional archaeology.[11]

As early as 1975 Americanist archaeologists began to acknowledge the potential for political limits on their global historical explorations stemming from foreign nationalism.[12] Since such an admission implied that excavations would be limited in both their scope and content—if they were allowed at all—it was suggested that Americanist archaeologists, "who tend to be intensive excavators rather than observers of surface remains," begin systemically adopting two underemployed methods, one well established and one relatively new and emerging.[13]

The first was the British technique of noninvasive "field archaeology" espoused by O.G.S. Crawford. In the years before World War I Crawford "longed to see [archaeological sites] not obliquely but in plan, as would be possible in an aeroplane" or balloon, and after the war he went on to invent and refine the techniques of aerial photography of archaeological sites.[14] The second method, one that relied on modern high-technology inventions, was to adopt, adapt, and develop sophisticated scientific technologies, similar to those already employed by investigators in other "hard" sciences, for archaeological investigations.

In addition to Crawford's classic methods of field archaeology and aerial photogrammetry, these techniques included proton magnetometry to measure magnetic anomalies, soil resistivity to measure electrical resistance, and ground-penetrating radar. At the high end of the technological spectrum, advocated methods included thermal and infrared remote sensing by aircraft and satellites.

For underwater sites, exploration with submersibles such as Jacques-Yves Cousteau's *Soucoupe* or George Bass's *Asherah*, a submersible developed specifically for archaeological research in 1964, could be combined with manned undersea field stations such as the Conshelf Two station envisioned and constructed in the Red Sea by Cousteau and, since the 1960s, with unmanned remotely operated undersea research vehicles (autonomous underwater vehicles or AUVs) currently under development, testing, and deployment.[15] Remotely operated instruments have been placed around underwater artifact concentrations in northern Europe to monitor currents, salinity, and other processes affecting wreck sites.[16]

These "alternative[s] to the traditional approach to archaeological exploration, discovery and investigation . . . emphasize the acquisition and sophisticated analysis of a variety of remotely sensed imagery and data as the *primary* tools of exploration, discovery and recording."[17] With the biosphere, geosphere, and archaeosphere thus delineated, traditional field surveys and excavations would automatically revert to a status as secondary methods for verifying, or *ground-truthing,* the data collected with the primary remote sensors.

The dependence on massive technological infrastructure such as submarines and the bases and personnel they require will obtain until the perfection of independent undersea and space archaeology robotic probes. The array of such an "archaeoprobe," equipped with real-time telemetry capability and a miniature terrain rover, could be modified, like its oceanographic cousins, to meet virtually any exigency in the field. More, such a probe could be sent to a planetary site and operated remotely by a single explorer, independent of a massive science and technology bureaucracy. Such technological development will proceed alongside a persistent discussion in oceanographic technology circles over the course of subsea exploration, whether with submarines, submersibles, remotely operated vehicles (ROVs), or AUVs, or some combination of all of them.[18]

What seems clear is that there will likely remain a core of scientific explorers with no desire to leave exploration solely to robotic sensors. Willard Bascom, one of the most famous of American oceanographers, acknowledges this same human yearning when he writes in his autobiography of using satellites to study the oceans, remarking at one point that "in recent years my interest [in satellite oceanography] has waned again, probably because this is not a very adventurous form of oceanography. Although the scientific findings can be intellectually exciting, it takes a special sort of person to sit at a computer all day long sorting the data from a big dish antenna pointed at the sky or to spend years figuring out algorithms for converting the millions of data bits into useful information about what the ocean is doing."[19]

The equation for archaeologists is simple: either develop postgraduate programs at oceanographic and space research centers—to train students on the latest survey technology while simultaneously developing new hypotheses for archaeological research designs—or see archaeological exploration descend into arbitrary deconstructionism, "a kind of literary criticism, in which equally stimulating and internally consistent interpretations abound, but where no basis exists for deciding which one best approximates the historical reality of the past."[20] New and effective combinations of already available technologies, combined with the development of autonomous vehicles, employed in a research design that frees the archaeologist from reliance on the technological debates of oceanographers, will provide the necessary data for the application of the scientific method by archaeological explorers.

More than thirty years ago archaeologist George Bass entered the technological end of this controversy when the paradigm was manned versus unmanned exploration of space. He seemed to endorse the conception of technological archaeology—in this case a sonar or ROV-equipped long-range lock-out submarine for archaeology, one that could also serve either as a supply vessel for an underwater habitat for archaeologists or as the habitat itself. Bass wrote:

> Submarines will allow archaeologists to map the visible remains with stereophotography and to clear away the sand with portable, neutrally buoyant air lifts directed by remotely controlled manipulators attached to the submarines.
>
> Only one thing is missing, and that is the sure touch of the archaeologist's hand on the site. The present scientific controversy over whether manned or unmanned vehicles are more practical in the exploration of outer space is easily answered for the archaeological exploration of inner space: only a vast array of the most delicate manipulators imaginable could clean and raise the fragile and fragmentary pieces of wood which are so easily and gently handled by human divers.[21]

It has now been more than half a century since Bass commissioned *Asherah*, the first (and thus far only) submarine constructed specifically for archaeology. Since then, Robert Ballard, in his Black Sea research on board the nuclear submarine *NR-1*, has demonstrated that it is in fact possible to retrieve fragile artifacts from a submarine without harm. And while some might see a submarine for archaeology as an expensive luxury, Bass notes that more has been paid by museums for a single work of classical art than was spent on his submarine, which held the potential for revealing entire shiploads of such art (again, as Ballard subsequently demonstrated).

The twentieth century stands as the first in which the human species rose above the Earth to study both its own habitat and its capability to visit and potentially inhabit other worlds. Questions of where, how, and why humankind first sought to use air and space technology for scientific and geographic exploration have a direct bearing on behavioral questions of why we have become perhaps the "most inquisitive, exploring animal."[22] Defining the archaeological signatures by which this cultural transformation took place will provide a comparative model for similar cultural responses by extraterrestrial civilizations.

If remote survey technologies can be combined with techniques for identifying such surface remains in extreme environments, they will provide the basis for site evaluation without the requirements of surface survey. The current avenue for such remote evaluation of extreme environment sites is satellite photography on the order of high-altitude (150 miles perigee) advanced KH-11 satellite imagery.[23] The fine spatial resolution of KH-11 imagery and its use of metric markings for use as maps, combined with more recent Vega satellites that employ imaging radar for penetrating cloud cover, would make it possible to draw plans for virtually any small-scale site.

The current pathway of such research is clear. Part of the mission profile of the *Mars Reconnaissance Orbiter* was to search for archaeological traces of the lost *Mars Global Surveyor*, the *Mars Polar Lander*, and the British *Beagle 2*.[24] The expedition has thus far succeeded in capturing not only high-resolution images of the *Spirit* rover that has been exploring the surface of Mars since 2004 but also of the two Viking probes that reached Mars in the 1970s.[25]

This very human desire to search for archaeological traces of former expeditions becomes, in space, an almost spiritual requirement to relocate familiar human landmarks along expansionary pathways. It means that future space missions will devote significant energies not just toward pioneering new routes through space but to rediscovering

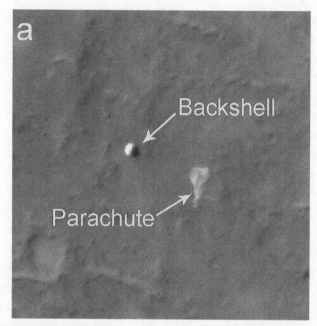

The bright irregularly shaped feature is *Spirit's* parachute, now lying on the Martian surface. Near the parachute is the cone-shaped backshell, which helped protect *Spirit's* lander during its seven-month journey to Mars. The backshell appears relatively undamaged by its impact with the Martian surface. Wrinkles and folds in the parachute fabric are clearly visible. Courtesy of NASA.

the techniques and technologies of earlier explorers. With the emerging capabilities of archaeologists to combine digital photography and photogrammetry in a regional GIS context in a Google Earth environment, it will be possible to delineate the exploratory archaeosphere, both topographically and, eventually, bathymetrically, in such a way as to enable provenance maps and charts of artifact clusters, sites, and site environments as well as site and regional archaeological histories.[26]

The requirement of life for water, along with the proposed mission to the potential frozen ocean of Europa, highlights the necessity to consider undersea sensing systems for archaeological research in a space context. Corollaries to human space missions, such as those that have established model Mars bases in the Arctic, should be developed to test the requirements for similar archaeological missions.[27]

Simultaneously, archaeologists can prepare theoretically for eventual fieldwork in space by using the extant volume of historical, technological, and planetary data to develop a combined pattern-recognition system and catalogue of structural signatures of intelligent life.

NASA alone has eight separate websites devoted exclusively to data just on its current missions, and each of these sites is further broken down into distinct descriptive pages on human aspects of exploration, emerging hardware and other technologies, spaceport and research facilities, and mission goals and accomplishments. Then there are the sites for the eleven separate federal space launch, control, or research centers. Nearly all this information is directly relevant to human evolution and cultural diversity. All of it is readily accessible over the Internet.

Even in terms of direct access, there are the earthbound challenges of archaeological surveys of abandoned rocket gantries in Florida or Kazakhstan. Such surveys, undertaken in part as corollaries to projected similar missions to extraterrestrial archaeological structures, could well provide the methodological and theoretical basis for future surveys of similar structures in space.

Given the vastness of space, the chances of real-time communication with other civilizations are small; on the other hand, the chances of excavating or otherwise remote-sensing traces of other civilizations seem, by comparison, rather high. The role of archaeology in space exploration in the near term, then, is twofold.

The first aspect is to shape the currently available raw material of historical, technological, and planetary data into a catalogue of analogues for defining the presence of extraterrestrial civilizations. This catalogue should be both methodological and theoretical and should center on notions of *Homo sapiens* as an exploratory, migratory species.

Second, a department of archaeological engineering, co-located perhaps with university departments with similar mission sets, such as those for ocean engineering, should develop a model of a remote probe to be employed throughout the galaxy to explore for traces of these signatures of civilization. With this mixture of anthropological theory and technological experience, an archaeoprobe can be designed and developed even though it might not see its first deployment for several generations. Operating in a sense as medieval monks, we can at least prepare a sort of illuminated manuscript for the edification of researchers not yet born, and within it a blueprint for the machine required to explore for the traces of galactic civilization defined by that manuscript.

15

Measuring the Mountains of the Moon

Any new form of archaeological research necessarily develops its own particular approach to method and theory, and aerospace archaeology is no different. The human archaeology of space will need to adopt and adapt many of the techniques long familiar to departments of ocean engineering, and from these will come the access to extraterrestrial sites that will provide the Baconian data for hypotheses of the human exploration and colonization of space.

By the end of the 2000s the notion of archaeological research in space had matured from its quasi–science fiction origins two decades earlier to a recognized subfield of archaeology, fully accepted at such august venues as the meetings of the World Archaeology Congress and the Society for Historical Archaeology. This next piece was the preface of my 2010 book *The Human Archaeology of Space: Lunar, Planetary and Interstellar Relics of Exploration*, which sought to provide an introduction to the field, a catalogue of potential cultural resources in extraterrestrial environments, and a theoretical basis upon which to organize this archaeology subfield.

On June 18, 2009, an Atlas V rocket launched the *Lunar Reconnaissance Orbiter* (LRO) from Cape Canaveral Air Force Station in Florida. Four days later the unmanned spacecraft entered orbit around the polar regions of the Moon. For a year, hovering 30 miles (50 km) above

The equatorial landing sites of *Apollo 11–17* (*Apollo 13* did not land on the Moon owing to an explosion in its oxygen system). The sites are all on the side of the Moon that faces Earth. Courtesy of NASA.

the surface, it undertook an intense series of photographic surveying and geophysical mapping in preparation for future manned polar base camps on the Moon and Mars.

Passing from pole to pole and crossing and re-crossing the Moon's equator, the lunar orbiter also took the first pictures of the landing areas of the manned Apollo spacecraft missions since the last Apollo mission in 1972. This use of the orbiter as an archaeological platform, searching for abandoned relics of the first era of human exploration of space, continues an intermittent interest by the National Aeronautics and Space Administration (NASA) in the archaeology of space exploration.

In a press release, NASA calls this element of the LRO mission "nostalgia." It is in fact much more than historical curiosity. In the realm of cultural oddities, even NASA admits that conspiracy theorists cling to the idea that the lunar landings were a hoax, designed to win the space race by clever use of television studio sets to simulate a lunar landing. Movies like 1978's *Capricorn One*, released in a post-Watergate environment of public distrust of the government, fueled such hoax theories.

Documenting these landing and research sites is impossible from Earth, even with the Hubble Space Telescope. In some of its first imagery returned to earth, LRO used relatively high-resolution cameras to document the landing areas of all Apollo missions save for that of *Apollo 12*. The resolution on the *Apollo 14* site, in particular, revealed not only the shadow thrown by the lunar module *Antares* but also the

Buzz Aldrin and Neil Armstrong practice for their lunar mission on a set designed to simulate the surface of the Moon. NASA: S69-32233. Courtesy of NASA.

footpath created when the mission's astronauts set up a remote research station nearby.

Later the probe relayed images of the *Apollo 12* landing area that
revealed artifacts and pathways in even greater detail. The major components of discarded expedition gear left behind on the lunar surface—such as the Lunar Excursion Module Descent Stages (LEM-DS)
and the earlier unmanned *Surveyor 3* probe explored by the *Apollo 12*
astronauts, are visible in the imagery. Perhaps more interesting are the
complex series of footpaths created by the astronauts as they placed an
instrument package on the moon and walked from the lunar module
to the *Surveyor* probe and then to nearby geological features.

Such imagery of walkways created by bipedal *Homo sapiens* exploring the surface of a place other than their home planet can offer interesting insights into the ways in which humans carry behavioral
patterns into space. Given a flat, largely unobstructed surface, the
walking paths are relatively straight. When confronted by a landscape

LRO's first look at the *Apollo 12* landing site with the associated *Surveyor 3*
probe. The footpaths created by the *Apollo 12* astronauts are shown by unnamed arrows. Courtesy of NASA.

As if reflexively displaying earth behavior by avoiding the middle of a roadway, *Apollo 15* astronaut Jim Irwin walks alongside a pathway created by a Lunar Roving Vehicle. The *Apollo 15* mission was the fourth to land humans on the Moon and the first to bring a Lunar Roving Vehicle to the Moon. In this way the humans could extend their range of exploration from a few hundred feet to tens of miles. Image AS15-86-11654. Courtesy of NASA.

of mounds and craters, the humans go around these obstacles rather that across or over them.

University of Hawai'i anthropologist Ben Finney once wrote that humankind "evolved as an exploratory, migratory animal."[1] Not only might the human exploration of space supersede the movement of *Homo erectus* out of Africa or *Homo sapiens* across the Wallace Line; Finney argued that it could "be studied directly without having to reconstruct and test the vehicles involved or interpret ambiguous texts."[2]

Leaving aside the earthbound challenges of archaeological surveys of abandoned rocket gantries in Florida or Kazakhstan, what space archaeology currently lacks in direct access for the archaeologist it more than makes up for in its sheer volume of historical, technological, and planetary data. The purpose of *The Human Archaeology of Space* is to gather into a single source the data on the artifacts that *Homo sapiens* has discarded in space and place them into the framework of archaeology. Because, as Finney implied and as the imagery mentioned reveals, nearly all this information is directly relevant to human evolution and cultural diversity, and today all of it is readily accessible on one's laptop or droid.

NASA alone has eight separate websites devoted exclusively to data just on its current missions, and each of these sites is further broken down into distinct descriptive pages on human aspects of exploration, emerging hardware and other technologies, space port and research facilities, and mission goals and accomplishments.

If you visit the Kennedy Space Center site, for example, and navigate to the history page, you will find this delicious little archaeological nugget: "[Scientists hope that the unmanned] Voyager [exploratory probe] will pass beyond the boundary of the Sun's influence before the onboard nuclear power supply wanes too low to tell us what's out there. *Voyager 1* is now the most distant human-made object." In anthropological terms, the artifact of human intelligence, *Voyager 1*, launched in 1977, is about to become the first tool fashioned by human hands to leave the boundaries of the Solar System.

The news release remarks on this event as an interesting bit of technological trivia, rather than as the immense cultural landmark that it most assuredly is. In fact, in November 2003, scientists began to debate whether *Voyager 1* had in fact reached the edge of the Solar System and begun to encounter a new region of unexplored space, where the wind from the Sun blows against the variety of gases that are diffused throughout interstellar space. At this point the *Voyager* spacecraft was more than 13 billion kilometers from the Sun.

For our archaeological purposes, it must be remembered that the two *Voyager* spacecraft did not strictly become archaeological objects until very recently. Humans could still contact them until late in 2015, and until that moment they still existed as part of a living human cultural system. In archaeological terms they were in their systemic context. Once that contact was broken and the spacecraft no longer responded to the humans who launched it on its way, it became an object of archaeological concern, a discarded artifact freighted with the attributes of the culture that constructed it.

This was the case, for example, with the *Pioneer 10* space probe, launched in 1972 on a mission to investigate Jupiter. *Pioneer 10* completed its mission and then continued, following an escape trajectory away from the Solar System. A final attempt to contact the spacecraft was made on February 7, 2003, a few weeks after a command was sent to it to shut down its final working experiment. In return, nothing was heard. After thirty-one years the probe had entered its archaeological context, even as it was still in motion—only now as a dead satellite. It remains headed toward the red star Aldebaran, the vicinity of which it is scheduled to reach in approximately two million years, or roughly the same amount of time that members of the bipedal, large-brained, tool-making and tool-dependent genus *Homo* have walked the Earth.

In this example it becomes clear how much longer a tool created by humans exists in its archaeological as opposed to its systemic context. The *Pioneer 10* continues to exist well past its original mission—the rendezvous with Jupiter. By human lights, such performance is likely at the limits of expectation. After all, thirty-one years of active life would occupy the majority if not the totality of a space scientist's active career. A young Ph.D. of, let's say, thirty-three years at the start of the mission would be close to retirement after the final attempt to communicate had been made more than three decades later.

But *Pioneer 10* has just begun its archaeological lifespan. It will long outlive our theoretical Ph.D. and perhaps even his or her gravestone. If *Pioneer 10* is not intercepted by an advanced civilization, or destroyed in a collision with an asteroid in some distant star system, it will likely complete its two-million-year journey to Aldebaran. There it will perhaps be caught in the star's gravitational pull. It will then begin to orbit that faraway star until the end of the history of the galaxy several billion years in the future. These are vast and bracing considerations. For it is the very possibility of one of the composite tools fashioned by

Homo sapiens undergoing study by another intelligence in the universe that ties the method and theory of lunar, planetary, and interstellar archaeology to the far more speculative archaeology of extraterrestrial civilizations.

The sheer volume and variety of anthropological hypotheses ready to be spun from the mountain of data collected by the exploration of space is enough to awaken even the most sluggish or jaded brains. "More Data than Ever!" as the *Mars Reconnaissance Orbiter* website proudly announces, almost as if it were a grocery store. Need to visualize a multispectral scanner Earth survey from space? Check the *SkyLab* Mission archives at the Johnson Space Center. Want to study how the *SkyLab* astronauts had to be positioned to conduct their Earth Resources Experiment? There is a picture of that, too. How about a cultural analysis of the type of humans NASA employed for *SkyLab* (exclusively white male engineers with fixed smiles and names of two syllables or less)? Or look at a map of the Moon showing the distribution of unmanned U.S.-U.S.S.R. probe landings. Why was NASA fixated on the Sea of Tranquility while the Russians obsessed over the Sea of Storms? Why did both bunch their landings within a few degrees of the lunar equator? Were the lunar poles uninteresting, dangerous, or difficult, or were human explorers of the Moon simply echoing several million years of equatorial adaptation on earth, where the poles were the last place human explorers managed to plant their flags?

Finally, there is the incomparable National Space Science Data Center (NSSDC), with its historic mission profiles and technical synopses of each spacecraft. I added the NSSDC technical specifications on artifacts located on moons and other planets (as well as those artifacts in heliocentric orbit and those heading away from the Solar System) in *The Human Archaeology of Space*. The book was enhanced with brief notes on the archaeological relevance of each mission, the goal being to create something approaching a foundational work in aerospace archaeology.

Widening our field of vision even farther, archaeologists can now see the whole of space—its contemplation as well as its exploration— as part of a new field of investigation. Just as the Scandinavian archaeologist Christer Westerdahl argued two decades ago for consideration

of a "maritime cultural landscape" to encompass the study of the human use of maritime space by boat, so too did Australian archaeologist
Alice Gorman propose a similar cultural landscape of space. This, she
argues, would follow a trend in cultural heritage management away
from the notion of archaeological sites as discrete locations and see
them instead as "a cultural landscape forged by the organic interaction
of the space environment and human material culture."[3]

The 500-metric-ton gorilla in all discussions of archaeology in space,
of course, is the question of nonhuman intelligence in the universe.
Like a sliver of space junk that becomes impossibly heavy the faster
it goes, it seems that the closer archaeologists get to the question of
potentially nonhuman artifacts of intelligence, the more they fear the
career-killing consequences of embracing the subject too closely.

But this feeling, too, is beginning to fade. The idea of archaeology
in space has long been accepted by the World Archaeological Congress,
which formed a Space Archaeology Task Force in 2003. And if one accepts the idea of archaeological research on sites from the history of
human exploration in space, it is hardly a giant leap to consider the potential for archaeological fieldwork on the evidence of extraterrestrial
civilizations. The very fact that *Homo sapiens* has made a deliberate
decision to launch unmanned spacecraft equipped with a variety of
symbolic messages intended for another potential intelligence opens
the door for archaeology to consider the possible forms and structures
such intelligence might take, and what artifacts and archaeological features such an intelligence might create in the wake of its history.

If Darwinian natural selection, as evolutionary biologist Richard
Dawkins suggests, is the only game in the universe, then we should expect to find systems of increasing complexity (though without any easily predictable cultural outcomes) throughout the universe. We should
also anticipate that such systems, like our own, may have advanced
to the point where they have left behind artifacts of their particular
intelligence in response to their individual selective environmental
pressures.

The subfield of "exobiology" is now a commonplace and consistently
generates news from what were originally hypothetical undertakings
but now enjoy data from moons of the outer planets that suggest

plausible regions for extraterrestrial life. The icy Jovian moon of Europa, with an apparent frozen ocean similar to Earth's Arctic Ocean, is now under intensive consideration by such biologists and intensive planning by spacecraft engineers who seek to burrow an oceanographic-style probe through Europa's pack ice in search of microbial life. The Saturnian moon of Titan has a dense atmosphere and liquid hydrocarbon lakes in its polar regions, which suggest a colder version of the early formation of Earth and possible microbial extraterrestrial life. (And, in true *Homo sapiens* fashion, the two missions now compete for funding.)

But what if what we eventually find in space is not life but traces of past life; not a living civilization but traces of a past civilization? Landforms inviting speculation, like the unexplained linear markings on the Tharsis Plateau of Mars or "The Face" and the nearly pyramidal shapes in the Cydonia region of Mars—which recent imagery suggest are likely no more than ancient mountains abraded by eons of sandstorms—were advanced by the late astronomer Carl Sagan and others as sites to be examined by future missions to Mars as potential artifacts of intelligence. Fossil life is apt to be a far more common discovery in the galaxy than living life.

In one sense, the issues of planetary archaeology and extraterrestrial civilizations proceed hand in hand. In October 2009 astronomers from the European Southern Observatory announced that, after an examination of 2,000 nearby stars, they had located 32 different "exoplanets," planets that exist beyond our Solar System. This raised to 400 the number of such planets discovered since the first exoplanet was announced in 1995. Given the billions of stars in the galaxy, the odds seem much better than even that numerous exoplanets are orbiting at the right distance from a star—the so-called Goldilocks distance: not too far, not too close—to allow for the formation of water, amino acids, oceans, life, and, potentially, intelligent life.

One such planet—Gliese 581c within the constellation Libra and approximately twenty light years from Earth—was discovered in 2007 by a team led by Stéphane Udry of the University of Geneva. Both 581c and a nearby Earth-like planet, Gliese 581d, lie within the habitable zone where water can exist without either freezing or vaporizing. This makes them both potential waterworlds, covered entirely by oceans and possibly inhabited by living forms.

At the very least, these 400 exoplanets, along with those certainly to be discovered in the years to come, will be among the first locations in the universe where *Homo sapiens* will aim unmanned *Voyager*-like spacecraft in future galactic exploring expeditions. If current practice is any guide to future missions, humans will send both orbiting platforms and surface landers and probes to these exoplanets. This means that these planets will one day hold the most widely scattered collection of hominid composite tools that it is possible to imagine.

Sagan, who believed there were more than a million currently active galactic civilizations, once wrote an article entitled "Is There Intelligent Life on Earth?" He argued that if one viewed satellite imagery of one-mile resolution, one could stare at the entire eastern seaboard of the United States for hours and see no sign of life, intelligent or otherwise. If structures similar to Hadrian's Wall in northern England exist on another planet, would we be able to recognize them as the artifacts of intelligence? If Dawkins is correct and Darwinian evolution is a process without any particular purpose or ultimate goal, would intelligent life on an exoplanet even construct tools or features in the landscape, and if so would we recognize them as such? If intelligent life exists on a waterworld, would it exist in a form closer to whales than humans? How would terrestrial archaeological science categorize intelligent life that produced no concomitant material culture?

16

Mobile Artifacts in
the Solar System and Beyond

We began this exploration of archaeology with the discussion of the artifact, in that case the much-transformed remains of an artifact of a Hollywood movie fixed upon a beach on an island. We can end with the consideration of a new form of artifact, one that never comes to rest.

There is one final notion in the archaeology of space that requires some not inconsiderable thought, and it is the idea of the study of artifacts that are still in motion. It is one thing to conceive of field research at sites of human exploration at fixed sites on Moon, asteroids, or planets, but what of all those many artifacts designed to continue in motion for hundreds, thousands, even millions of years? The Acheulian hand axe is easily the most long-lived artifact, both systemically and archaeologically, ever invented by humans. A space probe destined for an essentially infinite journey carries the possibility of durability at least as long as that of any Acheulian hand axe on Earth. This final essay, from the final chapter of *The Human Archaeology of Space: Lunar, Planetary and Interstellar Relics of Exploration*, seeks to define the nature of artifacts of human ingenuity as they travel through space in a variety of archaeological contexts.

It feels a bit odd for an archaeologist to consider objects that are still in motion as part of the material culture database, since the image we have of archaeological research centers upon the careful excavation of artifacts or fossils fixed within the soil or rock of the Earth, often for millions of years. Whole new categories of archaeological methodology seem to be called for if we are to consider the possibilities of fieldwork on the now dead—or soon-to-be dead—spacecraft we have launched on their way to distant stars.

But there is first the issue of whether a mobile artifact is in fact an object for archaeological study. This definition rests on the seminal work of Michael B. Schiffer, *Formation Processes of the Archaeological Record*, in which he sought to pin down whether an artifact was still in use for that which it was designed. By these lights, several distant-travelling spacecraft have only recently become strictly archaeological objects. These include the two *Voyager* probes, the *Galileo* probe to Jupiter, and the *New Horizons* probe to Pluto. Each of these spacecraft was scheduled to break contact with Earth in the year 2015. Until then they still existed as part of a living human cultural system.

Once such a spacecraft no longer responds to signals from or returns data to Earth, it ceases to be used for the original mission for which it was designed and transforms into a discarded, and hence archaeological, object. This is the case with the *Pioneer 10* space probe, which ceased "speaking" with Earth in 2003 and is now headed on a two-million-year journey toward the red star Aldebaran.

But in space as on Earth, these strict categories of systemic and archaeological context are not absolute. It is possible for an object to move in and out of context. For example, a ship that wrecks along a coastline and breaks apart has ceased to do the things humans designed it to do. It has entered its archaeological context. But pieces of the ship can be salvaged by people on shore, by the company that owned the ship, by salvors and insurance companies. These fragments can be reused in other systemic contexts, like the hut that Walter Wellman's crew built from timbers and sailcloth salvaged from his ship before it sank off the coast of Waldenøya in 1894. The shipwreck itself can return in a different form to a systemic context, like the wreck of the SS *Ethie* that I photographed along the western coast of Newfoundland

The wreck of the SS *Ethie* photographed along the western coast of Newfound-land in 2006, in archaeological context as a shipwreck, which in turn is in systemic context as a historic site and tourist spot.

in 2006. This site is now in systemic context as a tourist spot, complete with wayside plaque, parking lot, and viewing platform.

Within the general category of mobile artifacts in the Solar System and beyond, there are a few subcategories. The first would be those artifacts that are on their way from Earth to some undetermined place in interstellar space; the second would be those objects that, either deliberately or as the result of a mission failure, now orbit around the Sun (heliocentric orbit); and, finally, the vast archaeological space "midden" that currently encircles the Earth.

For our purposes, we will largely leave aside the third category, but I offer here a few words on it. A "midden" in archaeological terms is a feature of an archaeological site where one finds a collection of the waste products produced during the course of normal human daily life. Such features can and do accumulate for generations, and can be studied as the material signature of an entire culture. The midden of space junk that encircles Earth can similarly be thought of as a dump for domestic waste, but in this case the domestic waste of a whole planetary community.

The orbital midden is thought to include tens of millions of separate artifacts, none of them in systemic context. The vast majority of these artifacts are chips of paint from orbital satellites and spacecraft, slag from solid rocket motors, coolant from nuclear power plants, and other such small debris. Some of this material will fall from its Earth orbit and burn up in the atmosphere. But collisions between these small fragments create more small fragments, an increasing problem for attempts to track these objects so that they do no damage to new space missions.

Spacecraft can largely be protected from collisions with such debris by shielding the craft with metal foil. When a small object collides with the foil, the speed of the collision causes the debris to vaporize. However, NASA estimates that larger objects, those of ten centimeters or bigger, now number some 19,000. Objects of this size coming at a spacecraft at eight kilometers per second would destroy it.

In February 2009 a functioning (systemic) satellite, *Iridium 33*, collided at a speed of more than 42,000 kilometers per hour with a defunct (archaeological) Russian Space Forces satellite, *Kosmos-2251*. The combined weight of the two satellites was about a ton and a half. Both were destroyed instantly, but at the same time produced potentially thousands of new bits of orbital debris, each of which is a potential hazard to other orbiting satellites and spacecraft.

The second category of mobile artifacts in the Solar System is those in heliocentric orbit; that is, in orbit around the Sun. There are more than fifty such objects, including twenty-nine launched from the

United States, fifteen from the Soviet Union or Russian Federation, five from the European Space Agency, and five from Japan. Only seven of these missions are still active and therefore in systemic context. The remainder are artifacts that were lost through communications failures or technical problems; that were deliberately abandoned after their systemic use was finished, such as the *Apollo 10* Lunar Module *Snoopy*; or that missed their original targets, such as the Moon or Venus or Mercury, and were subsequently captured by the gravitational pull of the Sun.

Artifacts in this category include:

Luna 1 (USSR; lunar exploration; launch January 2, 1959)

Pioneer 4 (US; lunar exploration; launch March 3, 1959)

Pioneer 5 (US; destination interplanetary space; launch March 11, 1960)

Venera 1 (USSR; destination Venus; launch May 19, 1961)

Ranger 3 (US; lunar exploration; launch January 26, 1962)

Ranger 5 (US; lunar exploration; launch October 18, 1962)

Mariner 2 (US; destination Venus; launch August 27, 1962)

Mars 1 (USSR; destination Mars; launch November 1, 1962)

Mariner 3 (US; destination Mars; launch November 5, 1964)

Mariner 4 (US; destination Mars; launch November 28, 1964)

Zond 2 (USSR; destination Mars; launch November 30, 1964)

Zond 3 (USSR; destination Moon; launch July 18, 1965)

Venera 2 (USSR; destination Venus; launch November 12, 1965)

Pioneer 6 (US; solar research; launch December 16, 1965)

Pioneer 7 (US; solar research; launch August 17, 1966)

Mariner 5 (US; destination Venus; launch June 14, 1967)

Pioneer 8 (US; solar research; launch December 13, 1967)

Pioneer 9 (US; solar research; launch November 8, 1968)

Mariner 6 (US; destination Mars; launch February 24, 1969)

Mariner 7 (US; destination Mars; launch March 27, 1969)

S-IVB upper stages for *Apollo 8, 9, 10, 11* and *12* (1968–69)

Lunar Module *Snoopy* from *Apollo 10* (1969)

Mars 4 (USSR; destination Mars; launch July 21, 1973)

Mars 7 (USSR; destination Mars; launch August 9, 1973)

Mariner 10 (US; destination Venus and Mercury; launch November 3, 1973)

Helios 1 (Joint US-ESA; solar research; launch December 10, 1974)

Helios 2 (Joint US-ESA; solar research; launch January 15, 1976)

Venera 11 (USSR; destination Venus; launch September 9, 1978)

Venera 12 (USSR; destination Venus; launch September 14, 1978)

Venera 13 (USSR; destination Venus; launch October 3, 1981)

Venera 14 (USSR; destination Venus; launch November 4, 1981)

Vega 1 (USSR; destination Venus; launch December 15, 1984)

Vega 2 (USSR; destination Venus; launch December 21, 1984)

Sakigake (Japan; destination Halley's Comet; launch January 7, 1985)

Sakigake (Japan; destination Halley's Comet; launch August 18, 1985)

Giotto (ESA; destination Halley's Comet; launch July 2, 1985)

Phobos 1(USSR; destination Martian moon of Phobos; launch July 21, 1988)

Ulysses (Joint US-ESA; destination Jupiter; launch October 6, 1990)

Nozomi (Japan; destination Mars; launch July 3, 1998)

Hayabusa/Minerva mini-lander (Japan; destination asteroid Itokawa; launch May 9, 2003)

The first category of mobile artifacts in the Solar System is that of those objects that were deliberately launched from Earth into a journey into interstellar space. These special artifacts of human intelligence hold a particular fascination for archaeologists, as they represent *Homo sapiens*'s attempts to fashion a tool that can cross the barrier of space on a hopeful mission to communicate with other forms of intelligent life that may or may not exist in the galaxy. There are five such composite tools: *Pioneer 10, Pioneer 11, Voyager 1, Voyager 2,* and *New Horizons*. Each initially had a specific scientific mission to carry out within the Solar System (*New Horizons* is still in its active mission phase; it reached its target of the planet Pluto in 2015, and now that it has flown by Pluto its mission has been extended. The spacecraft has begun an extended mission in the Kuiper Belt, making distant observations of

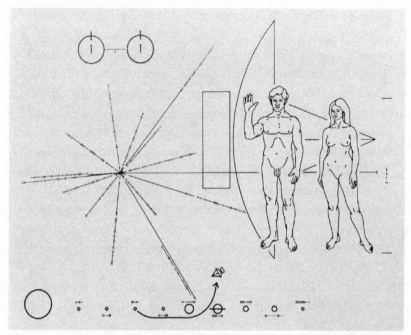

The plaque placed on the *Pioneer 10* spacecraft is meant to communicate to an extraterrestrial intelligence that another species of intelligence exists in the universe who built this particular artifact and sent it on a very long voyage that would almost certainly outlive the species that sent it. Courtesy of NASA.

several Kuiper Belt objects in advance of a close flyby scheduled for January 1, 2019, of an object known as 2014 MU69, and sampling the space environment in the outer reaches of the solar system). Once these primary missions concluded, the spacecraft were then directed toward the boundaries of the Solar System with the expectation that they would eventually enter interstellar space and become the representatives of *Homo sapiens* to the rest of the galaxy.

In a NASA history of the Pioneer expeditions, there is an epilogue titled "Interstellar Cave Painting." It recounts how Eric Burgess of the *Christian Science Monitor* looked at the *Pioneer 10* spacecraft as it was being tested and conceptualized it as the first human object that might reach other intelligent species. This observation led to a chain of events culminating in the design and placement on the spacecraft of "a special message from mankind."[1] Carl Sagan and others designed a plaque that would attempt in symbols to represent where the object had come from and the kinds of beings who had constructed it and sent it into space.

The human representations are slender, bipedal, and naked. An accompanying scale matched to the overall size of the spacecraft itself is supposed to allow an alien intelligence to discover that the woman is 162.56 centimeters—about 5'4"—tall, the male a bit taller (presumably our alien intelligence will recognize this as the long-term sexual dimorphism of the species). The male has his right arm uplifted at a right angle with the palm of his hand facing outward in what is hoped will be interpreted as a sign of greeting. Both figures have full heads of hair but otherwise no body hair, clothes, shoes, scars, deformities, tattoos, piercings, or other adornments or much in the way of body fat. The man's penis and scrotum are shown, but not the woman's vulva. Ethnically they appear white. They are relatively young, perhaps no more than twenty-five years old. They appear friendly and unthreatening; there is no suggestion of the endemic violence of their home world. There are no other representations of any other life on Earth, present or past, or any suggestion that the form of human on the plaque was the product of millions of years of evolution through natural selection and therefore constantly changing along with all other forms of life on the planet and, in fact, the planet itself. It has been said that the scientific contents of the plaque are difficult even for scientists to understand.

The NASA history explains that the "radial pattern to the left of center of the plaque represents the position of the Sun relative to 14 pulsars and to the center of the Galaxy. . . . The binary digits on the [pulsar] lines denote time.

This can be deduced because they represent precision to 10 decimal digits, which is unlikely for distances to stellar objects but quite feasible for measurements of time. And from the unit of time established from the hydrogen atom, the extraterrestrial intelligence should be able to deduce that all the times are about one tenth of a second . . . pulsars! Since the periods of pulsars run down at well established rates they act as galactic clocks. An advanced civilization would be able to search its galactic records and identify the star system from which the spacecraft originated, even if Pioneer is not intercepted for billions of years.[2]

It is a wonderfully comforting conceit, this idea of an advanced civilization of galactic record keepers. One envisions a planet of thoughtful Dutch archivists, as in a painting by Rembrandt, calmly discoursing on the meaning of the plaque as they examine the probe—now displayed atop the circular mahogany table of an ornate special collections room in a vast and eclectic library. It is revealing, as well, of the designer's apparent view of the essential loneliness of the human condition: *Homo sapiens* waving hopefully across a billion years of a cold universe on the infinitesimal chance someone might wave back.

A further orientation on the plaque shows our Solar System, with the spacecraft leaving from the third planet from the sun and with its antenna pointing backward toward that planet. Presumably from this an extraterrestrial intelligence would be able to infer that only this planet held the remarkable species that sent the artifact. Would they also conclude that no life existed on any other planets in our system? Or merely that these particular beings did not communicate, or had no ability to communicate, or did not *want* to communicate, with life on other planets in the system? What if humans launched a similar probe from the surface of Mars in, say, 100 or 1,000 years from now, equipped with a similar plaque but a different point of origin? Would this be interpreted by others as representing cooperation or conflict within our Solar System? Or even the death of the third planet?

Of course, all such questions rely on the intercepting extraterrestrials having a similar level of intelligence to that of humans, combined with a similar visual anatomy, physiology, and cognitive processing apparatus—a point that the NASA history itself makes. "If that [extraterrestrial] life possesses sufficient intelligence to detect the Pioneer spacecraft . . . it may also have the curiosity and the technical ability to pick up the spacecraft and take it into a laboratory to inspect it. Then the plaque with its message from Earth people should be found and hopefully deciphered."[3] If an extraterrestrial intelligence took an oceanic form—like whales, for example—then our message would not find an audience capable of even an attempt at decipherment.

As tool-using, bipedal organisms with stereoscopic vision, we have fashioned our space probes almost strictly for scientific purposes. When there is a thought given to cultural or archaeological implications of our exploration of space, as with the *Pioneer 10* plaque, the result can be seen as almost cursory—or illusory, depending on your interpretation of the *Pioneer 10* plaque. We are asking for an intelligence elsewhere in the galaxy to possess the ability to detect our lifeless probe and the technical skill to intercept it as it moves at perhaps ten kilometers per second or faster. The very concept of intercepting an object that appears on a set course might not be one that would even occur to another species. Or perhaps their interception would take the form of a defensive or offensive measure, such as that seen in the Hollywood film *Star Trek V: The Final Frontier*, when the Klingons indeed intercept a Pioneer probe with its attached plaque—only to blow it to smithereens immediately.

Assuming that the *Pioneer 10* probe and its unique representation of *Homo sapiens* are not destroyed by another species possessing some of our own aggressive tendencies, it should survive well beyond the age of humans on Earth. More than that, as the NASA history puts it, this modern cave painting "might survive not only all the caves of Earth, but also the Solar System itself. It is an interstellar stela that shows mankind possesses a spiritual insight beyond the material problems of the age of human emergence."[4]

Epilogue

Back Down to Earth, in Search of Pedro

So that is that. A bit more than a quarter century of thoughts and adventures in archaeology, all sprung from childhood walks along a meandering creek. These explorations introduced me to some of the world's most creative, skilled, and accomplished historians, archaeologists, archivists, pilots, and divers and transported me from that languid local waterway all the way to the North Pole, to airfields in equatorial Indonesia and Arctic Russia, to Cuba and the Middle East, and, if only in imagination, to Outer Space.

As if to reinforce the point, I have now returned from the human archaeology of space all the way back down to the local ground, to very much earthbound research that returns me to those childhood wanderings. Two summers on byways and highways in the United States and Canada, pulling onto narrow and less than comfortable verges as SUVs and eighteen-wheelers whip noisily by, have allowed for the hurried recording of vernacular billboards and other roadside archaeology attractions.

The famous billboards directing I-95 traffic to the South of the Border roadside attraction in Dillon, South Carolina, are less numerous now, and their range has shrunk considerably. No longer can one find them north of the Mason-Dixon Line, or even north of the Virginia–North Carolina border. The innocent "Pedro-speak," a hacked version of Spanglish ("Sommtheeng Deeferent!") has also toned down, as parts of the I-95 corridor since the 1960s have transformed from rural white poor to suburban Hispanic poor. Of course, such transformations are precisely what make the study of roadside material culture so inviting to an archaeologist.

Martin Rudwick reminds us how long it took for a generally accepted meaning of the word "fossil" to emerge—and just how critical the establishment of museums was—to the eventual definition of a fossil as "the preserved remains of a thing once alive."[1] Death, preservation, discovery, recovery, conservation, study, and display: these familiar stages of paleontology tend to blur when applied to human material culture. The "time of death" is almost never obvious, and preservation is unlikely, discovery uncertain, recovery problematic, conservation difficult, study fragmented, and display costly.

Whether consisting of the still undiscovered wreck of the USS *Akron*, the sandy fragments of the *Orca II*, a lost space probe on the Moon, or an original South of the Border billboard now lost to time, weather, and memory, modern human material culture is very often large, unwieldy, and ultimately impossible to preserve. Far better to be a tidy *Triceratops* fossil, a gigantic preserved remnant of living life 68 million years old, carefully recovered, lovingly rearticulated, and permanently preserved in a modern air-conditioned museum gallery.

So it can seem. Yet for an archaeologist of the recent past, it is far more interesting to be a member of a living human culture as it transforms before our brief lives, winding back on itself to emerge as something entirely new. That is how I begin my next quarter century of archaeological exploration—not in the recording of the remains of childhood aspirations and excitements but in their profound and awkward transformations. And in ours.

NOTES

Preface: Time and the River

1. Miles Russell, *The Piltdown Man Hoax: Case Closed* (Gloucestershire, UK: History Press, 2012), 143.

Chapter 1. The Last Logbook of the *Orca II*

1. Carl Gottlieb, *The Jaws Log*, expanded edition (New York: Newmarket Press, 2012), 9.

2. Ibid., 11.

3. Ibid., 45.

4. Ibid., 48.

5. Matt Taylor, *Jaws Memories from Martha's Vineyard* (London: Titan Books, 2011), 23.

6. Peter Brannen, "Once Bitten: Islanders Reveal More Jaws," *Vineyard Gazette*, May 26, 2011.

7. Mark Alan Lovewell, "The Salvor: In Menemsha, Lynn Murphy Marks 50 Years," *Vineyard Gazette*, September 2, 2004.

8. Jack Shea, "For Chilmarker Lynn Murphy, No Reverse Needed," *Martha's Vineyard Times*, June 1, 2016.

9. Christopher Balogh, "Farewell and Adieu in Menemsha," *Marlin* Magazine, May 20, 2015, http://www.marlinmag.com/farewell-and-adieu-in-menemsha (accessed August 24, 2016).

10. Taylor, *Jaws Memories*, 282.

11. Ibid., 284.

12. Marcus Errico, "Universal Studios' Jaws: The Fintastic Inside Story of George, Carrot Tooth, and the Ride that Ate Hollywood," n.d., http://marcuserrico.tumblr.com/post/121955806433/universal-studios-jaws-the-fintastic-inside (accessed August 23, 2016).

13. See, for example, theStudioTour, "*Jaws*," n.d., http://www.thestudiotour. com/wp/studios/universal-studios-hollywood/theme-park/attractions/the-studio-tour/current-studio-tour/jaws/ (accessed August 24, 2016). For an excellent history of the *Jaws* theme attraction at Universal Studios Florida, which ultimately revealed as many technical difficulties as the original movie shark, see Nick Sim, "*Jaws*: How Universal's Shark Ride Turned into Real-Life Disaster," 2015, http://www.themeparktourist.com/features/20150414/30158/jaws-how-universal-s-shark-ride-turned-real-life-disaster (accessed May 24, 2017).

14. Errico, "Universal Studios' Jaws."

15. Ibid.

16. theStudioTour, "Jaws," http://www.thestudiotour.com/wp/studios/universal-studios-hollywood/theme-park/attractions/the-studio-tour/current-studio-tour/jaws/ (accessed August 24, 2016).

17. Ibid.

18. Errico, "Universal Studios' Jaws."

19. Taylor, *Jaws Memories*, 305.

20. Ibid., 304–5.

21. "The 'Orca' from Jaws," Woodenboat.com, March 3, 2012, http://forum. woodenboat.com/showthread.php?144679-The-quot-Orca-quot-from-Jaws (accessed August 24, 2016).

22. David Hamblen, personal communication, May 24, 2017.

23. The full version of the BBC documentary, *In the Teeth of Jaws*, is on You-Tube at https://www.youtube.com/watch?v=9MiVtavjD8w. A one-minute clip containing just the visit to the *Orca II* remains, and a few glimpses of the rest of the archaeology at Lynn Murphy's *Jaws* beach is at https://www.youtube.com/watch?v=oHQx59rifrE.

24. Nick Freand Jones, "In the Teeth of Jaws," British Broadcasting Corporation (BBC2), 1997, https://www.youtube.com/watch?v=9MiVtavjD8w (accessed August 24, 2016).

25. "*Jaws*: Behind the Scenes on Martha's Vineyard," Boston.com, June 11, 2015, http://www.boston.com/culture/movies/2015/06/11/jaws-behind-the-scenes-on-marthas-vineyard (accessed August 24, 2016).

26. Taylor, *Jaws Memories*, 305.

27. "Does anyone know anything about boats??? 'Jaws Question,'" Horror-Domain.com, 2009, http://horrordomain.com/forums/topics/posts/index.cfm?t=5315 (accessed on August 24, 2016).

28. Ibid.

29. Ibid.

30. Ibid.

31. Ibid.

32. Ibid.

33. Ibid.

34. Ibid.

35. Michael B. Schiffer, *Formation Processes of the Archaeological Record* (Salt Lake City: University of Utah Press, 1987). There does not appear to be a specific formation process identified with the remains of a human cultural process such as movie making. However, sites such as Tozeur in Tunisia, where many desert scenes from the original *Star Wars* were filmed in 1976, have since become destinations for film fans and other tourists, at least when actual human conflicts have not intervened to prevent such visits. See, for example: http://www.daily-mail.co.uk/travel/travel_news/article-3348004/Disused-toilets-free-standing-vaporators-Luke-Skywalker-s-home-Haunting-images-abandoned-Star-Wars-sets-deep-Tunisian-desert.html (accessed May 31, 2017).

36. Schiffer, *Formation Processes*, 75.

37. See http://www.smithsonianmag.com/arts-culture/hollywood-on-exhibit-128925023/#zz5U1qRHUL7E62mG.99 (accessed May 30, 2017).

38. See http://www.laweekly.com/arts/10-geeky-hollywood-artifacts-sold-at-auction-over-the-weekend-from-empire-strikes-back-star-trek-willy-wonka-walt-disney-and-others-2374165 (accessed May 30, 2017).

Chapter 2. The Throwaway Society in the Mudflats

1. For more on the Glen Foerd estate, see Anonymous, *Welcome to Glen Foerd*, n.d., on file at Glen Foerd estate; see also http://www.glenfoerd.org/. For more on the history of Philadelphia and its northeastern suburbs and waterways, see Jean R. Soderlun, ed., *William Penn and the Founding of Pennsylvania, 1680–1684* (Philadelphia: University of Pennsylvania Press, 1983); Alicia M. Freitag and Harry C. Silcox, *Historical Northeast Philadelphia: Stories and Memories* (Holland, Pa.: Brighton Press, 1994); Albert Cook Myers, ed., *Narratives of Early Pennsylvania, West New Jersey, and Delaware, 1630–1707* (New York: Barnes and Noble, 1912); and Adrian C. Leiby, *The Early Dutch and Swedish Settlers of New Jersey* (Princeton: D. Van Nostrand Company, 1964). For a discussion of the potential archaeology of the Delaware and its waterfront, see J. L. Cotter, D. G. Roberts, and Michael Parrington, "Archaeological Resources of the Delaware River: Submerged Sites and Shipwrecks," in *The Buried Past: An Archaeological History of Philadelphia* (Philadelphia: University of Pennsylvania Press, 1994), 460–65. For background on the geological and hydrological forces at work on the Poquessing Creek and their archaeological implications, see A. G. Brown, *Alluvial Geoarchaeology* (Cambridge: Cambridge University Press, 1997); and Michael B. Schiffer, *Formation Processes of the Archaeological Record* (Salt Lake City: University of Utah Press, 1987.

2. Marion Shoard, "Edgelands," in *Remaking the Landscape: The Changing Face of Britain* (London: Profile Books, 2002).

3. Cotter et al., "Archaeological Resources of the Delaware River," 465.

4. The pipe stem diameter of 5/16 of an inch is a size that gives the unmarked bowl an approximately 72 percent chance of dating from 1680–1710. However, given its provenience, above the components of a carpet sweeper, there are other more plausible explanations. It could be a later deposition of an earlier artifact, or a contemporary (ca. 1920) copy of an earlier clay pipe bowl style. It could also be an actual ca. 1700 pipe bowl brought to the surface by the action of the dense concentration of water plants, which appear to be pushing plate and bottlework to the surface as they reappear each spring.

5. Particularly valuable volumes consulted during our laboratory work included Ralph and Terry Kovel, *Kovel's New Dictionary of Marks, Pottery and Porcelain, 1850 to the Present* (New York: Crown, 1986); Gene Florence, *Pocket Guide to Depression Glass and More, 1920s–1960s*, 11th edition (Paducah, Ky.: Collector Books, 1999); Mary Frank Gaston, *The Collector's Encyclopedia of Limoges Porcelain*, 2nd rev. edition (Paducah, Ky.: Collector Books, 1991); and most especially Bill and Betty Wilson, *19th Century Medicine in Glass* (Amador City, Calif.: 19th Century Hobby and Publishing, 1971); and Betty Zumwalt, *Ketchup, Pickles, Sauces: 19th Century Food in Glass* (Fulton, Calif.: Mark West, 1980).

Chapter 3. Airship Underwater: In Search of the USS *Akron*

1. Quote from Henry Cord Meyer, *Airshipmen, Businessmen and Politics 1890–1940*, Smithsonian History of Aviation and Spaceflight Series (Washington, D.C.: Smithsonian Institution Press, 1991), 248. For a general history on airships and their operations, see John Toland, *The Great Dirigibles: Their Triumphs & Disasters* (New York: Dover Publications, 1972). For specific references to lighter-than-air operations in the navy, see Roy A. Grossnick, ed., *Kite Balloons to Airships: The Navy's Lighter-than-Air Experience* (Washington, D.C.: Deputy Chief of Naval Operations, 1987). See also Douglas H. Robinson, *Giants in the Sky: A History of the Rigid Airship* (Seattle: University of Washington Press, 1973); Douglas H. Robinson and Charles L. Keller, *"Up Ship!" A History of the U.S. Navy's Rigid Airships 1919–1935* (Annapolis: Naval Institute Press, 1982); and Richard K. Smith, *The Airships Akron and Macon: Flying Aircraft Carriers of the U.S. Navy* (Annapolis: Naval Institute Press, 1965).

2. Charles E. Rosendahl, "The Loss of the Akron," *Naval Institute Proceedings* 60, no. 7 (1934): 921–33.

3. Associated Press, "Doomed Men of *Akron* Shouted Cheery Farewells Before Dying," *Evening Star* (Washington, D.C.), April 5, 1933, Richard E. Deal Papers, National Air and Space Museum Archives.

4. "Roosevelt Grieves at Loss to the Nation," *New York Times*, April 5, 1933, 1.

5. A Junior Officer's Widow, "Even the Birds," *Naval Institute Proceedings* 60, no. 1 (January 1934): 44–45.

6. Anonymous, "Wreck of 1930s Airship Surveyed Off New Jersey," *Naval History* 16, no. 6 (2002): 64–66.

7. John Davis, "Lost at Sea: The Great U.S. Navy Airships Akron and Macon" (film), *The Sea Hunters* (Halifax, Nova Scotia: Eco-Nova Productions, 2005).

8. Henry S. Rawdon, *Corrosion Embrittlement of Duralumin II: Accelerated Corrosion Tests and the Behavior of High-Strength Aluminum Alloys of Different Compositions* (Washington, D.C.: National Advisory Committee for Aeronautics, Technical Note, 1928).

Chapter 4. The Archaeological Shorelines of the High North

1. Prior to 2016, accounts of the American attempts to reach the North Pole from the European and Russian High Arctic were episodic and infrequent. See, for example, E. B. Baldwin, *The Franz Josef Land Archipelago: E. B. Baldwin's Journal of the Wellman Polar Expedition, 1898–1899*, ed. P. J. Capelotti (Jefferson, N.C.: McFarland, 2004); Susan Barr, "Virgohamnas historie: Et øde, uhyggelig sted, en ukoselig bukt [Virgohamna's history: A desolate, uncomfortable, unpleasant bay]," *Svalbardposten* 17, no. 80–81 (1980): 6–7; P. J. Capelotti, *The Wellman Polar Airship Expeditions at Virgohamna, Danskøya, Svalbard: A Study in Aerospace Archaeology*, NPI Meddelelser no. 145 (Oslo: Norwegian Polar Institute, 1997); P. J. Capelotti, *By Airship to the North Pole: An Archaeology of Human Exploration* (New Brunswick, N.J.: Rutgers University Press, 1999); P. J. Capelotti, "E. B. Baldwin and the American-Norwegian Discovery and Exploration of Graham Bell Island, 1899," *Polar Research* 25, no. 2 (2006): 155–71; P. J. Capelotti, "A 'Radically New Method': Balloon Buoy Communications of the Baldwin-Ziegler Polar Expedition, Franz Josef Land, June 1902," *Polar Research* 28 (2008): 52–72; and P. J. Capelotti, Herman Van Dyk, and Jean-Claude Cailliez, "Strange Interlude at Virgohamna, Danskøya, Svalbard, 1906: *The Merkelig Mann*, the Engineer and the Spy," *Polar Research* 26 (2007): 64–75. For the first comprehensive history of the American attempts on the North Pole from this area, see P. J. Capelotti, *The Greatest Show in the Arctic: The American Exploration of Franz Josef Land, 1898–1905* (Norman: University of Oklahoma Press, 2016).

2. Capelotti, *Greatest Show*, 149–83.

3. Ibid., 330–47.

4. P. J. Capelotti, "The 'American Supply Trail': Archaeological Notes on the Remains of the Ziegler Polar Expedition in Zemlya-Frantsa Iosifa, 1903–05," *Polar Record* 47, no. 3 (2011): 193–201.

5. See, for example, Barr, "Virgohamnas historie," 6–7; and Capelotti, *Wellman Polar Airship Expeditions*.

6. Peter Schmidt Mikkelsen, *North-East Greenland, 1908–1960: The Trapper Era* (Cambridge: Scott Polar Research Institute, 2008), 82–85, 195–97.

7. Andreas Umbreit, "Franz Josef Land: Possible Discovery of the Kane Lodge Depot of the Baldwin-Ziegler Expedition (1901/02)," *Report to the Russian Arctic National Park*, 2012, http://www.franz-josef-land.info.

8. Susan Barr, "Soviet-Norwegian Historical Expedition to Zemlya Frantsa-Iosifa," *Polar Record* 27, no. 163 (1991): 297–302. The geographic and archival dispersal of the expeditions and their records has also seen a gap of more than sixty years since an attempt to synthesize their results by Caswell. See John Edwards Caswell, *The Utilization of Scientific Reports of the United States Arctic Expeditions, 1850–1909* (Stanford: Stanford University Press, 1951).

9. C. Michael Hall and Jarkko Saarinen, "Tourism and Change in Polar Regions," in *Tourism and Change in Polar Regions: Climate, Environment and Experience*, ed. C. Michael Hall and Jarkko Saarinen, 1–41 (London: Routledge, 2010), 1.

10. Arvid Viken, "Svalbard, Norway," in *Extreme Tourism: Lessons from the World's Cold Water Islands*, ed. Godfrey Balddacchino, 129–44 (Oxford: Elsevier, 2006), 129.

11. Walter Wellman, *The Aerial Age* (New York: A. R. Keller, 1911), 152.

12. "Wellman Not Very Hopeful," *New York Times*, May 25, 1907, 4.

13. Swedish Society for Anthropology and Geography, *Andrée's Story: The Complete Record of His Polar Flight, 1897* (New York: Viking Press, 1930), 43.

14. William Martin Conway, John Walter Gregory, Aubyn Trevor-Battye, and Edmund Johnston Garwood, *The First Crossing of Spitsbergen: Being an Account of an Inland Journey of Exploration and Survey, with Descriptions of Several Mountain Ascents, of Boat Expeditions in Ice Fjord, of a Voyage to North-East-Land, the Seven Islands, down Hinloopen Strait, Nearly to Wiches Land and into most of the Fjords of Spitsbergen and of Almost Complete Circumnavigation of the Main Island* (London: J. M. Dent, 1897).

15. William Martin Conway, *No Man's Land: A History of Spitsbergen from Its Discovery in 1596 to the Beginning of the Scientific Exploration of the Country* (Cambridge: Cambridge University Press, 1906), 302.

16. Translated from Fridtjof Nansen, *En Ferd Til Spitsbergen* [A Journey to Spitsbergen] (Kristiania: Jacob Dybwads Forlag, 1920), 144.

17. Ibid., 145.

18. John H. Stubbs and Emily G. Makas, *Architectural Conservation in Europe and the Americas* (Hoboken, N.J.: John Wiley, 2011), 185–87.

19. Callum and Jane Sproull Thomson, "Arctic Cruise Ship Island Tourism," in

Extreme Tourism: Lessons from the World's Cold Water Islands, ed. Godfrey Balddacchino (Oxford: Elsevier, 2006), 171.

20. Susan Barr, "The History of Western Activity in Franz Josef Land," in *Franz Josef Land*, ed. Susan Barr (Oslo: Norsk Polarinstitutt, 1995), 98.

21. Yevgeny Federov, *Polar Diaries* (Moscow: Progress, 1983), 106.

22. Ibid.

23. "Find Arctic Cairn Left by American," *New York Times*, August 5, 1930, 18.

24. Personal communication, May 19, 2008. The writer asked to remain anonymous.

25. Conway, *First Crossing of Spitsbergen*, 65.

26. Thomson and Thomson, "Arctic Cruise Ship," 174.

27. http://northpolevoyages.com/franz_josef/voyage.php (accessed May 2006).

28. P. J. Capelotti, "A Preliminary Archaeological Survey of a Tupolev TB-3 (ANT-6) Aircraft on Ostrov Rudol'fa, Zemlya Frantsa-Iosifa, Russia," *Polar Record* 43, no. 2 (2007): 173–77.

29. Robert Finch, *The Iambics of Newfoundland: Notes from an Unknown Shore* (New York: Counterpoint, 2007), 19.

30. Ibid.

31. Capelotti, *Wellman Polar Airship Expeditions*, 98.

32. Ibid., 88.

33. Hall and Saarinen, "Tourism and Change," 32.

34. Emma J. Steward, Dianne Draper, and Jackie Dawson, "Monitoring Patterns of Cruise Tourism across Arctic Canada," in *Cruise Tourism in Polar Regions: Promoting Environmental and Social Sustainability?* (London: Earthscan, 2010), 133.

35. R. Roura, "Cultural Heritage Tourism in Antarctica and Svalbard: Patterns, Impacts, and Policies," in *Tourism and Change in Polar Regions: Climate, Environment and Experience*, ed. C. Michael Hall and Jarkko Saarinen (London: Routledge, 2010), 196.

36. Hein B. Bjerck and Leif Johnny Johannessen, *Virgohamna: In the Air Toward the North Pole* (Longyearbyen: Governor of Svalbard, 1999).

37. Ibid., 11.

38. Bjørn Fossli Johansen, Kristen Prestvold, and Øystein Overrein, *Cruise Handbook for Svalbard* (Tromsø: Norwegian Polar Institute, 2011), http://cruise-handbook.npolar.no/en/ index.html.

39. Ibid.

40. Lori E. A. Bradford and Norman McIntyre, "Off the Beaten Track: Messages as a Means of Reducing Social Trail Use at St. Lawrence Islands National Park," *Journal of Park and Recreation Administration* 25, no. 1 (2007): 9–11.

41. Urban Wråkberg, "Presentations of Nature, Heritage and Geopolitics in the Arctic Visitor Industry: Reflections on Some Cases from Svalbard (Norway) and North-West Russia," presentation at the International Conference of Arctic Social Science (ICASS IX), Umeå, Sweden, June 9, 2017.

42. Atle Staalesen, "Rescue Mission for Baldwin's Historical Refuge on Franz Josef Land," *Independent Barents Observer*, August 4, 2017, https://thebarentsobserver.com/en/arctic/2017/08/rescue-mission-baldwins-historical-refuge-franz-josef-land#.WYR1sZh4yRc.twitter (accessed August 9, 2017).

43. Governor of Svalbard, *Reiselivsstatistikk for Svalbard 2006* [Travel Statistics for Svalbard 2006] (Longyearbyen: Governor of Svalbard 2006), 5.

44. Ibid., 7.

45. Roura, "Cultural Heritage Tourism," 196.

Chapter 5. The Elusive Island

1. Thor Heyerdahl, "Did Polynesian Culture Originate in America?" New York: *International Science* 1 (May 1941): 15–26.

2. Ibid.

3. Heyerdahl commented extensively on his reasons for choosing to build a raft of *balsa* wood for his the *Kon-Tiki* experiment, prominently in *Kon-Tiki: Across the Pacific by Raft* (New York: Rand McNally, 1950): 30–35, and in *American Indians in the Pacific: The Theory Behind the Kon-Tiki Expedition* (London: George Allen and Unwin, 1952), see esp. 585–620; 1971, 17; 1979, 193–95, 201–18.

4. Karl H. Rensch, "Polynesian Plant Names: Linguistic Analysis and Ethnobotany, Expectations and Limitations," in *Islands, Plants, and Polynesians: An Introduction to Polynesian Ethnobotany: Proceedings of a Symposium*, edited by Paul Alan Cox and Sandra Anne Banack (Portland, Ore.: Dioscorides Press, 1991), 98.

5. Alfred Métraux, *Easter Island: A Stone-Age Civilization of the Pacific* (London: Andre Deutsch, 1957), 227.

6. See Thor Heyerdahl and Edwin N. Ferdon Jr., eds., *The Archaeology of Easter Island: Reports of the Norwegian Archaeological Expedition to Easter Island and the East Pacific, Volume 1*, Monographs of the School of American Research and the Museum of New Mexico (Santa Fe), no. 24, 2 vols. (New York: Rand McNally, 1961).

7. See, for example, David Lewis, *We, the Navigators: The Ancient Art of Land-finding in the Pacific* (Honolulu: University Press of Hawai'i, 1972); and David Lewis, "Hokule'a Follows the Stars to Tahiti," *National Geographic* 150, no. 4 (October 1976). See also Andrew Sharp, *Ancient Voyagers in Polynesia* (Berkeley: University of California Press, 1963).

8. See R. Gerard Ward, John W. Webb, and M. Levison, "The Settlement of the

Polynesian Outliers: A Computer Simulation," in *Pacific Navigation and Voyaging*, edited by Ben R. Finney (Wellington, New Zealand: Polynesian Society, 1976).

9. See, for example, Ben R. Finney, Paul Frost, Richard Rhodes, and Nainoa Thompson, "Wait for the West Wind," *Journal of the Polynesian Society* 98 (1989). For further readings see Ben R. Finney, ed., *Pacific Navigation and Voyaging* (Wellington, New Zealand: Polynesian Society, 1976); Ben R. Finney, *Hokule'a: The Way to Tahiti* (New York: Dodd, Mead and Company, 1979); and Ben R. Finney, *From Sea to Space* (Palmerston North, New Zealand: Massey University, 1992).

10. Lewis, *We, the Navigators*, 269.

Chapter 6. The Origins of the Raft

1. The Joseph Birdsell excerpt comes from his article "The Recalibration of a Paradigm for the First Peopling of Greater Australia," in J. Allen et al., *Sunda and Sahul: Prehistoric Studies in Southeast Asia, Melanesia and Australia* (London: Academic Press, 1977). Many of the questions related to the varying geographic distribution of the human population and arrival in Sahul, including Birdsell's article, are included in this excellent volume.

2. See Kuno Knöbl, *Tai Ki: To the Point of No Return* (New York: Little Brown, 1976).

3. These included especially the happy discovery of C. Hartley Grattan's dusty yet still magisterial *The Southwest Pacific to 1900* and *The Southwest Pacific since 1900*, published in 1963 by the University of Michigan Press.

4. The discoveries and very recent dating of the *Homo erectus* skulls to between 27,000 and 53,000 years ago were reported in C. C. Swisher III et al., "Latest *Homo erectus* of Java: Potential Contemporaneity with *Homo sapiens* in Southeast Asia," *Science* 274, no. 5294 (December 13, 1996): 1870–74.

5. Birdsell, "Recalibration of a Paradigm," 123.

6. Ibid., 144.

7. This episode with the bamboo raft in the Maldives occurs in one of Heyerdahl's lesser-known classics, *The Maldive Mystery* (Bethesda, Md.: Adler and Adler, 1986), 187–90. An interesting ethnological fieldtrip, indeed, would trace the course of this bamboo vessel back to Burma and recount the lives of the raft builders there. Is there any local tradition of using such large cargo-carrying rafts on deep-water voyages over several thousand miles employing, as Heyerdahl speculated, the winds of the Northeast Monsoon to propel the raft across the waters of the Bay of Bengal?

Chapter 7. Thor Heyerdahl and the Theory of the Archaeological Raft

1. Eric de Bisschop, *Tahiti Nui* (New York: McDowell, Oblensky, 1959), 7.

2. Vital Alsar, *La Balsa* (New York: Reader's Digest Press, 1973), 23.

3. DeVere Baker, *The Raft Lehi IV* (Long Beach, Calif.: Whitehorn Publishing, 1959), vii.

4. Santiago Genovés, *The Acali Experiment: Five Men and Six Women on a Raft Across the Atlantic for 101 Days* (New York: Times Books, 1980), xv.

5. William Willis, *Whom the Sea Has Taken* (New York: Meredith, 1966).

6. Ibid., 59.

7. Bengt Danielsson, *From Raft to Raft* (London: George Allen and Unwin, 1960), 133.

8. Bisschop, *Tahiti Nui*, 133.

9. Alain Bombard, *The Bombard Story* (London: Andre Deutsch, 1953), 30.

10. Arne Skjølvold, personal communication, March 14, 2000. If Skjølsvold is correct, then it is possible that the *moai* 263 carving shows not humans on the deck of a three-masted ship, but flames, and represents the burning of a European vessel. Depending on the amount of time it took for the downslope movement of soil to cover the lower part of the monolith, it is perhaps even a representation of the destruction of HMS *Bounty* by Fletcher Christian and his fellow mutineers on nearby Pitcairn Island in 1789, a representation by someone who either witnessed the event or later heard of it.

11. John Haslett, *Voyage of the Manteño* (New York: St. Martin's, 2006; republished in 2013 as *The Lost Raft*).

12. Leslie Dewan and Dorothy Hosler, "Ancient Maritime Trade on Balsa Rafts: An Engineering Analysis," *Journal of Anthropological Research* 64, no. 1 (2008).

13. Robert G. Bednarik, "Seafaring in the Pleistocene," *Cambridge Archaeological Journal* 13, no. 1 (2003): 41–66. See also Bruce Bower, "Erectus Ahoy: Prehistoric Seafaring Floats into View," *Science News* 164 (October 18, 2003): 248–50.

Chapter 8. Eric de Bisschop and the Response to *Kon-Tiki*

1. Eric de Bisschop, *Tahiti Nui* (New York: McDowell, Oblensky, 1959), , 34–35.

2. Ibid. 57.

3. Ibid., 60–61.

4. Bengt Danielsson, *From Raft to Raft* (London: George Allen and Unwin, 1960), 61.

5. Bisschop, *Tahiti Nui*, 68.

6. Ibid., 109.

7. Ibid., 79.

8. Ibid., 105.

9. Ibid., 93.

10. Ibid., 102.

11. Danielsson, *From Raft to Raft*, 63.

12. Bisschop, *Tahiti Nui*, 185–86.

13. See Edmund Fanning, *Voyages Round the World* (New York: Collins and Hannay, 1833).

14. For the full story of the *Essex*, see Owen Chase, *Narrative of the Most Extraordinary and Distressing Shipwreck of the Whale-Ship Essex* (New York: W. B. Gilley, 1821).

15. Danielsson, *From Raft to Raft*, 117.

16. Ibid., 126.

17. Michael E. Moseley, *The Inca and Their Ancestors* (London: Thames and Hudson, 1992), 94.

18. Danielsson, *From Raft to Raft*, 128.

19. Ibid., 129.

20. Ibid., 139.

21. Ibid., 154.

22. Ibid., 244.

23. Ben R. Finney et al., *Voyage of Rediscovery* (Berkeley: University of California Press, 1994), 272.

Chapter 12. The Tupolev TB-3 on Rudolf Island

1. On Otto Schmidt see William Barr, "Discovery of the Wreck of the Soviet Steamer *Chelyuskin* on the Bed of the Chukchi Sea," *Polar Record* 43, no. 1 (2007): 67–70.

2. John McCannon, *Red Arctic: Polar Exploration and the Myth of the North in the Soviet Union, 1932–1939* (New York: Oxford University Press, 1998), 70–78.

3. L. Brontman, *On the Top of the World: The Soviet Expedition to the North Pole, 1937* (1938; reprint, New York: Greenwood Press, 1968), 30–31.

4. A. N. Krenke, "Russian Research in Franz Josef Land," in *Franz Josef Land*, edited by S. Barr (Oslo: Norsk Polarinstitutt, 1995).

5. L. Andersson, *Soviet Aircraft and Aviation, 1917–1941* (Annapolis: Naval Institute Press, 1994), 251.

6. Brontman, *On the Top of the World*, 35.

7. Andersson, *Soviet Aircraft*, 255.

8. McCannon, *Red Arctic*, 70–71.

9. Ibid., 160.

10. Susan Barr, ed., *Franz Josef Land* (Oslo: Norsk Polarinstitutt, 1995). See also Susan Barr, "Soviet-Norwegian Historical Expedition to Zemlya Frantsa-Iosifa," *Polar Record* 27, no. 163 (1991): 297–302.

11. "The Flights in the Soviet Arctic in 1938," *Problems of the Arctic* (Leningrad), vols. 5–6 (1938): 142–49.

12. McCannon, *Red Arctic*, 159.

13. M. I. Belov, *Nauchnoye i khozyaystvennoye osvoyeniye Sovetskogo Severa 1933–1945: Istoriya otkrytiya I osvoyenya Severnogo morskogo puti, tom 4* (Leningrad: Gidrometeorologicheskoye izdatel'stvo, 1969), 390.

14. McCannon, *Red Arctic*, 162. Arctic researcher and ornithologist Eugene Potapov makes the point: "In colloquial language, 'pidor' does not exactly mean homosexuality. Usually this means reckless behavior. However, the strict dictionary definition means 'homosexual.' Placing the accusation in the context of Stalin's time: if there was any proof of indecent behavior, Chukhnovsky would have ended up handcuffed immediately. At the time in the crime code it was 25 years in gulag" (Eugene Potapov, personal communication, January 29, 2018).

15. Mazuruk to Schmidt, July 14, 1938. Report communicated in e-mail to UK amateur radio operator Mike Hewitt by G. Weston DeWalt, October 2, 2002. "The radio engineer who worked at the station at Rudolfa described in his diaries: 'April, 14 . . . Was breaking H-210 with the tractor and steel rope. Then transported the wings to the station. Sunny,'" diary note provided to the author by Eugene Potapov from the diaries of Vitaliy Belikovich, which have been published online by Belikovich's granddaughter at http://ukhtoma.ru/belikovich.htm (Eugene Potapov, personal communication, January 29, 2018).

Chapter 14. Surveying Fermi's Paradox, Mapping Dyson's Sphere

1. E. M. Jones, *"Where Is Everybody?" An Account of Fermi's Question* (Los Alamos, N.M.: Los Alamos National Laboratory Report LA-10311-MS, 1985).

2. F. D. Drake, "The Radio Search for Intelligent Extraterrestrial Life," in *Current Aspects of Exobiology*, ed. G. Mamikunian and M. H. Briggs, 323–46, Jet Propulsion Laboratory Technical Report (London: Pergamon Press, 1965).

3. Isaac Asimov, *Extraterrestrial Civilizations* (New York: Crown, 1979).

4. F. J. Dyson, "Search for Artificial Stellar Sources of Infrared Radiation," *Science* 131 (1960): 1667–68.

5. K. A. Seaver, *The Frozen Echo: Greenland and the Exploration of North America, ca. A.D. 1000–1500* (Stanford, Calif.: Stanford University Press, 1996).

6. J. Trefil, "Ah, but There May Have Been Life on Mars," *Smithsonian* 26, no. 5 (1995).

7. C. Sagan, *Pale Blue Dot: A Vision of the Human Future in Space* (New York: Random House, 1994), 59–70.

8. R. Blom, "Space Technology and the Discovery of Ubar, " *P.O.B.* 17, no. 6 (1992): 11–20.

9. Thor Heyerdahl, *Aku-Aku: The Secret of Easter Island* (London: George Allen and Unwin, 1958).

10. T. R. Lyons and D. H. Scovill, "Non-Destructive Archaeology and Remote Sensing: A Conceptual and Methodological Stance," in *Remote Sensing and*

Non-Destructive Archaeology, ed. T. R. Lyons and J. I. Ebert (Washington, D.C.: National Park Service, 1978).

11. For example, see S.L.H. Madry, "A Multiscalar Approach to Remote Sensing in a Temperate Regional Archaeological Survey," in *Regional Dynamics: Burgundian Landscapes in Historical Perspective* (New York: Academic Press, 1987).

12. T. R. Hester, R. F. Heizer, and J. A. Graham, *Field Methods in Archaeology* (Mountain View, Calif.: Mayfield Publishing Company, 1975), 309.

13. Ibid., 309.

14. O.G.S. Crawford, *Archaeology in the Field* (London: Phoenix House, 1953), 46.

15. J.-Y. Cousteau, "At Home in the Sea," *National Geographic* 125, no. 4 (1964). See also A. Falco, "The Soucoupe," *Calypso Log* 15, no. 2 (1988).

16. J. Whitfield, "Shipwreck Network Launched: Three-Year European Project Aims to Safeguard Shipwrecks," *Nature News*, published online, January 23, 2002.

17. Lyons and Scovill, "Non-Destructive Archaeology."

18. J. Travis, "Deep-Sea Debate Pits Alvin Against *Jason*," *Science* 259 (1993).

19. W. Bascom, *The Crest of the Wave: Adventures in Oceanography* (New York: Harper and Row, 1988), 314.

20. R. A. Gould, *Recovering the Past* (Albuquerque: University of New Mexico Press, 1990), 239.

21. Bass, *Archaeology Under Water*, 152.

22. B. R. Finney, *From Sea to Space* (Palmerston North, New Zealand: Massey University, 1992), 105.

23. J. T. Richelson, *U.S. Satellite Imagery, 1960–1999*, National Security Archive Electronic Briefing Book no. 13, 1999, http://nsarchive.gwu.edu/NSAEBB/NSAEBB13/.

24. Leonard David, "Orbiter to Look for Lost-to-Mars Probes," Space.com, November 1, 2006, http://www.space.com/3059-orbiter-lost-mars-probes.html. See also "NASA Uses Space Probe to Search for Missing Global Surveyor in Orbit around Mars," Associated Press, November 18, 2006, http://www.newson6.com/story/7648552/nasa-uses-space-probe-to-search-for-missing-global-surveyor-in-orbit-around-mars.

25. "NASA Mars Orbiter Photographs *Spirit* and *Vikings* on the Ground," December 4, 2006, https://www.nasa.gov/mission_pages/MRO/news/mro-20061204.html.

26. See, for example, Brian Handwerk, "Google Earth, Satellite Maps Boost Armchair Archaeology," *National Geographic News*, November 7, 2006, http://news.nationalgeographic.com/news/2006/11/061107-archaeology.html.

27. William L. Fox, *Driving to Mars: In the Arctic with NASA on the Human Journey to the Red Planet* (Emeryville, Calif.: Shoemaker and Hoard, 2006).

Chapter 15. Measuring the Mountains of the Moon

1. Ben Finney, *From Sea to Space* (Palmerston North, New Zealand: Massey University Press, 1992), 105.
2. Ibid.
3. Alice Gorman, "The Cultural Landscape of Interplanetary Space," *Journal of Social Archaeology* 5, no. 1 (2005): 86.

Chapter 16. Mobile Artifacts in the Solar System and Beyond

1. R. O. Fimmel and William Swindell, *Pioneer Odyssey* (Washington, D.C.: NASA, 1977), 183.
2. Ibid., 184.
3. Ibid.
4. Ibid., 186.

Epilogue: Back Down to Earth, in Search of Pedro

1. Martin J. S. Rudwick, *The Meaning of Fossils* (New York: Science History Publications, 1976).

INDEX

P.J. Capelotti is professor of anthropology at Penn State Abington. He is the author or editor of several books, including *The Greatest Show in the Arctic: The American Exploration of Franz Josef Land, 1898–1905*, and *Life and Death on the Greenland Patrol, 1942*.

CPSIA information can be obtained
at www.ICGtesting.com
Printed in the USA
BVHW081007120123
655895BV00011B/629